Computers For Seniors For Dummi...

Purchasing a PC C...

When you're purchasing your computer, check for ... ...ered in more detail in Chapter 1):

- **Memory:** Your computer should have at least 1 gigabyte (GB) of RAM.

- **Processor speed:** Look for a minimum of 1.6 GHz processor speed.

- **Size/footprint:** If you're short on space, a minitower or laptop might be better.

- **Price:** Set a budget.

- **Keyboard:** Make sure the keyboard feels comfortable to you.

- **Monitor:** Monitors come in different sizes and quality of resolution. A 15-inch monitor is comfortable for most people, but if you do work with higher-end images or watch videos, consider a larger monitor.

- **Input ports and drives:** Computers might come with CD or DVD drives, USB ports for connecting peripherals and USB sticks, and ports to connect to monitors and printers.

- **Wireless capability:** To connect to some wireless devices and networks, you need wireless capability.

- **Included software:** Some computers come with utility programs such as antivirus software or productivity software such as Microsoft Works.

- **Manufacturer support:** Check the warranty and technical support available.

- **Graphics and sound cards:** If you want to use multimedia or game software, ask for more sophisticated sound and video features.

Tips for Efficient Searching

Whether you're searching your computer for a file or the Internet for a document or Web site, here are some tips that can help you get appropriate results faster (however, note some search engines use slightly different approaches):

- Avoid search terms that are too general. The term *golden retriever* would get you more specific results than *dog*, for example.

- By default, if you type two keywords such as *Vacation Italy*, search engines generally look first for sites that contain both words.

- Most search engines generally don't take into account words such as *and, or,* and *a.*

- Some search engines such as Ask.com allow you to type in questions as sentences rather than using keywords.

- If you want to find an exact phrase, such as *"To be or not to be"*, put it in quotes.

Computers For Seniors For Dummies®

Ten Keystroke Shortcuts

Use these Windows keyboard short-cuts to handle common activities, such as cutting and pasting text, quickly and easily.

Key or Keystroke Combination	Effect
Ctrl+X	Cuts the selected text or object
Ctrl+C	Copies the selected text or object
Ctrl+V	Pastes copied or cut text or object
F1	Displays help
F2	Opens the selected item (folder or file) for renaming
Ctrl+Z	Undoes the previous action
Alt+Tab	Displays a list of currently open applications
Prt Scr	Prints a copy of current screen to the Windows Clipboard
Window Logo Key	Displays the Start menu
F3	Displays a search window

Ten Useful Web Sites

As you begin to use your computer, you might find the following sites to be good starting points for various types of online activities.

Description	Address
www.cnn.com	News site
www.fool.com	Financial news and advice
www.tucows.com	Shareware download site
www.dowjones.com	Stock prices
www.britannica.com	Online encyclopedia (fee based)
www.consumerreports.org	Consumer advice and comparisons
www.flickr.com	Photo sharing
www.ancestry.com	Genealogy database
www.doityourself.com	Do-it-yourself home projects
www.movies.com	Information on current movies and stars

For Dummies: Bestselling Book Series for Beginners

Computers For Seniors
FOR
DUMMIES®

by Nancy Muir
Foreword by Sir Stirling Moss

WILEY

Wiley Publishing, Inc.

Computers For Seniors For Dummies®

Published by
Wiley Publishing, Inc.
111 River Street
Hoboken, NJ 07030-5774

www.wiley.com

Copyright © 2008 by Wiley Publishing, Inc., Indianapolis, Indiana

Published by Wiley Publishing, Inc., Indianapolis, Indiana

Published simultaneously in Canada

For general information on our other products and services, please contact our Customer Care Department within the U.S. at 800-762-2974, outside the U.S. at 317-572-3993, or fax 317-572-4002.

For technical support, please visit www.wiley.com/techsupport.

Wiley also publishes its books in a variety of electronic formats. Some content that appears in print may not be available in electronic books.

Library of Congress Control Number: 2008922654

ISBN: 978-0-470-24055-7

Manufactured in the United States of America

10 9 8 7 6 5 4 3 2 1

About the Author

Nancy Muir has written over 50 books on topics ranging from desktop applications to distance learning. She has contributed articles to several national magazines, and teaches a college course in Internet Safety at Washington State University. Together with her husband, Earl Boysen, she maintains two informational Web sites: `www.BuildingGadgets.com` about electronics; and `www.understandingnano.com` focused on clear explanations of nanotechnology topics. Nancy also holds a certificate in distance learning design.

Author's Acknowledgments

Thanks to the people at Wiley Publishing for continuing to come to me to work with them. Special thanks go to Greg Croy, Acquisitions Editor, and Rebecca Huehls who made it all come together with her able project editing skills. Thanks also to the copy editor, Virginia Sanders, for making sure my text made sense.

Dedication

To all those seniors who are brave enough to take the leap into the brave new world of computing. And, to my husband Earl, who provides support, love, and understanding at all times. He's the perfect partner in every sense.

Publisher's Acknowledgments

We're proud of this book; please send us your comments through our online registration form located at `www.dummies.com/register/`.

Some of the people who helped bring this book to market include the following:

Acquisitions and Editorial

Project Editor: Rebecca Huehls

Executive Editor: Greg Croy

Copy Editor: Virginia Sanders

Technical Editor: Allen Wyatt

Editorial Manager: Leah P. Cameron

Editorial Assistant: Amanda Foxworth

Sr. Editorial Assistant: Cherie Case

Cartoons: Rich Tennant
(`www.the5thwave.com`)

Composition Services

Project Coordinator: Katherine Key

Layout and Graphics: Lissa Auciello-Brogan, Alissa D. Ellet, Erin Zeltner

Proofreaders: Cynthia Fields, Caitie Kelly, Sossity R. Smith

Indexer: Broccoli Information Management

Cover Photo of Sir Stirling Moss: Patrick Crew

Publishing and Editorial for Technology Dummies

Richard Swadley, Vice President and Executive Group Publisher

Andy Cummings, Vice President and Publisher

Mary Bednarek, Executive Acquisitions Director

Mary C. Corder, Editorial Director

Publishing for Consumer Dummies

Diane Graves Steele, Vice President and Publisher

Joyce Pepple, Acquisitions Director

Composition Services

Gerry Fahey, Vice President of Production Services

Debbie Stailey, Director of Composition Services

Contents at a Glance

Table of Contents

Foreword

The first time I heard the term "computer crash," I started worrying about the challenge of mastering these machines. Frankly I had all the gear but little or no idea on how to even get started. With no accelerator, no brake, not even a steering wheel, how was I going to control and do something useful with this computer?

It doesn't have to be that way as long as you have the proper instruction. Get your first computer driving lessons from *Computers For Seniors For Dummies*. The *For Dummies* team is known for making even the most difficult subjects easy — and fun — to master. In this book, you find the ideal road map for finding your way around a personal computer, your PC (learnt something new already!) for the first time.

Using *Computers For Seniors For Dummies*, you discover how to set up and fine tune your PC. You find out how to use Windows Vista — the petrol for your machine. Then the fun really begins! You can surf the vast world of the Internet to do anything from catching up on the latest news to finding out about a new hobby. (Be sure to visit me at www.stirlingmoss.com!) You can put your photos on the computer and share them with friends and family. You can play games. You can play music. You can shop for anything and everything under the sun. You can send greetings and gifts and join in online discussions. You can plan your vacations and print maps to your destination so you can get there without a wrong turn! And if you run into trouble, *Computers For Seniors For Dummies* has a repair shop — a section on working out and fixing the problem.

Computers open up a great world of possibilities. You should be a part of it. With *Computers For Seniors For Dummies*, you have the power to participate in that world.

If I can learn to drive a computer, although I still have my "L" plates on, so can you! Lose your fear and take control of your new machine with *Computers For Seniors For Dummies* — the book that is easy and fun to use and prepared especially for you.

Sir Stirling Moss,
Legendary British Racing Driver

www.stirlingmoss.com

Introduction

Computers have come a long way in just 20 years or so. They're now at the heart of the way many people communicate, shop, and learn. They provide useful tools for tracking information, organizing finances, and being creative.

During the rapid growth of the personal computer, you might have been too busy to jump in and learn the ropes, but you now realize how useful and fun working with a computer can be.

This book can help you get going with computers quickly and painlessly.

About This Book

This book is specifically written for mature people like you, folks who are relatively new to using a computer and want to discover the basics of buying a computer, working with software, and getting on the Internet. In writing this book, I've tried to take into account the types of activities that might interest a senior citizen discovering computers for the first time.

Foolish Assumptions

This book is organized by sets of tasks. These tasks start from the very beginning, assuming you know little about computers, and guide you through from the most basic steps in easy-to-understand language. Because I assume you're new to computers, the book provides explanations or definitions of technical terms to help you out.

All computers are run by software called an *operating system,* such as Windows. Because Microsoft Windows–based personal computers (PCs) are the most common type, the book focuses mostly on Windows functionality.

Why You Need This Book

Working with computers can be a daunting prospect to people who are coming to them later in life. Your grandchildren may run rings around you when it comes to technology, and you might have fallen for that old adage, "You can't teach an old dog new tricks." However, with the simple step-by-step approach of this book, you can get up to speed with computers and overcome any technophobia you might have experienced.

You can work through this book from beginning to end or simply open up a chapter to solve a problem or help you learn a new skill whenever you need it. The steps in each task get you where you want to go quickly, without a lot of technical explanation. In no time, you'll start picking up the skills you need to become a confident computer user.

Conventions Used in This Book

This book uses certain conventions to help you find your way around, including:

➡ When you have to type something in a text box, I put it in **bold** type. Whenever I mention a Web site address, I put it in another font, `like this`. Figure references are also in bold, to help you find them.

➡ For menu commands, I use the ⇨ symbol to separate menu choices. For example, choose Tools⇨Internet Options. The ⇨ symbol is just my way of saying "Open the Tools menu and then click Internet Options."

➡ Callouts for figures draw your attention to an action you need to perform. In some cases, points of interest in a figure might be circled. The text tells you what to look for, the circle makes it easy to find.

 Tip icons point out insights or helpful suggestions related to tasks in the step list.

How This Book Is Organized

This book is conveniently divided into several handy parts to help you find what you need.

➡ **Part I: Buying and Getting Started with Your Computer:** If you need to buy a computer or get started with the basics of using a computer, this part is for you. These chapters help you explore the different specifications, styles, and price ranges for computers and discover how to set up your computer out of the box, including hooking it up to a printer. These chapters provide information for exploring the Windows desktop when you first turn on your computer, customizing Windows to work the way you want it to, and getting the hang of the way Windows organizes files and folders. Finally, I provide information on using the Help system that's part of Windows.

➡ **Part II: Having Fun and Getting Things Done with Software:** Here's where you start working with that new computer. Using the popular and inexpensive Microsoft Works software, discover how to create documents in the Works Word Processor and work with numbers in the Spreadsheet. Chapters in this part also introduce you to built-in Windows applications you can use to work with digital photos, listen to music, and play games.

- ⟶ **Part III: Exploring the Internet:** It's time to get online! The chapters in this part help you understand what the Internet is and what tools and functions it makes available to you. Find out how to explore the Internet with a Web browser; how to stay in touch with people via e-mail, instant messaging, chat, blogs; and even how to make Internet phone calls.

- ⟶ **Part IV: Taking Care of Your Computer:** Now that you have a computer, you have certain responsibilities towards it (just like having a child or puppy!). In this case, you need to protect the data on your computer, which you can do using a program called Windows Defender. In addition, you need to perform some routine maintenance tasks to keep your hard drive uncluttered and virus free.

Get Going!

Whether you need to start from square one and buy yourself a computer or you're ready to just start enjoying the tools and toys your current computer makes available, it's time to get going, get online, and get computer savvy.

Part I
Buying and Getting Started with Your Computer

The 5th Wave   By Rich Tennant

AFTER SETTING UP THE COMPUTER, NED AND LORETTA SELECT THE COMPUTER'S BACKGROUND

© RICHTENNANT

"Oh – I like this background much better than the basement."

Buying a Computer

If you've never owned a computer and now face purchasing one for the first time, deciding what to get can be a somewhat daunting experience. There are lots of technical terms to figure out and various pieces of *hardware* (the physical pieces of your computer like the monitor and keyboard) and *software* (the brains of the computer that help you create documents and play games, for example) that you need to understand.

In this chapter, I introduce you to the world of activities your new computer makes available to you, and I provide the information you need to choose just the right computer for you. Remember as you read through this chapter that figuring out what you want to do with your computer is an important step in determining which computer you should buy. You have to consider how much money you want to spend, how you'll connect your computer to the Internet, and how much power and performance you'll require from your computer.

Get ready to . . .

Understand All You Can Do with Computers

In just a couple of decades, computers have moved from being expensive behemoths that lived in corporate basements to being personal productivity and entertainment tools. They have empowered people to connect around the world in unprecedented ways, and they've made common tasks much easier to handle.

The following list walks you through some of the things your computer will enable you to do. Depending on what activities are important to you, you can make a more informed purchasing choice.

⟼ **Keep in touch with friends and family.** The Internet has made it possible to communicate with other people via e-mail; share video images using webcams (tiny, inexpensive video cameras that capture and send your image to another computer); and make phone calls using a technology called VoIP (Voice over Internet Phone) that uses your computer and Internet connection to place calls. You can also chat with others by typing messages and sending them through your computer using a technology called instant messaging. These messages are exchanged in real time, so that you and your grandchild, for example, can see and reply to text immediately. Part III of this book explains these topics in more detail.

⟼ **Research any topic from the comfort of your home.** Online, you can find many reputable Web sites that help you get information on anything from expert medical advice to the best travel deals. You can read news from around the corner or around the world. You can visit government Web sites to find out information about your taxes, social security, and more, or even go to entertainment sites to look up your local television listings.

⟼ **Create greeting cards, letters, or home inventories.** Whether you're organizing your holiday card list or figuring out a monthly budget, computer programs can help. For example, **Figure 1-1** shows a graph that the Excel program creates from data in a spreadsheet.

➡ **Pursue hobbies such as genealogy or sports.** You can research your favorite teams online (see **Figure 1-2**) or connect with people who have the same interests. The online world is full of special interest chat groups where you can discuss these interests with others.

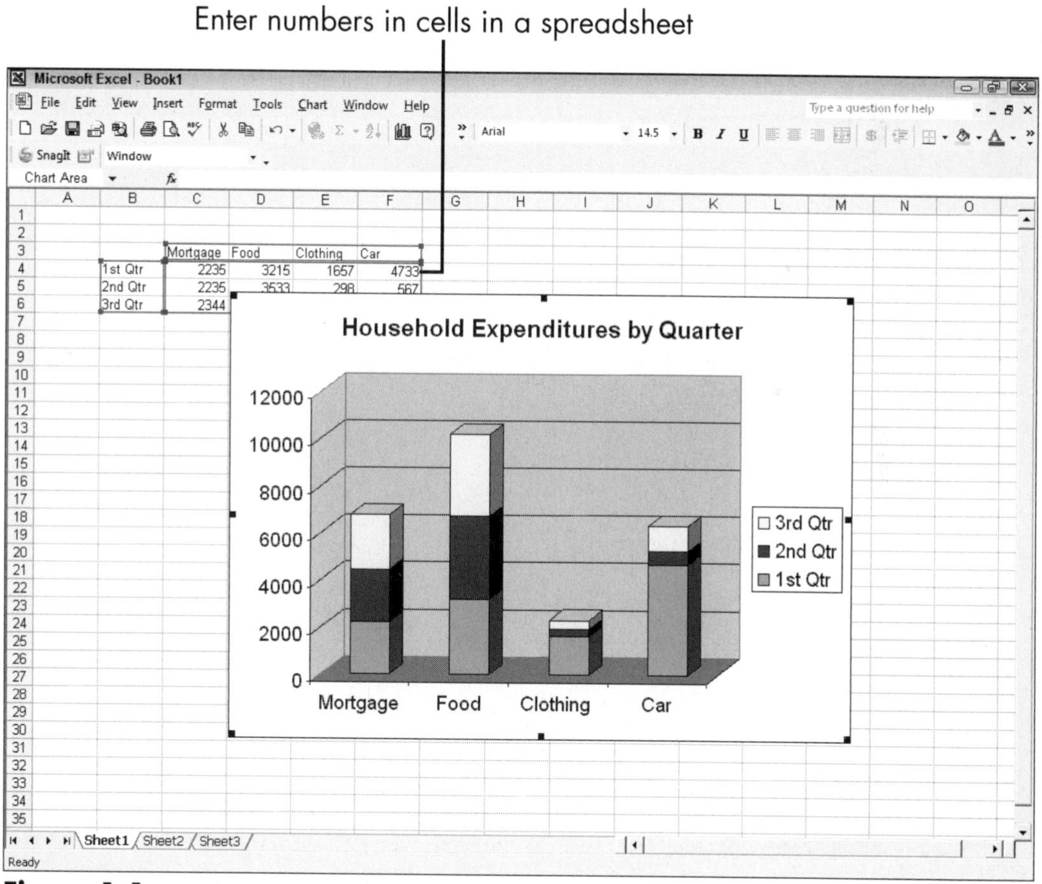

Enter numbers in cells in a spreadsheet

Figure 1-1

Click to view the game details

Figure 1-2

➠ **Play interactive games with others over the Internet.** You can play everything from shuffleboard to poker or action games in virtual worlds.

➠ **Share and create photos, drawings, and videos.** If you have a digital camera, you can transfer photos to your computer (called *uploading*) or copy photos off the Internet and share them in e-mails or use them to create your own greeting cards. If you're artistically inclined, you can create digital drawings. Many popular Web sites make sharing digital movies easy, too. If you have a digital video camera and editing software, you can use editing tools to make a movie and share it with others. Steven Spielberg, look out!

➡ **Shop online and compare products easily, day or night.** You can shop for anything from a garden shed to travel deals or a new camera. Using handy online features, you can easily compare prices from several stores or read customer product reviews. Web sites such as `www.nextag.com` list product prices from a variety of vendors on one Web page, so you can find the best deals. Beyond the convenience, all this information can help you save money.

➡ **Handle your financial life.** You can do your banking or investing online and get up-to-the-minute data about your bank account, credit card balances, and investments.

Understand Hardware and Software

Your computing experience is made up of hardware and software. The hardware is all the tangible computer equipment, such as the keyboard and mouse, and the software is what makes the hardware work or lets you get things done, such as writing documents with Microsoft Word or playing a Solitaire game. Think of the hardware as being like your television set and the shows that you watch as being like the software.

The hardware on your computer consists of

➡ **A central processing unit** (CPU), which is the very small, very high-tech semiconductor *chip* that acts as the brains of your computer. The CPU is stored in a computer tower along with the other nuts and bolts of your computer.

➡ **A monitor,** which displays images on its screen such as the Microsoft Windows Vista desktop or a document in a software program.

➡ **A keyboard,** which is similar to a typewriter keyboard. In addition to typing words, you can use a keyboard to give the computer commands.

➠ **A mouse,** which you also use to give your computer commands, but this little device is more tactile. You move the mouse around your desk with your hand, which moves a pointer around on-screen. Using this pointer, you can click on items like buttons that cause an action, or click on the screen and drag the mouse to select text or an object to perform an action on it (such as deleting it or making the text bold).

➠ **Peripherals,** such as a printer , speakers, webcams, and microphones. These might or might not come with your computer when you buy it, but your computer does come with slots (called *ports*) where you plug in various peripherals.

Software (also known as *programs* or *applications*) is installed on your computer hard drive, which resides in the computer tower. Here are a few basics about software:

➠ **You use software to get your work done, run entertainment programs, and browse the Internet.** For example, Quicken is a financial management program you can use to balance your checkbook or keep track of your home inventory for insurance purposes.

➠ **Some programs come preinstalled on your computer; you can buy and install other programs as you need them.** For example, there is always an operating system on a computer, because it runs all the other programs. Also some programs are included with your operating system, such as Solitaire, an electronic version of the old favorite card game, which comes with Windows Vista. Skype, a program that enables you to make online phone calls using your computer, is a popular program that you can find on the Internet and install on your computer yourself.

➠ **You can uninstall programs you no longer need.** Uninstalling unwanted programs helps to free up some space on your computer, which helps it perform better.

➠ **Some software programs called** *utilities* **exist to keep your computer in shape.** An antivirus program is an example of a utility used to spot and erase computer viruses from your system. Your *operating system* (such as Windows Vista, which you hear more about in the task, "Choose a Version of Windows") also includes some utilities, such as the Windows Defender program. Windows Defender protects your computer from unwanted intrusion by malicious programs called *spyware.* See Part IV for details about using utilities.

Explore Types of Computers

Just as there are many styles of shoes or mobile phones, you can find several styles of computer. Some are small and portable, some use different operating systems to make everything run, and some excel at certain functions such as working with graphics or playing games. This section explains some features you'll need to consider when choosing the type of computer you should buy.

Operating System: Windows Vista is probably the most common computer operating system, and this book mainly focuses on its features. However, Macintosh computers from Apple are also popular. These use Apple-specific software; however, many software applications written for Windows are also available for the Macintosh, and you can also set up your Mac to run the Windows operating system, which gives you the best of both worlds.

Computer Design: Two types of computer you can buy are a laptop and a desktop. Here's the difference:

➠ A *laptop* is portable, weighing anywhere from two to eight pounds. The monitor, keyboard, and mouse are built into the laptop. (Note that if the monitor is damaged, you have to pay quite a bit to have it repaired or hook it up to an external monitor.)

Figure 1-3 shows an example of a laptop, which is sometimes called a *notebook* computer. Choose a laptop if you want to use your computer mainly away from home or you have little space in your home for a larger computer.

➡ *Desktop* models typically have a large tower that contains the computer's processing system (called a CPU), such as the tower shown in **Figure** 1-4. The keyboard, mouse, and monitor are separate. Desktop computers take up more space than a laptop and are not portable, but they're usually less expensive.

Pictures and Sound: If you work with a lot of *visual elements* (for example, photographs, home movies, or computer games), consider a computer that has a better graphics card. Games often involve sound, so a high-end sound card might also be useful. Computers with more sophisticated sound and image capabilities are often referred to as *gaming* or *multimedia* models. Because the capabilities of these cards change all the time, I don't give you the specifications for what's high end; instead, ask the person you're buying the computer from whether the system can handle sophisticated sound and graphics.

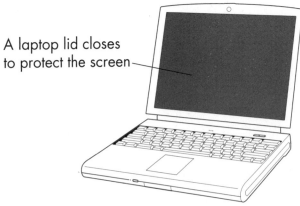

A laptop lid closes to protect the screen

Figure 1-3

A desktop takes up more space

Figure 1-4

Choose a Version of Windows

As mentioned in the previous task, your computer's *operating system* (software that runs all the programs and organizes data on your computer) will be one of your first choices. This book focuses on computers running the current version of Windows, which is called Windows Vista. Vista comes in different versions for home and business users. If you consider yourself primarily a home user, you should consider these two versions of Vista:

➡ **Home Basic** is less expensive but will work just fine for you if you mainly use a computer to send and receive e-mail, browse the Internet, create simple documents such as letters, or view photos. This version also includes important basic security features.

➡ **Windows Vista Home Premium** includes entertainment tools such as Windows Media Center for playing music and movies. If you want to do more than look at photos, you'll find that this version of Vista is better at working with design and image manipulation programs such as Photoshop. Also, if you choose a laptop, be aware that Home Premium includes great features for managing the battery power of your computer.

Before Windows Vista, there was Windows XP. Many people still use computers that run XP and get along just fine. However, Windows XP doesn't come with security tools such as Windows Defender. If you decide to use Windows XP, find a friend or family member who's knowledgeable about computers and can help you use XP features or other software programs that will help keep your computer secure. Note that if you're using XP, some of the steps for common tasks are different than they are if you use Windows Vista; however, you can still use this book to find out about many computer basics.

Choose a Price Range

You can buy a computer for anywhere from US $400 to $5,000 or more, depending on your budget and computing needs. You may start with a base model, but extras such as a larger monitor or higher-end graphics card can soon add hundreds to the base price.

You can shop in a retail store for a computer or shop online using a friend's computer (and perhaps get his or her help if you're brand new to using a computer). Consider researching different models and prices online and using that information to negotiate your purchase in the store if you prefer shopping at the mall. Be aware, however, that most retail stores have a small selection compared to all you can find online on a Web site such as Dell.com.

Buying a computer can be confusing, but here are some guidelines to help you find a computer at the price that's right for you:

➡ **Determine how often you will use your computer.**
If you'll be working on it eight hours a day running a home business, you will need a better quality computer to withstand the use. If you turn on the computer once or twice a week, it doesn't have to be the priciest model in the shop.

➡ **Consider the features that you need.** Do you want (or have room for) a 20-inch monitor? Do you need the computer to run very fast and run several programs at once, or do you need to store tons of data? (Computer speed and storage are covered later in this chapter.) Understand what you need before you buy. Each feature or upgrade adds dollars to your computer's price.

➡ **Shop wisely.** If you walk from store to store or do your shopping online, you'll find that the price for the same computer model can vary by hundreds of dollars at different stores. Also consider shipping costs if you buy online, and keep in mind that many stores charge a restocking fee if you return a computer you aren't happy with.

➡ **Buying used or refurbished is an option,** though new computers have reached such a low price point that this might not save you much. In addition, technology gets out of date so quickly, you might be disappointed buying an older model. Instead, consider going to a company that produces customized, non-name brand computers at lower prices — perhaps even your local computer repair shop. You might be surprised at the bargains you can find (but make sure you're dealing with reputable people before buying).

➡ **Online auctions** are a source of new or slightly used computers at a low price. However be sure you're dealing with a reputable store or person by checking reviews others have posted about them or contacting the Better Business Bureau. Be careful not to pay by check (this gives a complete stranger your bank account number) but instead use the auction site's tools to have a third party handle the money until the goods are delivered in the condition promised. Check the auction site for guidance on staying safe when buying auctioned goods.

Some Web sites, such as Epinions.com, allow you to compare several models of computers side by side, and others such as Nextag.com allow you to compare prices on a particular model from multiple stores.

Select a Monitor

Monitors are the window to your computer's contents. If you're buying a desktop computer, it may come with a monitor that suits your purposes, or you might upgrade to a better monitor. A good monitor can make your computing time easier on your eyes. The crisper the image, the more impressive your vacation photos or that highly visual golf game will be.

Consider these factors when choosing a monitor:

➡ **Size:** Monitors for the average computer user come in all sizes, from tiny 10-inch screens on smaller laptops to 22-inch desktop models. Larger screens are typically more expensive. Although a larger monitor can take up more space side to side and top to bottom, many don't have a bigger *footprint* (that is, how much space their base takes up on your desk) than a smaller monitor.

➡ **Image quality:** The quality can vary greatly. You will see terms such as LCD (liquid crystal display), CRT (cathode ray tube), flat screen, brightness, and resolution. Today CRT screens, though still available, are old technology.

 Look for an LCD monitor, preferably with a flat screen (see **Figure 1-5**) to ease glare.

➡ **Resolution:** A monitor's resolution represents the number of pixels that form the images you see on the screen. The higher the resolution, the crisper the image. You should look for a monitor that can provide at least a 1,024 x 768 pixel resolution.

➡ **Cost:** The least expensive monitor might be the one that comes with a computer package, and many of these are perfectly adequate. You can often upgrade your monitor when you buy if you customize a system from a company such as Dell or Gateway. Monitors purchased separately from a computer can range from around $100 to $3,000 or more. Check out monitors in person to really see whether their image quality and size are worth the money.

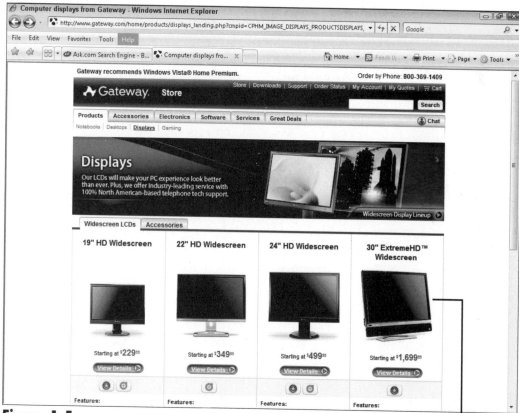

Figure 1-5

A flat screen monitor is trim and reduces glare

Choose an Optical Drive

You've probably used or seen a DVD used to play movies at home. Computers can also read data from or play movies or music from DVDs. Your computer is likely to come with at least one *optical drive*, which is a small drawer that pops out, allowing you to place a DVD in a tray, push the drawer back into the computer, and use the contents of the DVD. If you buy a software program, it will come on a CD or DVD, so you also need this drive to install software.

When you buy a computer, keep these things in mind about optical drives:

➡ **DVDs versus CDs:** DVDs have virtually replaced CDs as the computer storage medium of choice, but you might still find a CD floating around with music or data on it that you need to read. For that reason, you might want a DVD/CD combo drive.

➡ **DVD drives:** DVD drives are rated as Read (R) or Write (W). A readable DVD only allows you to look at data on it, but not save data to it. A writeable DVD allows you to save data (or images, or music) to it. A RW, or read-writeable, DVD drive lets you both read and write to DVDs.

➡ **DVD standards:** In the earliest days of DVDs, there were two different standards, + and -. Some drives could play DVDs formatted + but not those format-ted -, for example. Today, you should look for a DVD drive that is specified as +/- so it can deal with any DVD you throw at it.

Understand Processor Speed and Memory

You computer contains a processor contained on a computer chip. The speed at which your computer runs programs or completes tasks is determined in great measure by your computer processor speed. Processor speed is measured in *gigahertz* (GHz). The higher this meas-urement, the faster the processor. I won't quote the speed you should look for because these chips are constantly getting smaller and contain more and more power. However, when you shop, know that the higher numbers give the best performance and factor that into your decision depending on your needs.

In addition, computers have a certain amount of storage capacity for running programs and storing data. You'll see specifications for RAM and hard drive memory when you go computer shopping. Again the specific numbers will change so the guideline is to look for higher RAM numbers if you feel you need more storage capacity.

➡ RAM is the memory needed to simply access and run programs. RAM chips come in different types, including DRAM, SDRAM, and the latest version, DDR2. Look for a minimum of 1 gigabyte (GB) of RAM for everyday computing.

➡ RAM chips are rated by *clock rate*, which relates to how quickly they can make a request for data from your system. You might see RAM chip speed measured in megahertz (MHz). Today, 667 MHz could be considered an acceptable clock rate.

➡ Your hard drive has a certain capacity for data storage measured in gigabytes (GB). These days you should probably look for a minimum of a 80GB hard drive, but hard drives can come with a range of huge capacities, with the largest being measured in terabytes (TB, measure in thousands of gigabytes).

➡ Your computer will require some RAM to run the operating system; Windows Vista requires 512 megabytes (MB) of RAM and a 20GB hard drive.

Determine How You'll Connect to the Internet

You have to decide how you'll connect to the Internet. You can use a dial-up connection over a standard phone line or pay a fee to get a broadband connection such as DSL. However if you want a wireless connection that works like your cell phone to pick up a signal in certain *hotspots*, you have to be sure to buy a computer with wireless capabilities. Here's how these work:

- **Dial-up:** If you intend to use a dial-up connection (that is, connect over your phone line), your computer has to have a dial-up modem either built in or in an external model. Dial-up connections can be very slow, and while you're using them, you can't use your phone to make or receive calls.

- **Wireless:** Wireless connections require that you have a computer equipped with wireless capability. You can access the Internet wirelessly when you're near a wireless *hotspot* (a place that offers wireless service), and many hotspots are appearing at public places such as hotels, airports, and restaurants. You can also subscribe to a Wireless Wide Area Network (WWAN) service from a mobile phone provider, to tap into its connection. Check the model computer you want to be sure it is wireless-enabled. There are various techy standards for wireless such as 802.11a, b, or g. The very latest standard to look for is 802.11n, which delivers better wireless performance.

- **Broadband:** Broadband connections can be DSL (digital subscriber line) or cable modem. In both cases, you pay a fee to a provider, which might be your phone company or cable company. DSL works over your phone line but doesn't prohibit you from using the phone when you're online. Cable runs over your cable TV line and is a bit faster than DSL, though connections can be less dependable. Both are considered always-on connections, meaning that you don't have to wait to dial up to a phone connection or connect to a wireless network — you're always connected.

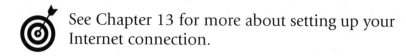 See Chapter 13 for more about setting up your Internet connection.

Buy a Customized Computer

You can buy prepackaged computer systems online or in an electronics store. An alternative is to buy a customized computer. Companies such as Dell and Gateway (see **Figure 1-6**) offer customized computer systems. When you buy the computer, you can pick and choose various features, and the provider will build the system for you.

Click a computer type to begin

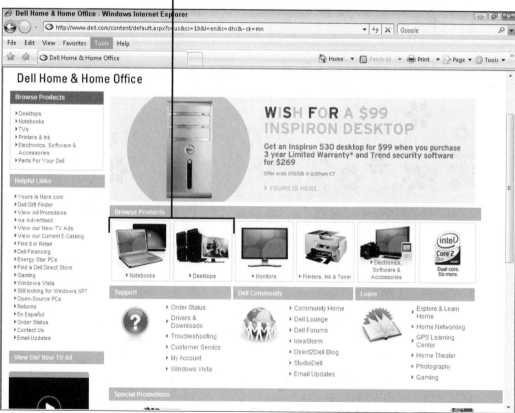

Figure 1-6

Here are some of the variables you'll be asked about when you purchase a customized system, many of which are discussed in this chapter:

➠ Type and speed of processor

➠ Amount of RAM or hard drive capacity

➠ Installed software, such as a productivity suite like Microsoft Office or Microsoft Works, or a premium version of an operating system

➠ More sophisticated graphics or sound cards

➠ Peripherals such as a printer or an upgrade to a wireless mouse or keyboard

➠ Larger or higher-end monitor

➠ Wireless capability

➠ Warranty and technical support

These all add to your final price, so be sure you need an option before you select it. Most of these companies provide explanations of each item to help you decide.

Setting Up Your Computer

*Y*our desktop computer might be a big tower, or perhaps it's built into a single unit with your monitor. It likely has multiple slots and places to plug things in (called *ports*) as well as indicator lights that tell you what's working and what's not.

When you get your personal computer, more often called a *PC*, out of the box, you'll probably find a handy document showing you just where to plug in things, such as your monitor, keyboard, and mouse. Today's computers often color-code plugs, so it's easy to spot where a particular item plugs in. Still, a basic overview of what your computer system is comprised of, how you turn your computer on and off, and how you set up things such as your computer's date and time is helpful to many people. And although all computer models differ somewhat, the information and illustrations in this chapter can help you locate various switches and connectors on your own computer.

If you've never handled a PC before, use the tasks in this chapter to do the following:

➡ Locate connections on the front and back of your computer. You use these connections to hook up your monitor, printer, mouse, keyboard, and more.

→ Turn on your computer, set up your mouse and keyboard functionality, and turn off your computer.

→ Set your computer's screen resolution.

→ Work with user accounts and passwords.

Connect the Monitor, Keyboard, and Mouse

Your computer comes with a monitor, keyboard, and mouse. You should connect these before turning on the computer. Your computer will offer several types of connection ports, though USB ports are becoming the most common for connecting equipment to your computer. Use the following table in conjunction with **Figure 2-1** to identify device-to-PC connector ports.

Connection	Location	What It's Good For
Serial port	1	Connect your monitor.
USB port	2	Connect various USB devices, such as a digital camera.
Parallel port	3	Connect a non-USB printer.
Audio	4	Connect speakers.

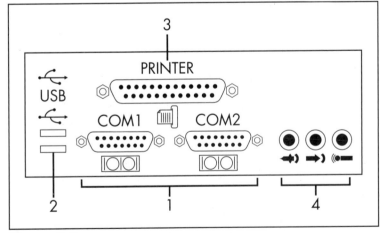

Figure 2-1

Understand Accounts and Passwords

Windows Vista allows you to set up any number of user accounts, if you like. Here's how accounts work:

➡ Accounts retain settings such as startup programs and desktop configuration. Also, each account holder has his or her own sets of folders for storing documents, pictures, and so on.

➡ If you set up one account for yourself and another for a family member, for example, when you log on to Windows with your account, all your settings and files are available to you. The other user can have his or her own settings and they won't affect yours.

➡ You can set up passwords for each account so that others can't access your files, though you aren't required to set up passwords for any account.

➡ You can set up accounts to have administrator privileges, which allows those people using such accounts to make certain system settings, such as changing the level of security or turning security features on and off. Users without such privileges cannot make system changes, which helps protect your computer from deliberate or inadvertent tampering.

Passwords are used both on computers and on the Internet as a way to authenticate a user's right to access an account. If you have set up a password for an account, you must enter a password before you can log on to your computer with that account. Here's some more information about passwords that will be useful:

➡ Passwords must be unique for each account on your computer.

➡ Strong passwords use a combination of letters, numbers, and punctuation. Weak passwords use words that can be found in the dictionary or personal information that is easy to discover, such as your car model, pet's name, or hometown. Nefarious people can use software to search for logical passwords that include common names or words to figure out your password.

➡ If you must write down your password to remember it, keep it in a safe place away from your computer so that others can't find it.

Turn On Your Computer and Log On to Windows

1. With your computer set up, you're ready to turn it on. Start by pressing the power button on your computer to begin the Windows Vista start-up sequence.

2. If this is the first time you've started your computer, you see a screen that guides you through initial setup, which usually includes items such as specifying your country, date and time, and username. Also, your computer manufacturer might have added additional setup steps, such as registering your computer via the Internet.

3. In the following Windows Vista Welcome screen, all user accounts are represented by labeled picture icons. Click the account you want to access.

4. In the following screen, enter your password if you have assigned one and then click the arrow button (or click the Switch User button to return to the previous screen and choose another user to log on as). Windows Vista verifies your password and displays the Windows Vista desktop, as shown in **Figure** 2-2. (**Note:** If you haven't set up the password protection feature when you click an account icon on the Welcome screen, you're taken directly to the Windows Vista desktop. You find out more about adding and changing passwords in the preceding task.)

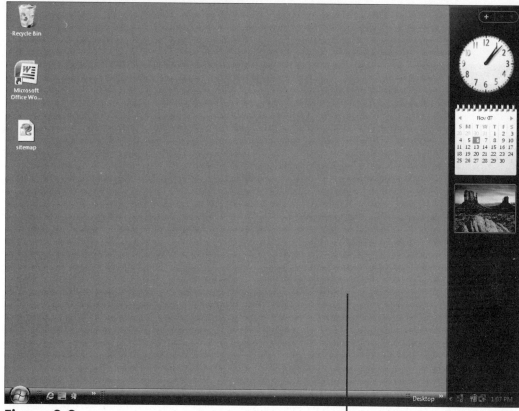

Figure 2-2

The Windows desktop

Use the Mouse

Unlike a typewriter, which uses only a keyboard to enter text into documents, with a computer you use both a keyboard and a mouse to enter text and give commands to the computer. Though you might have used a keyboard of some type before, a mouse might be new to you, and frankly, it takes a little getting used to. In effect, when you move your mouse around on your desk (or in some models, roll a ball on top of the mouse), a corresponding mouse pointer moves around your computer screen. You control the actions of that pointer by using the right and left buttons on the mouse.

Here are the main functions of a mouse and how to control them:

➡ **Clicking:** When people say "click," they mean "press the left mouse button." Clicking has a variety of uses. You can click while in a document to place your mouse cursor, a little line that indicates where your next action will take place. For example, you might click in front of a word you already typed and then type another word to appear before it in a letter. Clicking is also used in various windows to select check boxes or radio buttons to turn features on or off, or to select objects such as a picture or table in your document.

➡ **Right-clicking:** If you click the right mouse button, Windows displays a shortcut menu that is specific to the item you clicked. For example, if you right-click a picture, the menu that appears gives you options for working with the picture. If you right-click the Windows desktop, the menu that appears lets you choose commands that display a different view or change desktop properties.

➡ **Clicking and dragging:** To click and drag, you press and hold down the left mouse button and, while keeping it pressed down, move the mouse to another location. For instance, you can click in a document and drag your mouse up, down, right, or left to highlight contents of your document. This highlighted text is selected, meaning that any action you perform, such as pressing the Delete key on your keyboard or clicking a button for Bold formatting, is performed on the selected text.

➡ **Scrolling:** Many mouse models have a wheel in the center that you can roll up or down to scroll through a document or Web site on your screen. Just roll the wheel down to move through pages going forward, or scroll up to move backward in your document.

Customize the Mouse Settings

1. With your mouse plugged into the correct port, it should work with no further settings required on your part. If you'd like to customize the way your mouse works, choose Start➪Control Panel➪Hardware and Sound. In the resulting Hardware and Sound window, shown in **Figure 2-3**, click the Mouse link.

Click the Mouse link

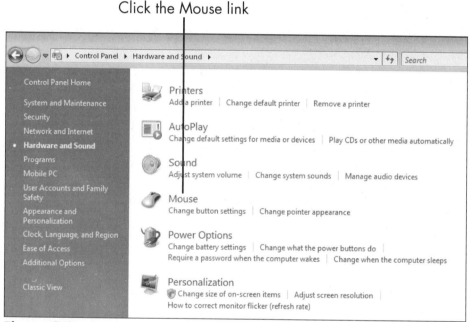

Figure 2-3

2. In the resulting Mouse Properties dialog box, click the Pointer Options tab, as shown in **Figure 2-4**. Then do any of the following:

- Click and drag the Select a Pointer Speed slider to adjust how quickly the mouse cursor moves across your computer screen.

- Select the Automatically Move Pointer to the Default Button in a Dialog Box check box to enable or disable the Snap To feature.

- Select the Display Pointer Trails check box to activate this feature and drag the slider to set the cursor trail style; these are essentially shadows that follow your cursor as it moves across the screen. You can choose to hide the cursor while you're typing.

3. Click OK to apply your changes and close the dialog box.

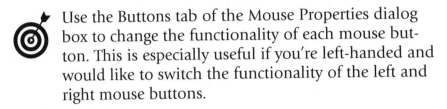 Use the Buttons tab of the Mouse Properties dialog box to change the functionality of each mouse button. This is especially useful if you're left-handed and would like to switch the functionality of the left and right mouse buttons.

Click the Pointer Options tab

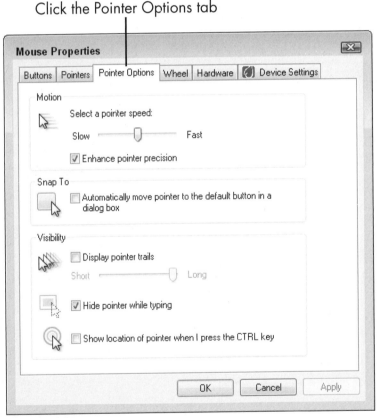

Figure 2-4

Set Up a Windows Password

1. You can assign a password to any account to keep others from being able to log on without your permission. Choose Start➪Control Panel➪User Accounts and Family Safety.

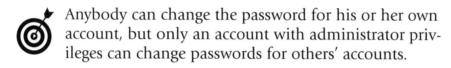 Anybody can change the password for his or her own account, but only an account with administrator privileges can change passwords for others' accounts.

2. In the resulting window shown in **Figure** 2-5, click the Change Your Windows Password link. Then, if you have more than one user account, click the account you want to add the password to. Click the Create a Password for Your Account link.

3. In the Create a Password for Your Account screen, shown in **Figure** 2-6, enter a password, confirm it, and add a password hint.

Click Change Your Windows Password

Figure 2-5

Enter a password

Figure 2-6

If you forget your password, Windows shows the hint you entered to help you remember it, but keep in mind that anybody who uses your computer can see the hint when it's displayed. So, if lots of people know that you drive a Ford and your hint is "My car model," your password protection is about as effective as a thin raincoat in a hurricane.

4. Click the Change Password button.

5. You see the Make Changes to Your User Account window again. If you want to remove your password at some point, you can click the Remove Your Password link here.

 6. Click the Close button to close the User Accounts window.

 After you create a password, you can go to the User Accounts and Family Safety window and change it at any time by clicking the Change Your Windows Password link. You can also change the name on your user account by clicking the Change Your Account Name link in the User Accounts and Family Safety window.

Set Up Additional User Accounts

1. When you set up your computer, you create your user account. If you want to create additional accounts, you can follow these steps. Choose Start⇨Control Panel.

2. In the resulting Control Panel window, click the Add or Remove User Accounts link.

3. In the resulting Manage Accounts window, shown in **Figure** 2-7, click the Create a New Account link.

4. In the Manage Accounts window that appears, shown in **Figure** 2-8, enter an account name and then select the type of account you want to create:

• **Standard user,** who can't do the tasks an administrator can.

- **Administrator,** who can do things like create and change accounts and install programs. Typically, it's a good idea to allow only one person to have administrator privileges to avoid confusion.

5. Click the Create Account button and then close the Control Panel.

 After you create an account, you can make changes to it, such as assigning a password or changing the account type, by double-clicking it in the Manage Accounts window you reached in Step 4 of the preceding step list and following the links listed there.

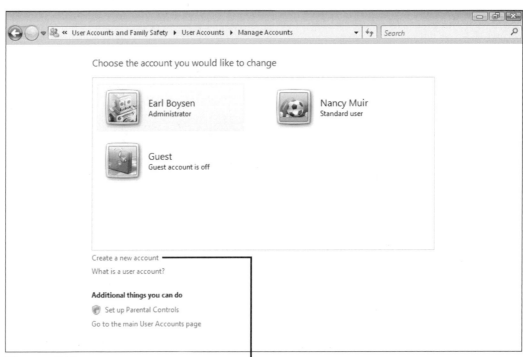

Figure 2-7

Click Create a New Account

Choose an account type

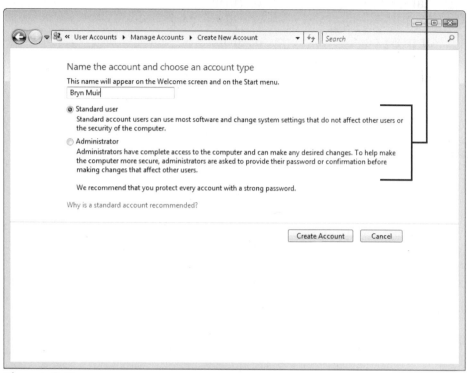

Figure 2-8

Switch User Accounts

1. If you're logged on to one account and then decide to open a different account (you can have only one open at a time), you use a simple process to switch accounts. Click Start and then click the arrow next to the Lock button (see **Figure 2-9**).

2. Choose Switch User. In the resulting window, click the username you want to log in as.

3. If the user account is password-protected, a box appears for you to enter the password. Type the password and then click the arrow button to log in.

If you forget your password and try to switch users without entering one, Windows shows your password hint, which you can create when you assign a password to help you remember it.

4. Windows logs you in with the specified user's settings.

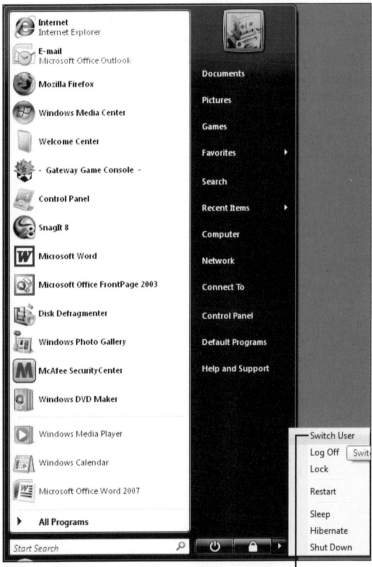

Figure 2-9

Choose Switch User

Change Your User Account Picture

1. If you don't like the picture associated with your user account, you can change it. Choose Start⇨Control Panel⇨Add or Remove User Accounts

2. Click the account you want to change.

3. In the resulting window, click the Change Your Picture link and click another picture (or browse to see more picture choices) to select it.

4. Click the Change Picture button; the dialog box closes.

Set the Date and Time

1. The date and clock on your computer keep good time, but you might have to provide the correct date and time for your location. To get started, press the Windows key on your keyboard to display the taskbar if it isn't visible.

2. Right-click the Date/Time display on the far right of the taskbar and then choose Adjust Date/Time from the shortcut menu that appears.

3. In the Date and Time dialog box that appears (see **Figure 2-10**), click the Change Date and Time button.

4. In the Date and Time Settings dialog box that appears (see **Figure 2-11**) click on a new date in the Date calendar. Enter a new time in the Time text box to change the time or use the spinner arrows to choose a different time.

5. Click OK twice to apply the new settings and close the dialog box.

If you don't want your computer to adjust for Daylight Saving Time, click the Change Time Zone button and deselect the Automatically Adjust Clock for Daylight Saving Time check box to turn off this feature.

 Another option for displaying the time or date is to add the Clock or Calendar gadget to the Windows Sidebar. You can also drag gadgets right onto your desktop if you prefer not to leave the Sidebar displayed. See Chapter 3 for more about using the Sidebar and gadgets.

Click the Change Date and Time button

Figure 2-10

Select a date   Set the time

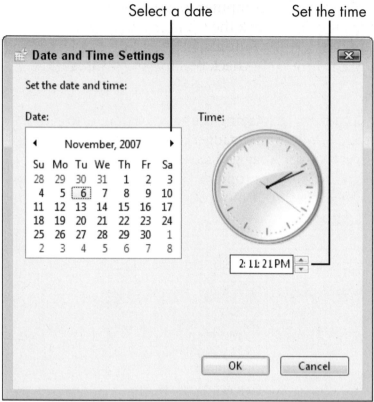

Figure 2-11

Set the Screen Size (Resolution)

1. Screen resolution controls the number of little dots (called *pixels*) that make up the images on your screen. Different screen resolution settings can also make what's on-screen look larger or smaller. Resolution is expressed with two numbers, such as 1,024 x 780. The smaller the resolution numbers, the bigger things appear on-screen, but the less space you have for placing windows side-by-side, for example. If you want to change your resolution, test a few settings until you find one you like. To start, right-click the desktop to display a shortcut menu and then choose Personalize.

2. In the resulting Personalization window, click the Display Settings link.

3. In the Display Settings dialog box that appears (as shown in **Figure 2-12**), move the Resolution slider to a higher or lower resolution. You can also choose how many colors your computer uses for display by making a choice in the Colors drop-down list.

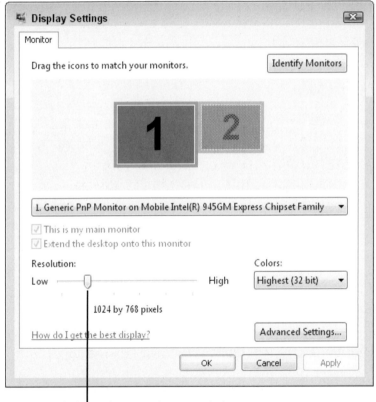

Click and drag the Resolutions slider
Figure 2-12

 Higher resolutions, such as 1,400 x 1,250, produce smaller, crisper images. Lower resolutions, such as 800 x 600, produce larger, somewhat jagged images. The upside of higher resolution is that more fits on your screen; the downside is that words and graphics can be hard to see.

The Color Quality setting on the Settings tab of the Display Properties dialog box offers two settings. The lower color quality is 16-bit; the higher is 32-bit. Essentially, the higher the bits, the more color definition you get.

4. Click OK to accept the new screen resolution.

 Remember that you can also use your View settings in most software programs to get a larger or smaller view of your documents without having to change your screen's resolution.

Set Up Your Keyboard

1. Adjusting your keyboard settings might make it easier for you to type, and it can be helpful to people with dexterity challenges. To see your options, choose Start⇨Control Panel⇨Hardware and Sound. In the resulting Hardware and Sound window, click the Keyboard link.

2. In the Keyboard Properties dialog box that appears, click the Speed tab (see **Figure 2-13**) and drag the sliders to adjust the two Character Repeat settings, which do the following:

• **Repeat Delay:** Affects the amount of time it takes before a typed character is typed again when you hold down a key.

• **Repeat Rate:** Adjusts how quickly a character repeats when you hold down a key after the first repeat character appears.

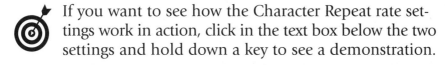 If you want to see how the Character Repeat rate settings work in action, click in the text box below the two settings and hold down a key to see a demonstration.

3. Drag the slider in the Cursor Blink Rate section. This affects cursors, such as the insertion line that appears in text.

4. Click OK to save and apply changes and close the dialog box.

 If you have trouble with motion (for example, because of arthritis or carpal tunnel syndrome), you might find that you can adjust these settings to make it easier for you to get your work done. For example, if you can't pick up your finger quickly from a key, a slower repeat rate might save you from typing more instances of a character than you'd intended.

Click and drag the sliders

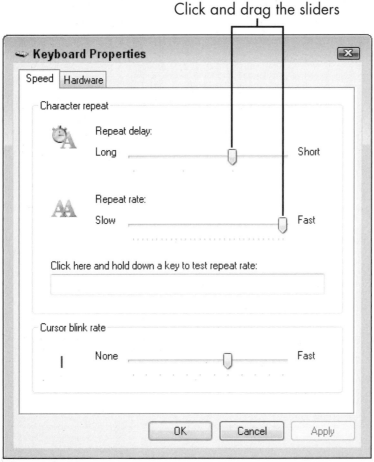

Figure 2-13

Turn Off Your Computer

1. To turn off your computer when you're done, you need to initiate a shut down sequence in your operating system instead of simply turning off the power. Choose Start and click the arrow to the right of the button with a lock on it at the bottom right of the Start menu.

2. In the resulting shortcut menu, as shown in **Figure 2-14**, choose Shut Down. Windows Vista closes, and the computer turns off. Turning off your computer through the shut down process helps your computer close out of any processes it's doing behind the scenes so you don't lose data or settings.

> You can also choose Restart to turn off and then immediately turn on your computer. You would use this setting if your computer is having problems and you want your system to reset or if you install new software or make new settings and are instructed to restart your computer.

> The Sleep option on the shortcut menu in Step 2 is like letting your computer take a nap. The screen goes dark, and in the case of laptops, power consumption lowers. By clicking your mouse button or pressing Enter on your keyboard, you can wake up your computer again with everything just as you left it.

> When you turn off your computer, peripherals such as your monitor or printer don't turn off automatically. You have to press their power buttons to turn each off manually.

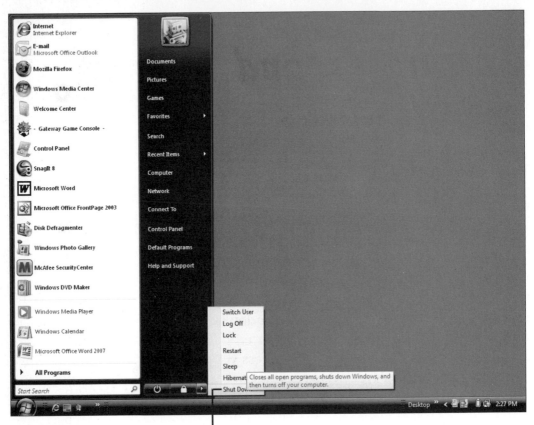

Figure 2-14

Click Shut Down

Getting around the Windows Desktop

*J*ust as your desk is the central area from which you do all kinds of work, the Windows Vista desktop is a command center for organizing your computer work. The desktop appears when you log on to a Windows Vista computer. The Start menu is located on the desktop; you use this menu to access your computer settings, files, folders, and software. On the desktop, there is also a taskbar that offers settings, such as your computer's date and time, as well as shortcuts to your most frequently accessed programs or files.

This chapter is an introduction to all the things you can do via the desktop. Along the way, you discover the Recycle Bin, where you place deleted files and folders, and the Quick Launch bar, which allows quick access to commonly used programs. You also find out how to work with application windows, create a desktop shortcut, and shut down your computer when you're done for the day.

Understand the Desktop

Think of the desktop as the mother of all the windows that you can open on your computer to get your work done. The desktop appears when you first turn on your computer. You can use various elements of the desktop to open or manage files, access settings for Windows, go online, and more. **Figure 3-1** shows the desktop and some of the elements on it, including the following:

➡ **The taskbar** is home to the Start menu. Currently open programs are listed here, and you can click on one to switch programs. Finally, you can work with various settings such as the volume control using icons displayed on the taskbar.

➡ **The Quick Launch bar** is a set of icons within the taskbar that you use to open frequently used programs. You can customize the Quick Launch bar to contain any programs you want. See the section "Customize the Quick Launch Bar" later in this chapter.

➡ **The Recycle Bin** holds recently deleted items. It will empty itself when it reaches its maximum size (which you can modify by right-clicking the Recycle Bin and choosing Properties), or you can do so manually. Check out the section "Empty the Recycle Bin" later in this chapter for more about this.

➡ **Desktop shortcuts** are icons that reside on the desktop and provide a shortcut to opening a software program or file. Your computer usually comes with some shortcuts, such as the Recycle Bin and a browser shortcut, but you can also add or delete shortcuts. Click a desktop shortcut to launch an associated program. See the "Create a Shortcut to a File or Folder" section later in this chapter.

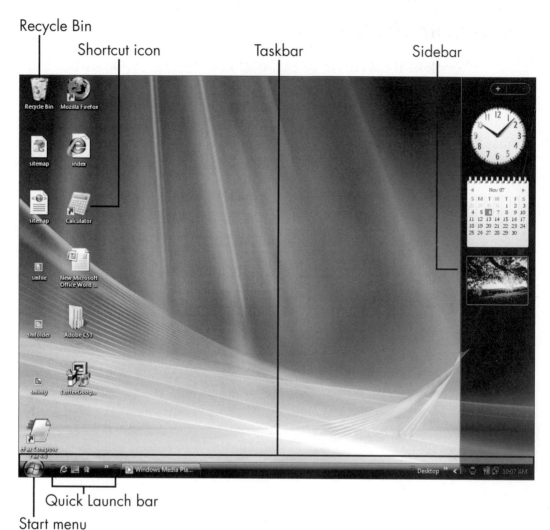

Recycle Bin

Shortcut icon

Taskbar

Sidebar

Quick Launch bar

Start menu

Figure 3-1

⟶ **The Sidebar** can be displayed on your desktop, providing you with handy little tools called *gadgets*. Some built-in gadgets include a stock ticker, a clock, and a calculator, but you can also download lots of other gadgets from the Office Web site. The section "Set Up Windows Sidebar," later in this chapter, explains how to get started with the Sidebar.

The desktop is always there as you open program windows to get your work done. If you make a program window as big as it can be (*maximize* it), you won't see the desktop, but you can go back to the desktop at any time by shrinking a window (minimize it) or closing windows. You can also press Alt+Tab simultaneously and choose the desktop from the open programs icons in the window that appears.

Work with the Start Menu

 1. Press the Windows key on your keyboard or click the Start button on the desktop to display the Start menu.

2. From the Start menu, you can do any of the following:

- Click a frequently used program in the left pane of the Start menu. (See **Figure 3-2**.)

- Click All Programs to display a list of all programs on your computer. You can click any program in the list to open it or click a program folder to see more options.

- Click any category in the upper-right section of the Start menu to display a Windows Explorer window with related folders and files (see **Figure 3-3**).

- Click the Power Button icon to put the computer to sleep but keep current programs running, or click the Lock icon to go to the log on screen; if your account requires password to open it, only somebody who knows the password can now open Windows.

- Click the arrow next to the Lock icon to display a menu of choices for shutting down or restarting your computer, for logging off, or for logging in as a different user.

3. When you move your cursor away from the Start menu, the menu disappears.

Click a frequently used program

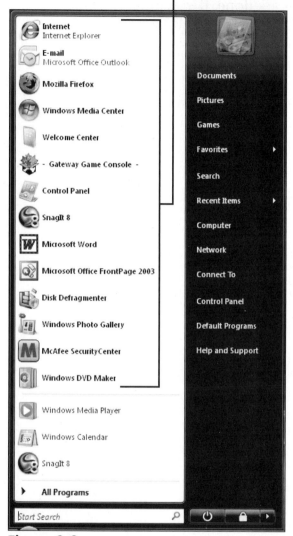

Figure 3-2

 If you open the Start menu and right-click in a blank
area of the menu, a shortcut menu pops up. Choose
Properties to display the Taskbar and Start Menu
Properties dialog box, where you can customize the
Start menu behavior. If you would rather use the look
and feel of the Start menu in older versions of
Windows, select Classic Start Menu in the Taskbar

and Start Menu Properties dialog box and then click OK. (Note that this book deals only with the Windows Vista style Start menu features.)

Files in the Picture folder

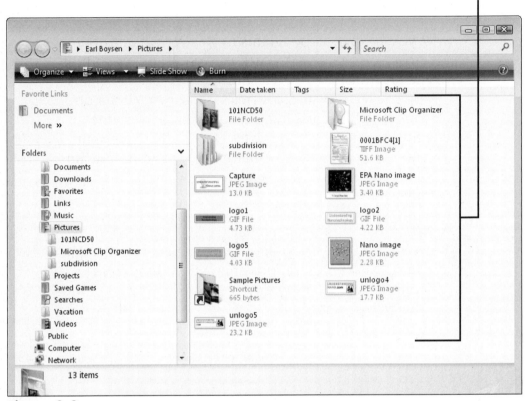

Figure 3-3

Customize the Quick Launch Bar

1. The Quick Launch bar can be a handy tool for starting programs, and you can customize it to contain the programs you use most often. Locate the Quick Launch bar on the taskbar just to the right of the Start button; if it's not visible, right-click the taskbar and choose Toolbars⇨ Quick Launch from the shortcut menu (see **Figure 3-4**).

2. To place any application on the Quick Launch bar, right-click that application in the Start menu or on the desktop (as shown in **Figure** 3-5) and then choose Add to Quick Launch. You can also click an icon, and while keeping the mouse button pressed, drag that icon to the Quick Launch bar.

If you have more programs in this area than can be shown on the taskbar, click the arrows to the right of the Quick Launch bar; a shortcut menu of programs appears. However, don't create too much clutter on your Quick Launch bar; if you do, it can become unwieldy. Logical candidates to place here are your Internet browser, your e-mail program, and programs that you use every day, such as a word processor or calendar program.

When the Quick Launch bar is displayed, the Show Desktop button is available. When you click this button, all open applications are reduced to taskbar icons. It's a quick way to view your desktop — or hide what you're up to!

Click Toolbars...   Then click Quick Launch

Figure 3-4

Right-click a program in the Start menu

Figure 3-5

Arrange Icons on the Desktop

1. After you use your computer for a while, you might find the desktop becomes cluttered with icons. You can sort the icons in neat rows based on a criterion, such as the most recently used to the least recently used. First right-click the desktop and choose View in the resulting shortcut menu; be sure that Auto Arrange isn't selected, as shown in **Figure** 3-6. (If it is selected, deselect it before proceeding to the next step.)

2. Right-click the Windows Vista desktop. In the resulting shortcut menu, choose Sort By and then choose the criterion for sorting your desktop icons (see **Figure** 3-7). For example, you can arrange them alphabetically by name or from smallest file to the largest file.

3. You can also click any desktop icon and drag it to another location on the desktop — for example, to separate it from other desktop icons so you can find it easily.

 If you've sorted or manually rearranged your desktop by moving items hither, thither, and yon and you want to instantly move your icons into orderly rows along the left side of your desktop, snap them into place with the Auto Arrange feature. Right-click the desktop and then choose View⇨Auto Arrange.

Auto Arrange should not be selected

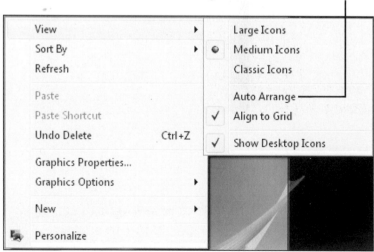

Figure 3-6

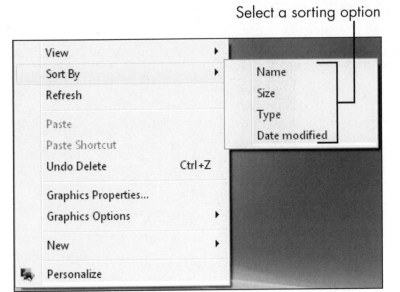

Select a sorting option

View	▶
Sort By	▶
Refresh	
Paste	
Paste Shortcut	
Undo Delete	Ctrl+Z
Graphics Properties...	
Graphics Options	▶
New	▶
Personalize	

Sort By submenu:
- Name
- Size
- Type
- Date modified

Figure 3-7

Empty the Recycle Bin

1. When you throw away junk mail, it's still in the house —
it's just in the trash bin instead of on your desk. That's the
idea behind the Windows Recycle Bin. Your old files sit
there, and you can retrieve them until you empty it or
until it reaches its size limit and Windows dumps a few
files. To empty the trash yourself, right-click the Recycle
Bin icon on the Windows Vista desktop and choose
Empty Recycle Bin from the shortcut menu that appears
(see **Figure** 3-8).

2. In the confirmation dialog box that appears, click Yes to
confirm that you want to delete the items. A progress dialog box appears indicating the contents are being deleted.
Remember that after you empty the Recycle Bin, all files
previously in it are unavailable to you. Chapter 5 has
more details about deleting files.

Choose Empty Recycle Bin

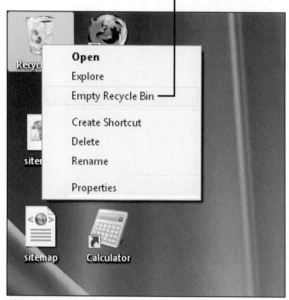

Figure 3-8

 Up until the moment you permanently delete items by performing the preceding steps or until Windows deletes files because the Recycle Bin has reached its capacity, you can retrieve items in the Recycle Bin. Start by right-clicking the desktop icon and choosing Open. Then select the item you want to retrieve and then click the Restore This Item link near the top of the Recycle Bin window.

 You can modify the Recycle Bin properties by right-clicking it and choose Properties. In the dialog box that appears, you can change the maximum size for the Recycle Bin, and where it should be stored on your hard drive. You can also deselect the option of having a confirmation dialog box appear when you delete Recycle Bin contents.

Set Up Windows Sidebar

1. To get started with the Sidebar and the useful gadgets that it holds, choose Start⇨Control Panel⇨Appearance and Personalization⇨Choose Whether to Keep Sidebar on Top of Other Windows (in the Windows Sidebar Properties category) to open the Windows Sidebar Properties dialog box.

2. Select the Sidebar Is Always on Top of Other Windows check box. If you like, you can also enable the Start Sidebar When Windows Starts option to ensure that the Sidebar always displays when you start your computer.

 If you're left handed or have some other propensity for things on the left, you can choose to have the Sidebar displayed on the left side of the screen by selecting the Left radio button in the Windows Sidebar Properties dialog box.

 3. Click OK and then click the Close button (the little red X in the upper-right corner) to close the Control Panel window. The Sidebar appears, as shown in **Figure 3-9**. (Note that you can also click the Sidebar icon on the Windows taskbar to instantly display the Sidebar at any time.)

4. Click a displayed gadget and drag it to the desktop if you want it to stay there even when the Sidebar is closed.

5. To display more gadgets, click the Gadgets symbol (a plus sign) at the top of the Sidebar.

6. In the resulting Add Gadgets dialog box (see **Figure 3-10**), double-click a gadget (or click and drag it to the Sidebar). If you need to view additional gadgets, click the Get More Gadgets Online link in the lower-right corner of the dialog box.

7. Click the Close button to close the dialog box.

 If you display gadgets and then click and drag them onto the desktop, even if you close the Sidebar, they stay visible. So if you want to save desktop space, find the gadgets you like, plop them on your desktop, and hide the Sidebar!

Click to display the Add Gadgets dialog box

Gadgets in the Sidebar

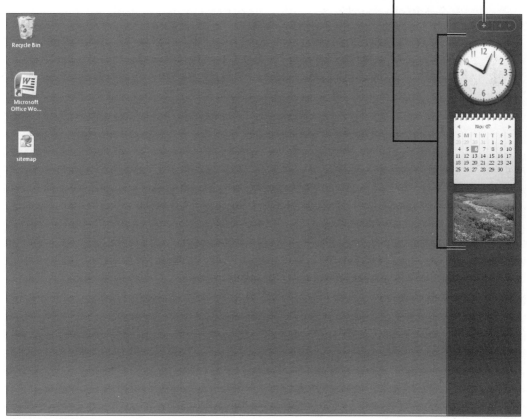

Figure 3-9

Figure 3-10

Double-click a gadget to add it

Find a File with Windows Explorer

1. Windows Explorer is a program you can use to find a file or folder by navigating through an outline of folders and subfolders. It's a great way to look for files on your computer. To get started, right-click the Start menu and choose Explore.

2. In the resulting Windows Explorer window, shown in **Figure 3-11**, double-click a folder in the Folder list on the left to open the folder.

3. The folder's contents are displayed in a pane on the right side of the window. If necessary, open a series of folders in this right pane until you locate the file you want.

4. When the file you want appears in the list of items in the Name column in the right pane, double-click its icon to open it.

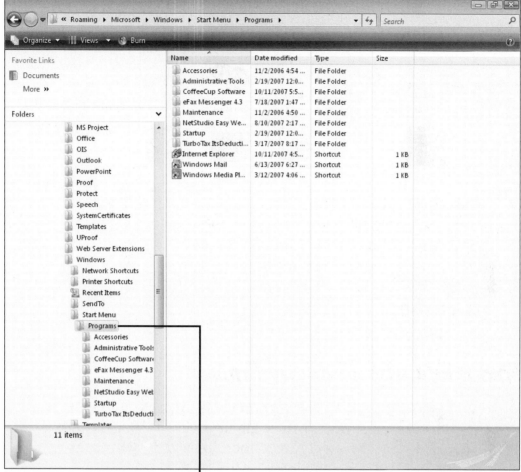

Figure 3-11

Double-click a folder to open it

To see different perspectives and information about files in Windows Explorer, click the arrow on the Views button at the top (it looks like series of columns) and choose one of the following menu options: Extra Large, Large, Medium, or Small Icons for graphical displays; Details to show details such as Date Modified and Size; and Tiles to show the file/folder name, type, and size. If you're working with a folder containing graphics files, the graphics automatically display as thumbnails unless you choose Details.

 You can open commonly used folders from the Start menu, including Documents, Pictures, and Music. Click one of these, and Windows Explorer opens that particular window.

Create a Shortcut to a File or Folder

1. Shortcuts are handy little icons you can put on the desktop for quick access to items you use on a frequent basis. (See this chapter's first section, "Understand the Desktop," for an introduction to shortcuts.) To create a new shortcut, first choose Start⇨All Programs and locate the program on the menu that appears.

2. Right-click an item, FreeCell for example, and choose Send To⇨Desktop (Create Shortcut) (see **Figure 3-12**).

3. The shortcut appears on the desktop (see **Figure 3-13**). Double-click the shortcut icon to open the application.

 You can create a shortcut for a brand new item by right-clicking the desktop, choosing New, and then choosing an item to place there, such as a text document, bitmap image, or contact. Then double-click the shortcut that appears and begin working on the file in the associated application.

 Occasionally, Windows Vista offers to delete desktop icons that you haven't used in a long time. Let it. The desktop should be reserved for frequently used programs, files, and folders. You can always re-create shortcuts easily if you need them again. To clean up your desktop manually, right-click the desktop and choose Personalize. In the Personalization window that appears, click the Change Desktop Icons link in the Tasks list on the left. In the Desktop Icons setting dialog box that appears, click the Restore Default button, which returns to the original desktop shortcuts set up on your computer.

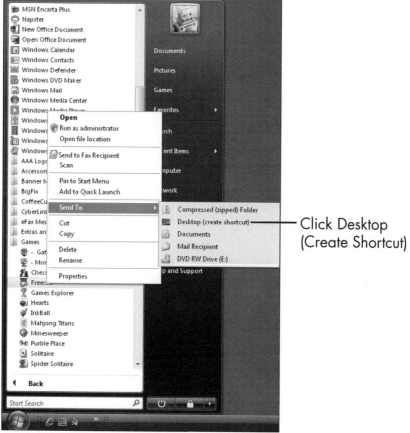

Click Desktop
(Create Shortcut)

Figure 3-12

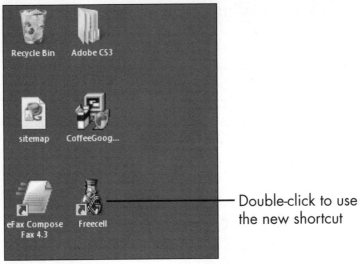

Double-click to use
the new shortcut

Figure 3-13

Start a Program

1. Before you can use a program, you have to start it (also
   called *launching* a program). Launch a program by using
   any of the following four methods:

   • Press the Windows key on your keyboard and choose
     All Programs. Locate the program name on the All
     Programs list that appears and click it. Clicking an item
     with a folder icon displays a list of programs within it;
     just click the program on that sublist to open it (as
     shown in **Figure** 3-14).

   • Double-click a program shortcut icon on the desktop
     (see **Figure** 3-15).

   • Click a program icon on the Quick Launch bar, located
     on the taskbar. The taskbar should display by default; if
     it doesn't, press the Windows key (on your keyboard) to
     display it, and then click an icon on the Quick Launch
     bar (refer to Figure 3-1), just to the right of the Start
     button. If the Quick Launch bar is not displayed, see

"Customize the Quick Launch Bar" earlier in this chapter for details.

- If you used the program recently and saved a document, choose Recent Items from the Start menu. Then click a document created in that program from the list that displays. (See Chapter 5 for information about displaying recently used files on the Start menu.)

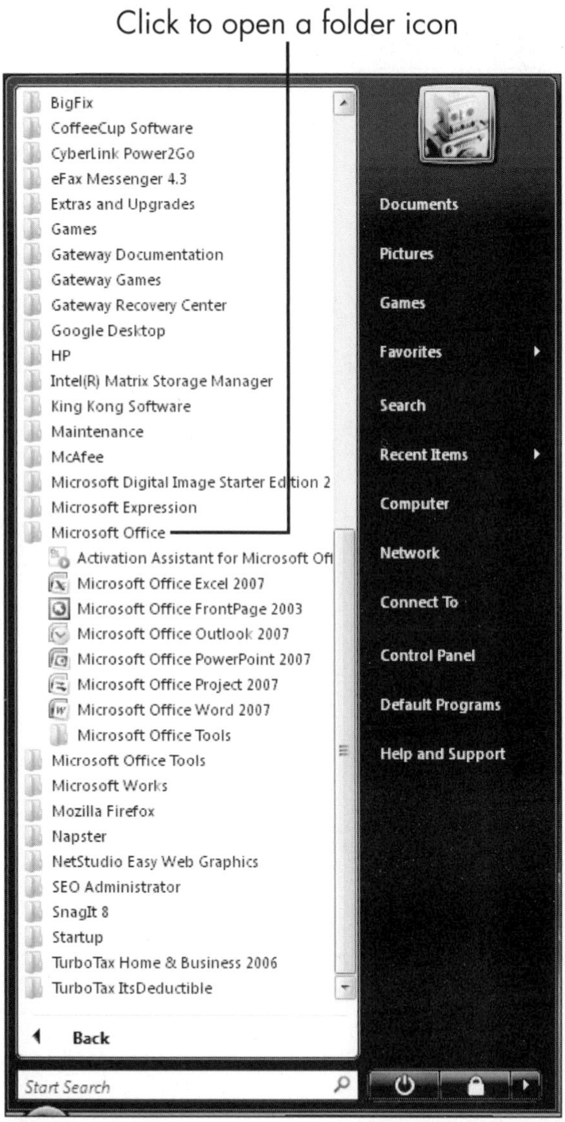

Click to open a folder icon

Figure 3-14

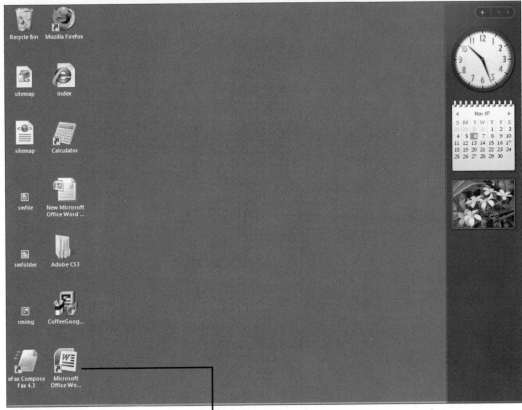

Figure 3-15

Double-click a desktop shortcut

2. When the application opens, if it's a game, play it; if it's a spreadsheet, enter numbers into it; if it's your e-mail program, start deleting junk mail. . . . You get the idea.

Switch between Programs

1. You can have two or more programs, or two or more windows in a single program, open on your desktop. The last program that you worked in is the active program. To switch between open programs easily, hold down the Alt key while pressing Tab.

2. A small box opens, as shown in **Figure 3-16**, revealing all opened programs.

Press tab to select another open program in this list

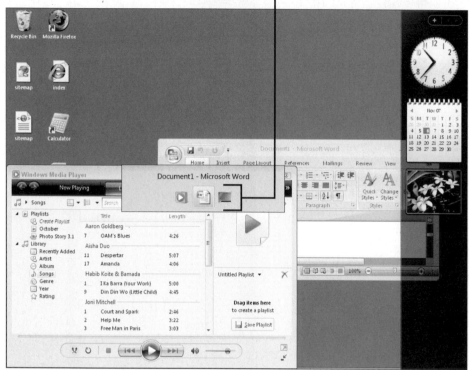

Figure 3-16

3. Release the Tab key but keep Alt pressed down. Press Tab to cycle through the icons representing open programs.

4. When you release the Alt key, Windows Vista switches to whichever program is selected. To switch back to the last program that was active, simply press Alt+Tab, and that program becomes the active program once again.

 All open programs also appear as items on the Windows Vista taskbar. Just click any running program on the taskbar to display that window and make it the active program. If the taskbar isn't visible, press the Windows key on your keyboard to display the taskbar.

Resize a Window

1. You can make windows bigger or smaller to focus on the one you're working in or to see more than one at a time. One way to resize windows is to click the Restore Down button (the icon showing two overlapping windows) in the top-right corner of a program window. The window reduces in size.

2. To enlarge a window that has been restored down to again fill the screen, click the Maximize button (see **Figure 3-17**). (*Note:* This button is in the same location as the Restore Down button; this button toggles to one or the other, depending on whether you have the screen reduced in size or maximized. A ScreenTip identifies the button when you pass your mouse over it.)

3. To size a window more precisely, click and drag any corner of a reduced window. By doing this, you can resize it manually.

With a window maximized, you can't move the window. If you reduce a window in size, you can then click and hold the title bar to drag the window around the desktop, which is one way to view more than one window on your screen at the same time.

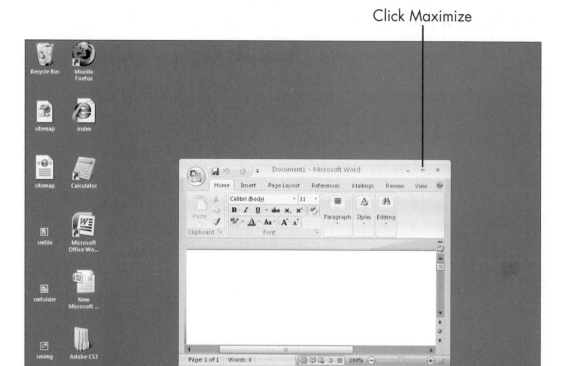

Click Maximize

Figure 3-17

Close a Program

1. When you're done with a program, you can close it. With an application open, first save any open documents and then close them by using one of these methods:

- Click the Close button in the upper-right corner of the window. If two or more instances of the program are open in separate windows, this closes the document and its current window but not the application.

- Choose File⇨Exit (see **Figure 3-18**).

Choose the Exit command

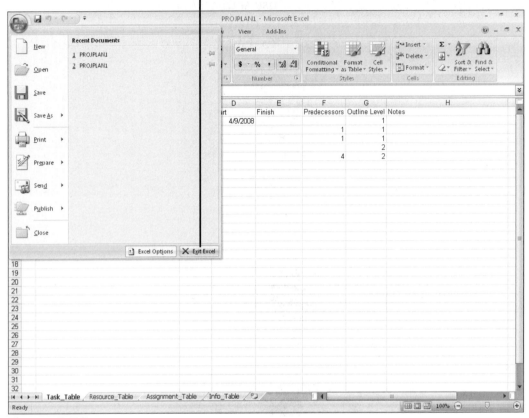

Figure 3-18

 Note that choosing File⇨Exit closes all open documents in an application as well as the application. Choose File⇨Close to close only the currently active document and keep the application and any other open documents open.

2. The application closes. If you haven't saved any documents before trying to close the application, you see a dialog box asking whether you want to save the document. Click Yes or No, depending on whether you want to save your changes.

To save a document before closing an application, choose File➪Save and use settings in the resulting Save dialog box to name the file and also specify which folder to save it to. Chapter 5 explains in more detail how to save files.

Customizing Windows

Chapter 4

*T*ake it from somebody who spends many hours in front of a computer: Customizing the way Windows looks and feels pays off by making your computer easier to use as well as decreasing eyestrain. In addition, you get a computer that looks and performs the way you want it to.

Not only can you change the appearance of your desktop to use colors and images that are pleasing to you, but you can also set up the way your keyboard and mouse work and turn on accessibility features that help you if you have vision, hearing, or mobility challenges.

To customize how Windows Vista appears or works, for example, you can do the following:

➡ Change the desktop background to show different colors or images. You can even pick a preset theme that combines a color scheme and desktop background image in pleasing combinations.

➡ Set up the sharpness with which Windows Vista displays images and colors.

➡ Use screen saver settings to display the photo from your bike trip through France or an interesting animation. You can set a screen saver to appear when you stop using your computer for a certain period of time, which is useful to keep whatever project you're working on private.

➟ Make things on the screen easier to see. For example, you can make the color contrast higher.

➟ Modify the way the mouse works for left-handed use, change the cursor to sport a certain look, or make the cursor easier to view as it moves around your screen.

➟ Work with keyboard settings that make typing and choosing computer commands easier for people who are challenged by physical conditions, such as carpal tunnel syndrome or arthritis. You can even use a Speech Recognition feature that enables the computer to type what you say so you can avoid using a keyboard or mouse entirely.

The Many Ways to Customize Windows

Windows comes with certain preset, or *default*, programs and settings such as the appearance of the desktop, how you use the mouse and keyboard to give your computer commands, and the software that's installed when you take your computer out of the box. Here are some of the things you can change about the Windows environment and why you might want to change them:

➟ As you work with your computer, you might find that changing the appearance of various elements on your screen not only makes it more pleasant to look at, but also helps you see the text and images more easily. Windows has built-in *themes* that you can apply quickly. Themes save sets of elements that include menu appearance, background colors or patterns, screen savers, and even mouse cursors and system sounds. If you choose a theme and then modify the way your computer looks in some way — for example, by changing the color scheme — that change overrides the setting in the theme you last applied.

➡ Screen savers are animations that appear after your computer has remained inactive for a time. In the early days of personal computers, screen savers helped to keep your monitor from burning out from constant use. That problem no longer exists, but many people like to use a screen saver to automatically conceal what they're doing from passers by.

➡ A mouse is set up by default to work best for right-handed users, but you can modify a mouse to work with your left hand and change how actions like clicking and dragging work (for example, if you have arthritis, you may not be able to click and drag quickly, so you can change the setting to work with your limitations).

➡ You can change how your keyboard works; for example, modifying how you hold down multiple keys for keystroke shortcuts such as Alt+Tab. If you're a slow typist, this setting can come in handy. You can also display an on-screen keyboard so you can click keys with your mouse, rather than your fingers.

➡ For people with manual dexterity challenges, you can use Speech Recognition, a feature of Windows that allows you to speak commands and text entries, rather than using your mouse and keyboard.

➡ If your challenge is in the hearing department, you can have Windows replace the sounds it plays to notify you of various actions it performs, such as closing a program, with visual clues.

➡ If your computer has certain software applications installed that you don't need, it's nice to be able to uninstall them so you have only the applications you

use on your system. This also saves some system
memory you can use for other software applications.

Change the Desktop Background

1. The desktop background can consist of a solid color or a
   photo or graphical image. You can choose your background and modify how it is displayed by accessing the
   Windows Control Panel. You can go to the desktop settings quickly by right-clicking the desktop and choosing
   Personalize from the shortcut menu.

2. In the resulting Personalization window, click the
   Desktop Background link to display the Desktop
   Background dialog box, as shown in **Figure** 4-1.

3. Select a category of desktop background options from the
   Picture Location drop-down list to display previews of
   certain types if images:

   • Windows Wallpapers are photos and graphical back-
     grounds Microsoft has built into Windows Vista.

   • Pictures opens your Pictures folder, allowing you to use
     one of your own images as your desktop background. In
     Figure 4-2, I've chosen a photo as a background.

   • Sample Pictures allows you to choose from samples
     included in your Sample Pictures folder, which is
     located in your Pictures folder.

   • Public Pictures allows you to browse to locate any
     image on your computer or computer network in the
     Public folder.

   • Solid Colors allows you to choose from a palette of pre-
     selected colors.

Select a location   Click a picture

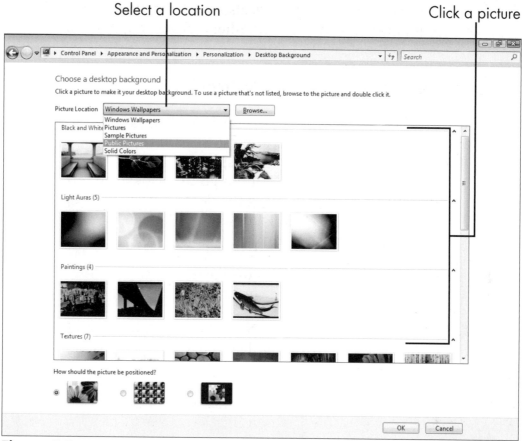

Figure 4-1

4. Click the image you want to use. The background is previewed on your desktop.

5. If you select an option other than Solid Colors, you can also control whether one large image or several smaller images appear and whether the image is centered. From the positioning options at the bottom of the dialog box, select one of the following:

- **Fit to Screen:** This option stretches one copy of the image to fill the screen, covering any background color completely.

- **Tile:** This choice displays multiple copies of the image filling the desktop. The number of images depends on the size and resolution of the original graphic.

- **Center:** Quite logically, this option centers the image on a colored background so that you can see a border of color around its edges. The background photo in Figure 4-2 is centered.

6. Click OK to apply the settings and close the dialog box.

A centered picture used as the background

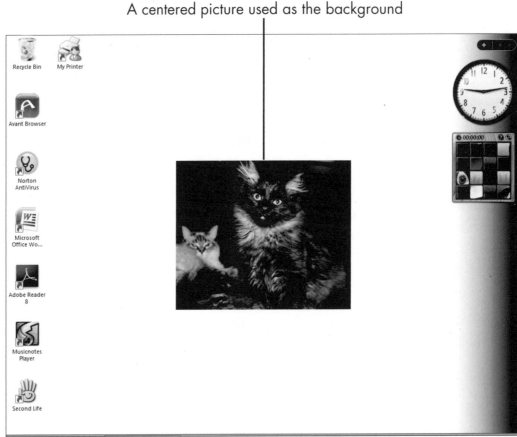

Figure 4-2

If you apply a desktop theme (see more about this in the next task), you overwrite whatever desktop settings you've made in this task. If you apply a desktop theme and then go back and make desktop settings, you replace the theme's settings. However, making changes is easy and keeps your desktop interesting, so play around with themes and desktop backgrounds all you like!

Choose a Desktop Theme

1. To apply a predesigned theme that controls your desktop appearance, first right-click the desktop and choose Personalize. The Personalization window opens. Click the Theme link.

2. In the resulting Theme Settings dialog box, as shown in **Figure 4-3**, select a theme from the Theme drop-down list. You have the following options:

- **Windows Vista** offers up a beautiful lake and mountains against a blue sky. The color scheme that this theme uses for various on-screen elements, such as window title bars, relies heavily on grays, blues, and reds.

- **Windows Classic** sports a plain blue background with silvery-blue and gray colors for screen elements.

- **My Current Theme** uses whatever settings you have and saves them with that name.

- **Browse** takes you to the Program Files folder of Windows, where you can look for any files with the .theme extension. It's not that Windows Vista comes with a lot of these waiting in this folder for you to use, but if you like, you can buy and install a program called Microsoft Plus!, which provides you with lots of extra graphic goodies, and those new themes will be stored here by default. If you find one you like, select it and click the Open button to make it available to select as your theme in the Theme Settings dialog box.

3. Click OK to apply the selected theme.

Select a theme from the drop-down list

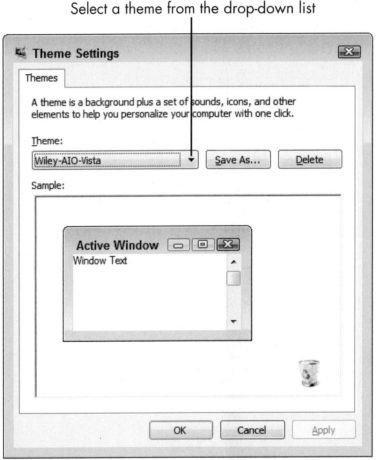

Figure 4-3

Set Up a Screen Saver

1. If you choose to use a screen saver, you can also set how long your computer is inactive before that screen saver appears. Right-click the desktop and choose Personalize. In the resulting Personalization window, click the Screen Saver link to display the Screen Saver Settings dialog box.

2. Click the downward-pointing triangle, as shown in **Figure 4-4**, to open the Screen Saver drop-down list and then choose a screen saver from the list. If you want to use the photos in your own Picture folder, choose the Photos option. Other choices are a mixture of purely graphical animations and short movies such as Nature; just pick the one that appeals to you.

3. Use the arrows in the Wait *xx* Minutes text box to set the number of inactivity minutes that Windows Vista waits before displaying the screen saver.

4. Click the Preview button (see Figure 4-4) to take a peek at your screen saver of choice. The new selection previews in a full screen view for a few moments and then disappears and continues to preview in the small screen window in the dialog box.

5. When you're happy with your settings, click OK.

 If you decide that you don't want a screen saver to appear, choose None from the Screen Saver drop-down list in the Screen Saver Settings dialog box.

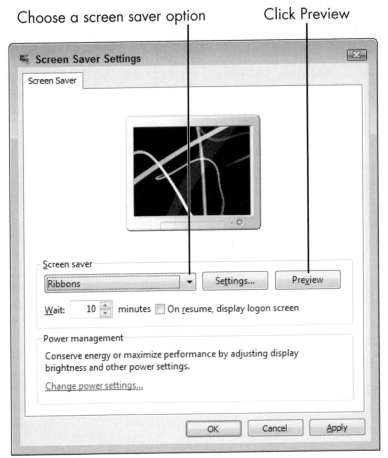

Choose a screen saver option   Click Preview

Figure 4-4

Modify How Your Keyboard Works

1. You can modify your keyboard so that it's easier to use if your fingers aren't as nimble as they used to be. To find these settings, choose Start⇨Control Panel⇨Ease of Access and then, in the Ease of Access window that appears, click the Change How Your Keyboard Works link.

2. In the resulting Keyboard dialog box (see **Figure 4-5**), select any of these settings by clicking a check box:

• Select the Turn on Mouse Keys check box to control your mouse by keyboard commands. If you turn on this setting, click the Set Up Mouse Keys link to specify settings for this feature. These settings include whether a message or sound notifies you that the feature has been turned on, and the pointer speed that's best for you when controlling mouse functions from your keyboard.

- Select the Turn on Sticky Keys check box to set up keystroke combinations to be pressed one at a time, rather than in combination. For example, a popular keyboard shortcut is the copy command, which you can perform by pressing the Ctrl key at the same time as you press the C key. Using sticky fingers, you can press first one key and then the other; this might be easier for slow typists or those with hand injuries or arthritis. (See Chapter 5 for more on copying files and similar commands.)

- You can use the Toggle Keys feature to set up Windows Vista to play a sound when you press Caps Lock, Num Lock, or Scroll **Lock** (which I do all the time by mistake!).

- If you sometimes press a key very lightly by accident or press it so hard it activates twice, you can select the Turn on Filter Keys check box to adjust *repeat rates* (or how rapidly a repeated touch on a key should be taken to invoke a second use of that key rather than a lengthy first press of the key). Use the Set Up Filter Keys link to fine-tune settings in the Set Up Filter Keys dialog box if you make this choice.

- To have Windows Vista underline keyboard shortcuts and *access keys* (you see access keys as underlined letters in menu commands; you can press those letters to choose the command from that menu) wherever these shortcuts appear, select the Underline Keyboard Shortcuts and Access Keys check box.

3. To save the new settings, click Save.

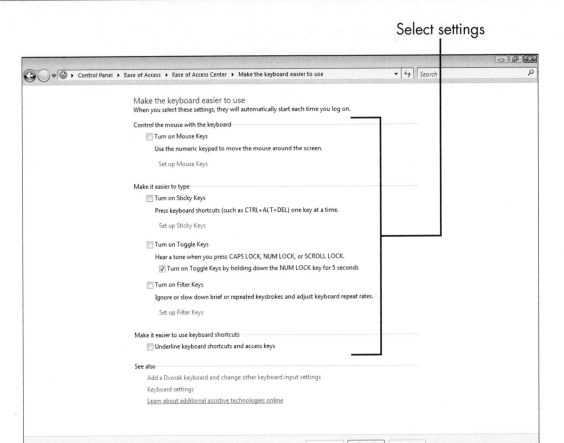

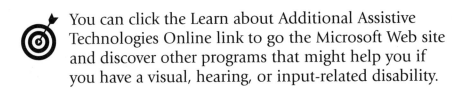

Figure 4-5

Click Save

You can click the Learn about Additional Assistive Technologies Online link to go the Microsoft Web site and discover other programs that might help you if you have a visual, hearing, or input-related disability.

Keyboards all have their own unique feel. If your keyboard isn't responsive and you have stiff fingers or a medical condition that makes using the keyboard challenging, you might also try different keyboards to see whether one works better for you than another.

Use the On-Screen Keyboard

1. If you find it easier to click on keys with a mouse rather than using your fingers, you might prefer the On-Screen Keyboard. Choose Start⇨Control Panel⇨Ease of Access to display the Ease of Access window and then click the Ease of Access Center link.

2. In the resulting Ease of Access Center window (see **Figure** 4-6), click the Start On-Screen Keyboard link. The On-Screen Keyboard appears.

Click Start On-Screen Keyboard

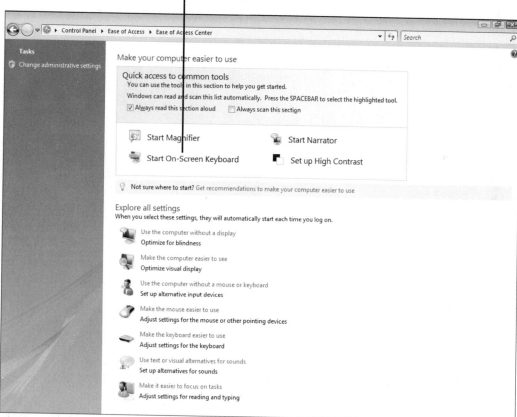

Figure 4-6

3. Open a document in any application where you can enter text and then click the keys on the On-Screen Keyboard to make entries.

4. To change settings, such as how you select keys (Typing Mode) or the font used to label keys (Font), choose Settings and then choose one of the four options shown in **Figure** 4-7.

- Choose Always on Top to keep the keyboard on top of applications, or choose Use Click Sound if you want to hear a plastic "click" whenever you press a key.

- If you choose either Typing Mode or Font a dialog box appears. Make settings and then click OK to close the dialog box.

Choose a setting from the menu

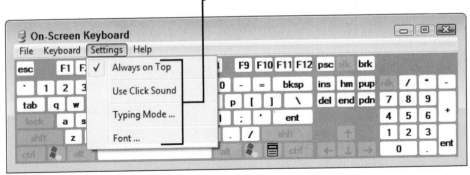

Figure 4-7

5. Click the Close button to stop using the On-Screen Keyboard.

 To use keystroke combinations (such as Ctrl+Z to undo your last action), click the first key (in this case, Ctrl) and then click the second key (Z). You don't have to hold down the first key as you do with a regular keyboard.

You can set up the Hover typing mode to activate a key after you hover your mouse over it for a predefined period of time (*x* number of seconds). If you have arthritis or some other condition that makes clicking your mouse difficult, this option can help you enter text. Choose Settings⇨Typing Mode⇨Hover to Select to activate the Hover mode.

Change Mouse Behavior

1. Choose Start⇨Control Panel⇨Ease of Access to display the Ease of Access window and then click the Change How Your Mouse Works link. The Make the Mouse Easier to Use dialog box opens (see **Figure** 4-8).

2. Click an item in the Mouse Pointers display to select a different style of mouse pointer.

3. If you want to use the numeric keypad to move your mouse cursor on your screen, select the Turn on Mouse Keys check box. If you turn on this feature, click the Set Up Mouse Keys link to fine-tune its behavior. In the dialog box that appears, make settings for keyboard shortcuts to turn this feature on and off, and settings that control the speed with which you can type mouse commands. Click OK to save these settings and return to the Make the Mouse Easier to Use dialog box.

4. Select the Activate a Window by Hovering Over It with The Mouse check box to enable this (pretty self-explanatory!) feature.

5. Click Save to save the new settings.

 You can swap the functionality of the left and right mouse button. This can be useful if you're left handed or if you want to change hands occasionally, which helps you avoid wrist injuries from repetitive motion with one hand. Open the Control Panel and click the Mouse link to display the Mouse Properties dialog box. On the Buttons tab, use the Switch Primary and Secondary Buttons feature to make the right mouse button handle all the usual left button functions, such as clicking and dragging, and the left button handle the typical right-hand functions, such as displaying shortcut menus.

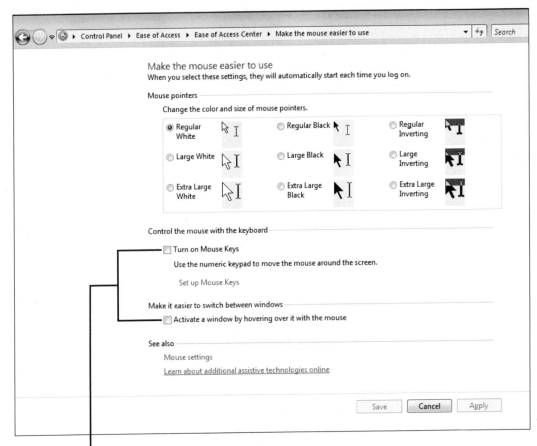

Click in a check box to activate a feature

Figure 4-8

If you have difficulty seeing the cursor on-screen experiment with the Windows Vista color scheme, discussed earlier in this chapter, to see if another setting makes your cursor stand out better against the background.

Optimize the Screen for Maximum Visibility

1. Windows Vista has a useful tool that helps improve the visibility of the screen for people who have poor eyesight or who suffer from frequent eyestrain. To see what this feature can do for you, begin by choosing Start⇨Control Panel.

2. In the resulting Control Panel window, click the Optimize Visual Display link under the Ease of Access tools.

3. In the resulting Make the Computer Easier to See dialog box (as shown in **Figure 4-9**), select the check boxes for features you want to use:

- **High Contrast:** Make settings for using greater contrast on screen elements.

- **Make Things on the Screen Larger:** If you select the Turn on Magnifier check box, you have two cursors on-screen. One cursor appears in the Magnifier window (see the area at the top of **Figure 4-10**), where everything is shown enlarged, and one appears in whatever environment you're working with on your computer (for example, your desktop or an open application). You can maneuver either cursor to work in your document, and the other cursor reflects your move. (They're both active, so it does take some getting used to.)

- **Make Things On Screen Easier to See:** Here's where you make settings that adjust on-screen contrast to make things easier to see, enlarge the size of the blinking mouse cursor, and get rid of distracting animations and backgrounds. You can also thicken the rectangle that appears to show the movement of a window when you drag it, which can help your eyes track it more easily. (This is called a *focus rectangle.*)

4. When you finish changing settings, click Save to apply them.

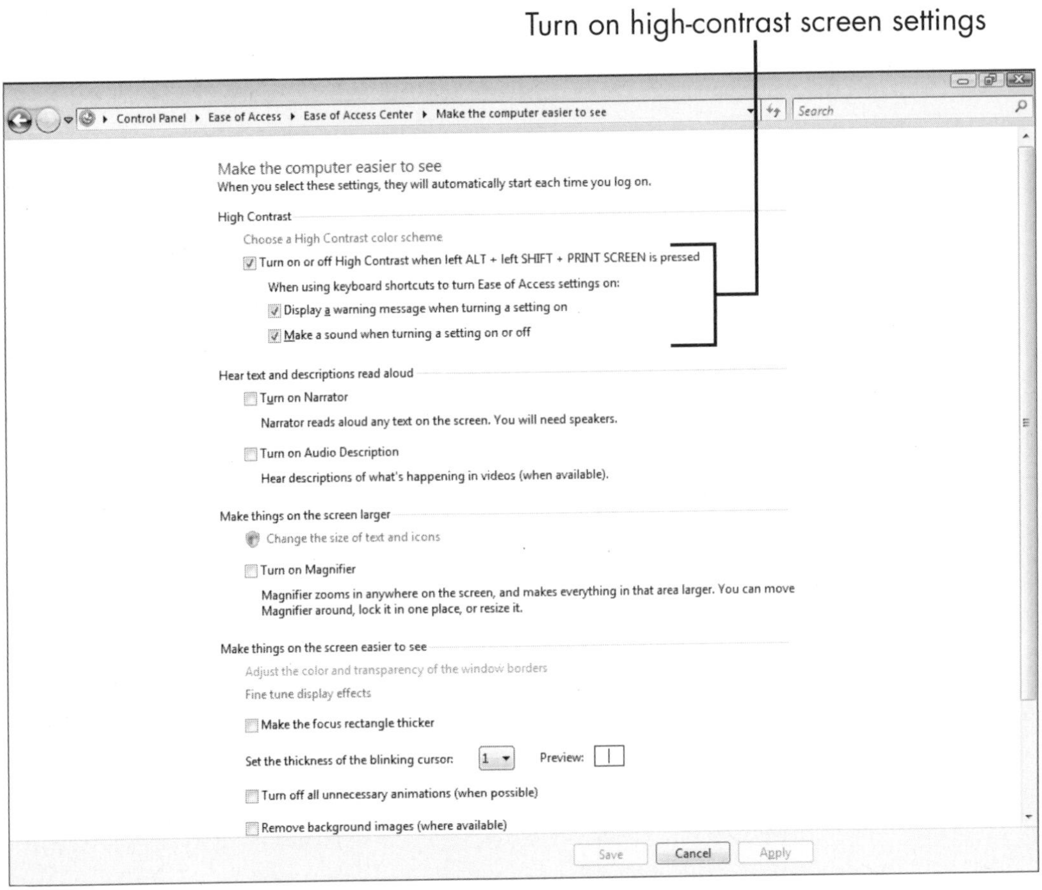

Turn on high-contrast screen settings

Figure 4-9

You can use the Magnifier window cursor

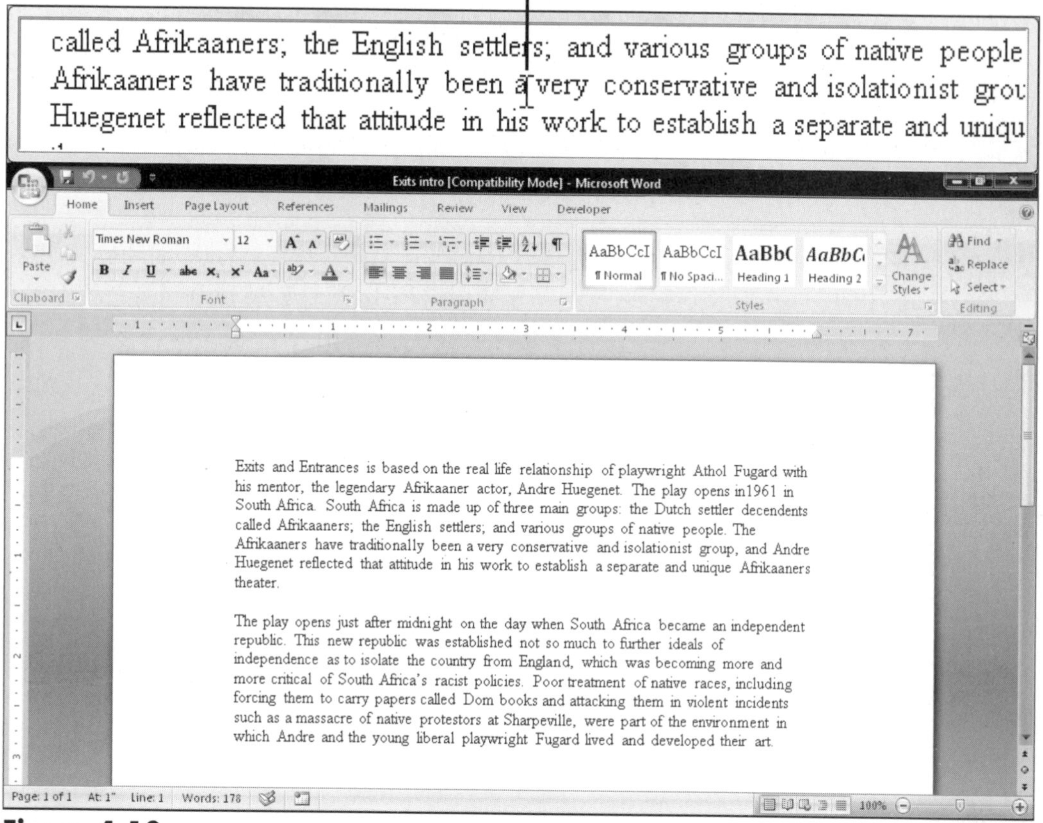

called Afrikaaners; the English settlers; and various groups of native people
Afrikaaners have traditionally been a very conservative and isolationist grou
Huegenet reflected that attitude in his work to establish a separate and uniqu

Figure 4-10

 To magnify more of the text, place the mouse pointer at the bottom of the Magnifier window (the mouse pointer changes to a line with an arrow at each end) and drag the cursor down. The size of the Magnifier window increases.

 To close the Magnifier window, press Alt+Tab and select the Magnifier item from the list of open programs. In the Magnifier dialog box, click the Close button.

Replace Sounds with Visual Cues

1. Windows plays sounds to signify some events, such as the appearance of a warning message or closing a program. If you're hard of hearing and want an alternative way for Windows to notify you of these events, you can change your computer settings to give you visual clues. To access these settings, choose Start⇨Control Panel⇨Ease of Access.

2. Click the Replace Sounds with Visual Cues link.

3. In the resulting Use Text or Visual Alternatives for Sounds dialog box (see **Figure 4-11**), make any of the following settings:

- If you select the Turn on Visual Notifications for Sounds (Sound Sentry) check box, Windows Vista will play sounds along with a display of visual cues.

- Select a setting for visual warnings. These warnings essentially flash a portion of your screen to alert you to an event.

- To have Windows display text captions whenever a sound occurs, select the Turn on Text Captions for Spoken Dialog (When Available) check box.

4. To save the new settings, click Save.

Visual cues are useful if you're hard of hearing and don't always pick up system sounds alerting you to error messages or a device disconnect. After the setting is turned on, it's active until you go back to the Use Text or Visual Alternatives for Sounds dialog box and turn it off.

This might seem obvious, but if you're hard of hearing, you might want to simply increase the volume for your speakers. You can do this by using the volume adjustment in a program such as Windows Media Player (see Chapter 11). Alternatively, you can modify your system volume by choosing Hardware and Sound in the Control Panel and then clicking the

Adjust System Volume. Click and drag the slider controls in the resulting dialog box to adjust the volume.

Select the check box for sound and visual notifications

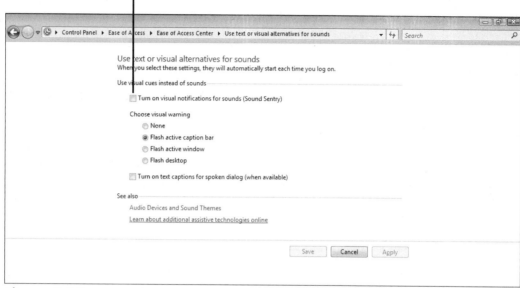

Figure 4-11

Set Up Speech Recognition

1. Speech Recognition is a Windows feature that allows you to speak commands and text into a microphone rather than clicking and typing. To use the feature, you have to set it up to recognize your unique speech inflections and accent. Though the program doesn't recognize every word perfectly, it can save you a lot of typing to spare your fingers and wrists some effort. Plug a desktop microphone or headset into your computer (the hole to plug into is typically labeled with a little headphone symbol) and choose Start➪Control Panel➪Ease of Access➪Start Speech Recognition.

2. The Set Up Speech Recognition message appears; click Next to continue. (*Note:* If you've used Speech Recognition before, this message doesn't appear.)

3. In the resulting Set Up Speech Recognition dialog box (as shown in **Figure** 4-12), select the type of microphone that you're using and then click Next. The next screen tells you how to place and use the microphone for optimum results. Click Next.

4. In the following dialog box (see **Figure** 4-13), read the sample sentence aloud. When you're done, click Next. If your voice didn't come through loud and clear, the next dialog box asks you to check the microphone connections and try again.

> During the Speech Recognition setup procedure, you're given the option of printing out commonly used commands. It's a good idea to do this because speech commands aren't always second nature!

5. In the resulting dialog box, choose whether to enable or disable document view. Document view allows Windows Vista to review your documents and e-mail to help it recognize your speech patterns. Click Next.

6. In the resulting dialog box, if you want to view and/or print a list of speech recognition commands, click the View Reference Sheet button, and then click the Close button to close that window. Click Next to proceed.

7. In the resulting dialog box, either click to deselect the Run Speech Recognition at Startup check box to disable this feature or leave the default setting. Click Next. The final dialog box informs you that you can now control the computer by voice, and it offers you a Start Tutorial button to help you practice voice commands. Click that button to start the tutorial or click Cancel to skip the tutorial and leave the Speech Recognition set up.

8. The Speech Recognition control panel appears (see **Figure** 4-14). Say, "Start listening" to activate the feature and begin using spoken commands to work with your computer.

Select a microphone type

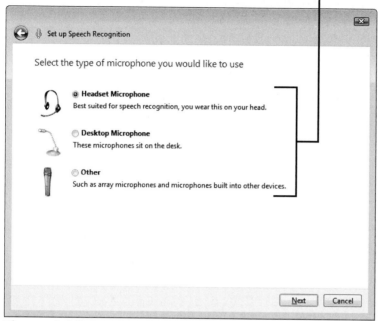

Figure 4-12

Read the sample sentence

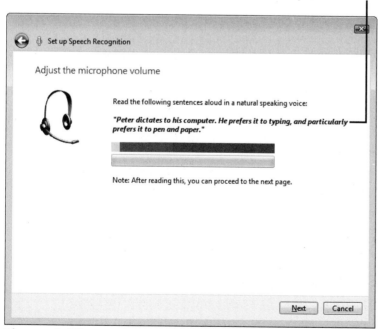

Figure 4-13

Click Close to stop Speech Recognition

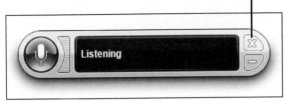

Figure 4-14

 To stop Speech Recognition, click the Close button on the Control Panel window. To start the Speech Recognition feature again, choose Start➪Control Panel➪Ease of Access and then click the Start Speech Recognition link. To find out more about Speech Recognition commands, click the Speech Recognition Options link in the Ease of Access window and then click the Take Speech Tutorials link in the Speech Recognition Options window.

Uninstall an Application

1. Your computer comes to you with certain programs prein-stalled, either by the manufacturer or a previous user. You won't necessarily want to keep every program and will want to install others that are useful to you, so it's handy to know how to uninstall unwanted software applica-tions. Choose Start➪Control Panel➪Uninstall a Program (under the Programs category).

2. In the resulting Uninstall or Change a Program window, as shown in **Figure 4-15**, select the program that you want to get rid of.

3. Click the Uninstall or Uninstall/Change button. (The but-ton you have to click will vary somewhat depending on the program you select.) Although some programs display their own uninstall screen that gives you instructions to follow for how to remove the program, in most cases, a confirmation dialog box appears (see **Figure 4-16**).

Select a program

Then click Uninstall

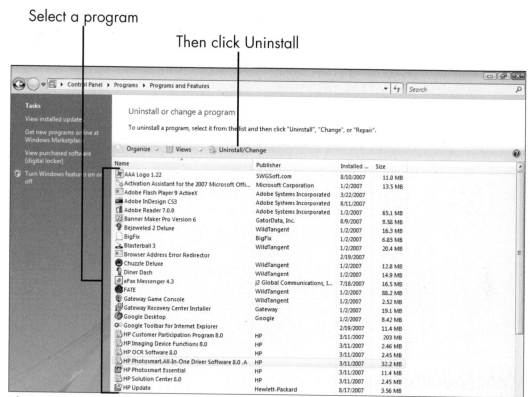

Figure 4-15

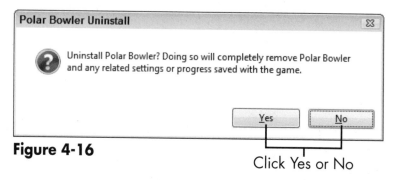

Figure 4-16

Click Yes or No

4. If you're sure that you want to remove the program, click Yes in the confirmation dialog box. A dialog box shows the progress of the procedure; it disappears when the program has been uninstalled.

5. Click the Close button to close the Uninstall or Change a Program window.

 With some programs that include multiple applications, such as Microsoft Office, you might want to remove only one program, not the whole shooting match. For example, you might decide that you have no earthly use for Access but can't let a day go by without using Excel and Word — so why not send Access packing and free up some hard drive space? If you have a program that you can modify in this way, you see a Change button in Step 2 of this task in addition to the Uninstall button. Click Change. A dialog box appears to allow you to select the programs that you want to install or uninstall or in some cases Windows might open the original installation screen from your software program.

 Warning: If you click the Uninstall button, some programs are simply removed with no further input from you. Be really sure that you don't need a program before you remove it or that you have the original software on a CD or DVD so you can reinstall it should you need it again.

Working with Files and Folders

Chapter 5

People have been using folders to store paperwork for years. When computers came into common use, some clever person adopted this model for the way that a computer stores files. *Files* are the individual documents that you create and save from within applications, such as Word and Excel. When you save a computer file, you can store it in a folder to organize your work logically. You can create folders and even subfolders and give them names, such as Household Inventory or Vacation Plans, to organize your files by project or topic.

You can also move files and folders around after you create them if you find you need to reorganize them, just as you might shuffle papers to different folders in the real world.

In this chapter, you find out how to organize and work with files and folders, including

➡ **Finding your way around files and folders:** This includes tasks such as locating and opening files and folders.

➡ **Manipulating files and folders:** These tasks cover moving, renaming, deleting, and printing a file.

➡ **Compressing a file:** This squeezes a file's contents to make larger files more manageable.

Understand How Windows Organizes Data

When you work in a software program, such as a word processor, you save your document as a file. Files can be saved to your computer hard drive; to removable storage media such as USB flash drives (which are about the size of a package of gum and you insert them into a USB port on your computer); or to DVDs (small flat discs you insert into a disc drive on your computer).

You can organize files by placing them in folders. The Windows operating system helps you to organize files and folders in the following ways:

➡ **Take advantage of predefined folders:** Windows sets up some folders for you. For example, the first time you start Windows Vista, you find folders for Documents, Pictures, Movies, and Music already set up on your computer. You can see them listed in Windows Explorer, as shown in **Figure 5-1**. (See Chapter 3 for an explanation of Explorer.)

The Documents folder is a good place to store letters, presentations for your community group, household budgets, and so on. The Pictures folder is where you store picture files, which you may transfer from a digital camera or scanner, receive in an e-mail message from a friend or family member, or download from the Internet. Similarly, the Movies folder is a good place to put files from your camcorder, and the Music folder is where you place tunes you download or transfer from a music player.

➡ **Create your own folders:** You can create any number of folders and give them a name that identifies the types of files you'll store there. For example, you might create a folder called *Digital Scrapbook* if you use your computer to create scrapbooks, or a folder called *Taxes* where you save e-mailed receipts for purchases and electronic tax filing information. The task "Create a New Folder" later in this chapter explains how to create a new folder.

Predefined folders help organize files

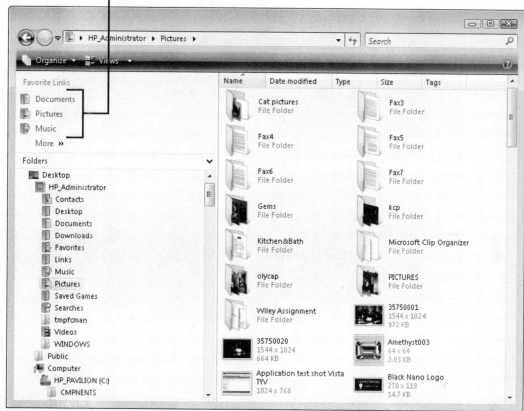

Figure 5-1

➡ **Place folders within folders to further organize files:** A folder you place within another folder is called a *subfolder*. For example, in your Documents folder, you might have a subfolder called *Holiday Card List* that contains your yearly holiday newsletter and address lists. In my Pictures folder, I organize the picture files by creating subfolders that begin with the year and then a description of the event or subject, such as *2005 Home Garden Project, 2005 Christmas, 2006 San Francisco Trip, 2006 Family Reunion, 2007 Pet Photos,* and so on. In **Figure 5-2**, you can see subfolders and files stored within the Documents folder.

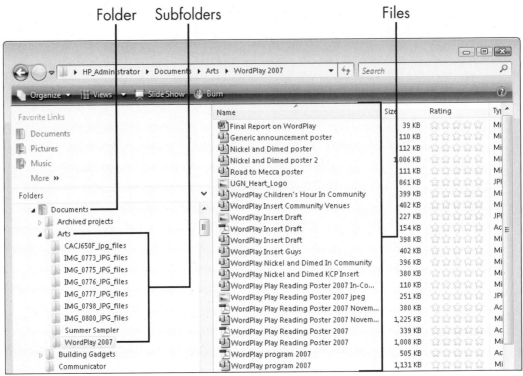

Figure 5-2

⟹ **Move files and folders from one place to another.**
Being able to move files and folders helps you if you
decide it's time to reorganize information on your
computer. For example, when you start using your
computer, you might save all your documents to your
Documents folder. That's okay for a while, but in
time, you might have dozens of documents saved in
that one folder. To make your files easier to locate,
you can create subfolders by topic and move files
into them.

Find and Open Files and Folders with Windows Explorer

1. To find and open a file, you use Windows Explorer, a feature of Windows that helps you locate files and folders
stored on your computer or discs. (Windows Explorer is

introduced in Chapter 3.) To open Windows Explorer, move your mouse pointer over the Start button and right-click. In the menu that appears, click Explore.

2. In the resulting Windows Explorer window, click the arrow to the left of any folder to display its contents in the left panel. This changes the arrow to point downward and reveals an outline of the hierarchy of folders, sub-folders, and files. You can click this arrow again to hide the folder contents in this list.

3. Click a subfolder in the left pane, as shown in **Figure 5-3**, and the subfolder opens to reveal its contents.

Click the arrow to see folder contents   Subfolder contents

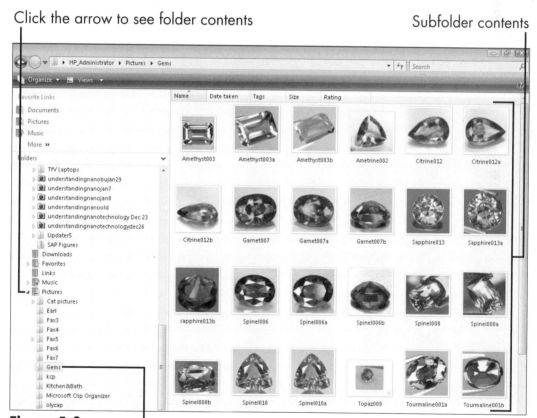

Figure 5-3

Then click a subfolder

4. If necessary, follow the procedure in Step 3 to open a series of folders until you locate the file you want.

5. When you find the file you want, double-click it, and it opens within the program used to create it.

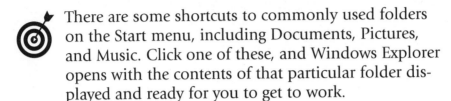 There are some shortcuts to commonly used folders on the Start menu, including Documents, Pictures, and Music. Click one of these, and Windows Explorer opens with the contents of that particular folder displayed and ready for you to get to work.

Choose a File or Folder View

1. You can use the Views menu to see different perspectives and information about files in Windows Explorer. For example, you can see a simple list or view files and folders as graphical icons. First open Windows Explorer. (See the preceding task for an explanation of how to do this.)

2. Click the arrow on the Views button to display the menu, as shown in **Figure 5-4**, and choose one of the following menu options:

- **List** displays a list of folder and file names with no further information.

- **Extra Large**, **Large**, **Medium**, or **Small Icons** displays a graphical symbol for each item (see **Figure 5-5**).

- **Details** shows a list of folders and files that shows information such as Date Modified and Size.

- **Tiles** shows the file/folder name, dimensions, and size.

If you're working with a folder containing graphics files, the graphics automatically display as thumbnails unless you choose Details. *Thumbnails* are small renditions of the actual graphic image contained in the file.

Choose a View option

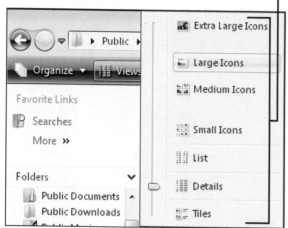

Figure 5-4

Display the Large Icons view

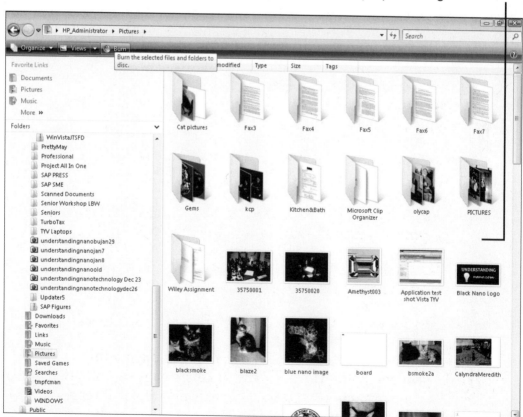

Figure 5-5

Launch a Recently Used File

1. Windows provides a shortcut to opening files you worked with recently. It provides a listing of the most recently used files that you access through the Start menu. Right-click the Start menu from the resulting shortcut menu, choose Properties.

2. In the Taskbar and Start Menu Properties dialog box that appears, click the Start Menu tab (if that tab isn't already displayed).

3. Make sure that the Store and Display a List of Recently Opened Files check box is selected (see **Figure 5-6**) and then click OK.

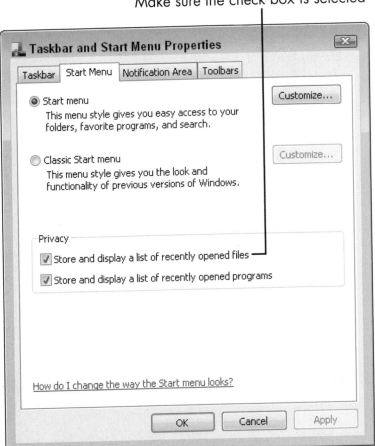

Make sure the check box is selected

Figure 5-6

4. Choose Start➪Recent Items and then choose a file from the resulting submenu (see **Figure 5-7**) to open it.

If a file in the Recent Items list can be opened with more than one application — for example, a graphics file that you might open with Paint or in the Windows Picture and Fax Viewer — you can right-click the file and use the Open With command to control which application is used to open the file.

If you open a new or recently used file and make changes, you should save the file. That procedure is covered in the first task in Chapter 8.

Select an item from the list

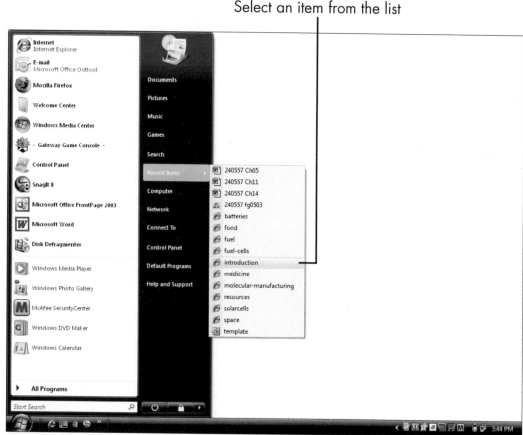

Figure 5-7

Create a New Folder

1. Earlier in this chapter, you discover how folders help you organize your files and that you can use existing Windows folders or create you own. To begin creating a new folder from Windows Explorer, right-click the Start button and choose Explore.

2. In the Windows Explorer window that appears, notice the Folders list on the left. Click the folder in which you want to create a new folder. For example, I selected the Music folder.

3. On the Explorer toolbar, click Organize (near the top-left of the window) and click New Folder in the menu. A new folder appears in the list of file/folder names, with the default name of New Folder. The folder name is highlighted, indicating that the name is open for you to edit with your specific folder name (see **Figure 5-8**).

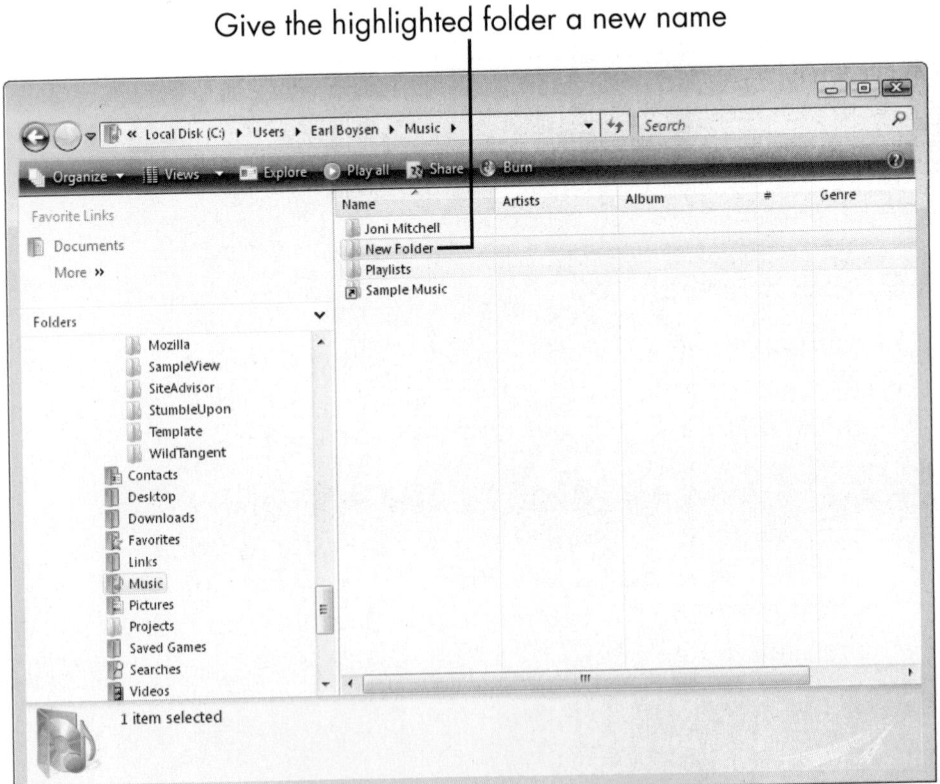

Give the highlighted folder a new name

Figure 5-8

4. Type a folder name; the words *New Folder* are replaced with the name you type. Click anywhere outside the folder name to save it.

 If you happen to click outside the folder name before you start Step 4 or if you want to rename a folder at some later time, simply perform the steps in the following task, "Rename a File or Folder."

Rename a File or Folder

1. Organizing files and folders helps you stay organized and makes finding the file you need easier. As you work with your computer and add more and more files, you may find that you want to rename a file. For example you may have named a file "Taxes" but the next year you realize that you would be better off with "2008 Taxes" and "2009 Taxes" folders. To rename a file or folder, open Windows Explorer by right-clicking Start and choosing Explore.

2. In Windows Explorer, locate the file or folder that you want to rename. (The task "Find and Open Files and Folders with Windows Explorer" earlier in this chapter explains how.)

3. Right-click a file or folder in any pane and choose Rename (see **Figure 5-9**).

4. The file/folder name is now highlighted, indicating that it is available for editing. Type a new name and then click anywhere outside the file/folder name to save the new name.

 You can't rename a file to have the same name as another file of the same format (for example, .doc for word processed documents or .jpeg for a picture) located in the same folder. Subfolders can't have the same name either.

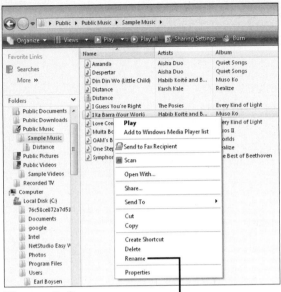

Figure 5-9

Right-click and choose Rename

Search for a File

1. Even if you've proven to be a whiz at organizing files within folders, there will be times when you can't locate a file because you forgot the name or where you saved it. To find a file, choose Start⇨Search.

2. In the Search Results window that appears, click the type of item for which you want to search along the top of the window (for example Pictures, Music, Documents, or E-mails) (see **Figure 5-10**). This helps to narrow down your search so it can happen faster. If you aren't sure of the type of file, leave the default setting of All.

3. Enter a search term in the Search field in the top-right corner. By default, all criteria for files are searched. In this example, I searched music, so any file with music in fields such as the filename, folder name, artist, album, or file type would be returned. The search begins, and results are displayed (see **Figure 5-11**). To open a file at this point, you can simply double-click it.

4. When you locate the file you want, you can double-click it to open it.

Click an item type

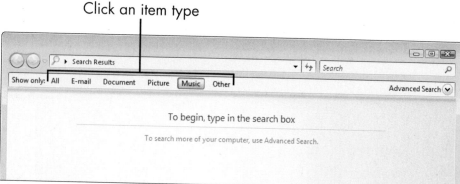

Figure 5-10

Type a search term here

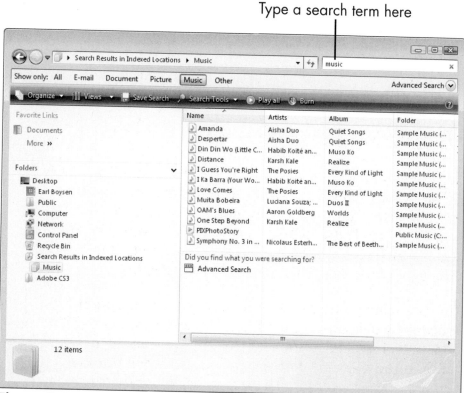

Figure 5-11

Add a File or Folder to Your Favorites List

1. The Windows Start menu offers a list of Favorites; these are Web sites, files, or folders that you like to work with often. Web sites are placed here when you add them as Favorites in Internet Explorer, which you read about in Chapter 14. You can add files and folders to Favorites so you can quickly access them from this list. Open Windows Explorer by right-clicking Start and choosing Explore.

2. In the resulting Windows Explorer window, locate the Web site, file, or folder that you want to make a Favorite. (The task "Find and Open Files and Folders with Windows Explorer" earlier in this chapter explains how.)

3. Click the file or folder and hold down the mouse button as you drag it to the Favorites folder in the Folders list on the left (see **Figure 5-12**). A copy of the item is placed in the Favorites folder.

4. To see a list of your Favorites, choose Start⇨Favorites.

5. In the resulting submenu (see **Figure 5-13**), click an item to open it.

Drag to the Favorites folder

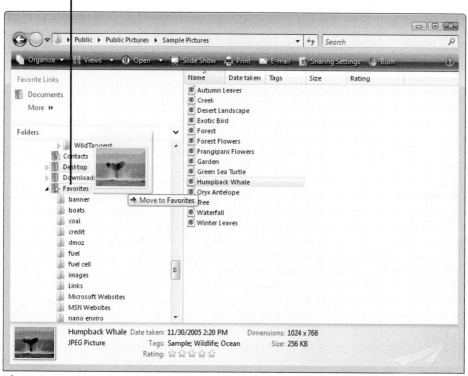

Figure 5-12

 If the Favorites item doesn't display on your Start menu, right-click the Start menu and choose Properties. On the Start Menu tab, select the Start Menu radio button, and then click the Customize button. In the list in the Customize Start Menu dialog box that appears, make sure that Favorites Menu check box is selected, and then click OK twice to save the setting.

Click an item to open it

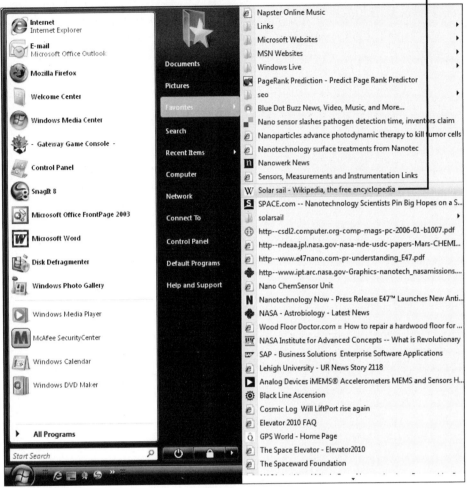

Figure 5-13

Copy a File or Folder

1. You might want to create a copy of a file for various reasons: to save a backup of it in case the first file is damaged, to use it in another project, or to provide the copy to somebody else to work with. You can also copy a set of files by copying an entire folder. To locate a file or folder to copy, right-click the Start button and choose Explore.

2. In the resulting Windows Explorer window (see **Figure 5-14**), notice the Folders list on the left. In that list, click the folder where the file you want to copy is located. If the file or folder you want is in a subfolder, click that to access it.

3. When you locate the file or folder you want to copy, right-click it and choose Copy from the shortcut menu that appears.

4. Navigate to the folder where you want to copy the file or folder (for example, a different folder in the Folder list).

5. Right-click in the Windows Explorer pane that lists files and folders and select Paste (see **Figure 5-15**). A copy of the file is pasted into that location.

Select the folder that holds the file

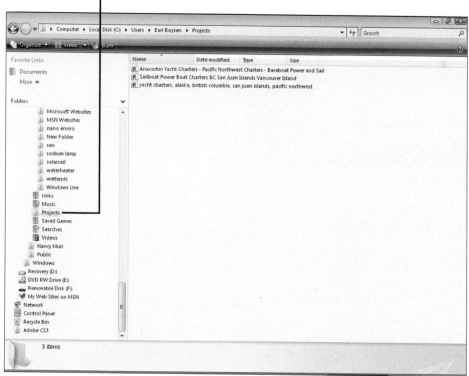

Figure 5-14

Then right-click and choose Paste

Select another folder

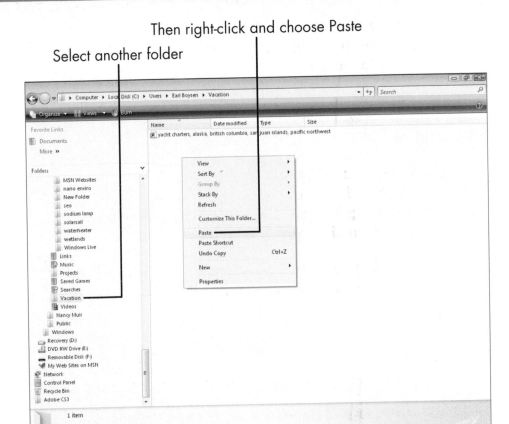

Figure 5-15

 You can also select a file and then, using the Explorer toolbar, choose Organize➪Copy to perform the copy function and Organize➪Paste to perform the paste function.

Move a File or Folder

1. If you decide a file or folder fits better in another location on your computer, you can simply move it. For example, perhaps you originally saved a file containing pictures of your cat in a Pets folder along with pictures of your dog and ferret, but then you decided to create a Cats folder and move all cat pictures there to make them easier to find. To get started, right-click Start and choose Explore.

2. In the resulting Windows Explorer window (see **Figure 5-16**), click a folder or series of folders to locate the file that you want to move.

3. Click and hold down the mouse button as you drag the file to another folder in the Folders list on the left side of the window.

If you right-click and drag the item to a new location, when you release the mouse button, you're offered the options of moving or copying the item when you place it via a shortcut menu that appears.

 If you change your mind about moving an item using the right-click-and-drag method, you can click Cancel on the shortcut menu that appears.

Click a folder to see its contents

Figure 5-16

4. Click the Close button in the upper-right corner of the Windows Explorer window to close it.

Create a Compressed File or Folder

1. If you have a large file or folder, it can take up lots of space on your computer or be too large to send as an e-mail attachment or store on a disc. To make it more manageable, you can *compress* it (much like using a trash compactor to minimize your trash). Open Windows Explorer by right-clicking Start and choosing Explore.

2. In the resulting Windows Explorer window, locate the files or folders that you want to compress. (The task "Find and Open files with Windows Explorer" earlier in this chapter explains how.)

3. Now you need to select what you want to compress. For this step, you can do either of the following:

- **Select a series of files or folders** (as shown in **Figure 5-17**): Click a file or folder, press and hold the Shift key, and then click another file or folder to select a series of items listed consecutively. The first and last items and all items in between are selected.

- **Select nonconsecutive items:** Press and hold the Ctrl key and click each item you want to include. All the individual items you clicked are selected.

4. Right-click any one of the selected items. In the resulting shortcut menu (see **Figure 5-18**), choose Send To⇨ Compressed (Zipped) Folder. A new compressed folder appears. The folder icon is named after the last file you selected in the series, and the name of the folder is left open for you to edit.

5. To rename your brand new compressed file, just type a new name and then click outside of the filename area.

(To rename the file at a later time, see the task "Rename a File or Folder," earlier in this chapter.)

Select a series of files

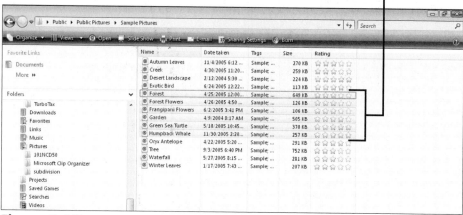

Figure 5-17

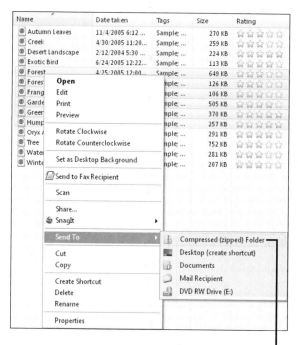

Choose Send To →
Compressed (zipped) Folder

Figure 5-18

Delete a File or Folder

1. Just as you sometimes clean out your kitchen drawers to get rid of old paper clips or cards, sometimes there's just no good reason to keep a file or folder around. In that case, you can delete it. Open Windows Explorer by right-clicking Start and choosing Explore.

2. In the resulting Windows Explorer window, locate the file or folder you want to delete. (The task "Find and Open Files and Folders with Windows Explorer" explains how.)

3. Right-click the file or folder to open a shortcut menu (see **Figure** 5-19) and then choose Delete.

4. The resulting dialog box asks if you're sure you want to delete the file. Click Yes to confirm the deletion.

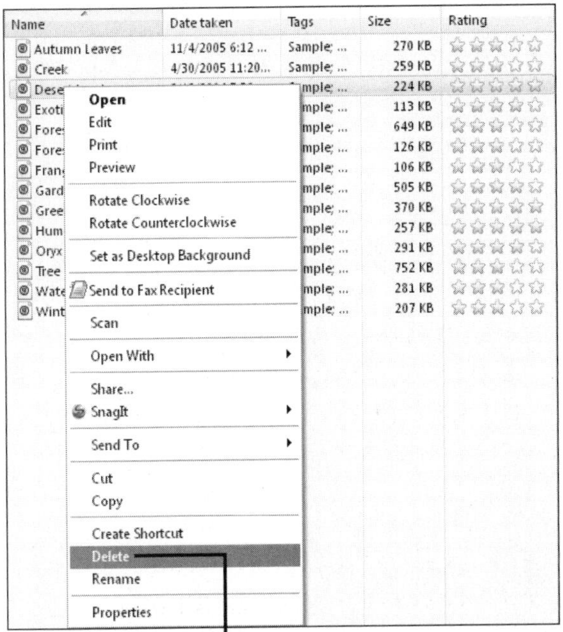

Select Delete from the menu

Figure 5-19

When you delete a file or folder in Windows Vista, it's not really gone. It's moved to the Recycle Bin folder. Windows Vista periodically purges older files from this folder when it gets too full, but you might still be able to retrieve recently deleted files and folders from it. To try to restore a deleted file or folder, double-click the Recycle Bin icon on the desktop. Right-click the file or folder and choose Restore. Windows Vista restores the file to wherever it was when you deleted it.

Store Copies of Files and Folders for Safekeeping

When you save a file, it's saved to your computer hard drive unless you choose a different location. Just as you can lose your car keys and that paper with your cousin's phone number, it's possible to lose files on your computer hard drive, either because you delete them by accident or because your computer is damaged in some way and loses data.

To help prevent loss of your valuable files, it's a good idea to save a copy of them, a procedure known as *backing up your files.* Here's what you need to know about backing up:

➡ **Using USB flash drives:** USB flash drives (also called just *flash drives* or *USB sticks*) are about the size of a thin package of gum. You plug these into the USB port on your computer. (See Chapter 1 for more about various plug-in spots on your computer, or check your computer manual for the location of your USB ports.) USB flash drives are great because they're small, extremely portable, and can hold a huge amount of computer data.

➡ **Understanding DVDs:** DVDs are round, flat metallic discs that you place in a DVD drive in your computer. Look for a small button on the front of your computer; when you press this button, a little tray pushes out. This is where you put your DVD. DVDs don't provide quite as much storage space as flash drives, they're bigger, and you have to store them in paper sleeves or plastic "jewel" cases to keep them from being damaged. But they cost a lot less than a flash drive.

➠ **Figuring out DVD formats:** DVD's come in different formats, such as DVD+, DVD-, and DVDs that can use either the + or - format. Check to see if your DVD drive in your computer can save to both formats or only one. If your manual tells you can only save to, say, DVD+ discs, then be sure to buy DVD+ discs at your office supply store. In addition, DVDs can be Read Only (labeled R), meaning you can read data from them but not save data to them; or Read/Write, meaning that you can both read the files on the disc and save data to it. A disc containing a software program might be read only, for example, so you can't overwrite the files saved there.

➠ **Viewing DVD and flash drive contents:** Just as you view files and folders on your hard drive using Windows Explorer, you can view files and folders saved to flash drives and DVD drives. The quickest way to display these is to choose Start➪Computer. The Windows Explorer window that displays lists all drives in your computer. The C: drive is usually your hard drive. Other drive letters represent built-in DVD drives or flash drives you've inserted in a USB port.

➠ **Backing up to a flash drive or DVD:** Backing up files to either a flash drive or DVD essentially involves saving a copy of those files. You can use either a simple copy and paste method to copy files to these storage media, or you can use the burn a disc procedure outlined in the next task.

Back Up Files to a Writable CD or DVD

1. To begin actually creating your backup, place a blank writable CD R/RW (read/writable) or DVD R/RW in your CD-ROM or DVD-ROM drive. You usually open the drive by pressing a button on the front of the drive and close it again by pressing the same button.

2. Choose Start⇨Documents.

3. In the resulting Documents window, select all the files that you want to copy to disc by clicking on one and then, while holding down the Ctrl key on your keyboard, clicking all other files one by one.

4. Right-click the files that you want and then choose Send To⇨Name of your writable CD-R/RW-ROM or DVD-ROM drive (see **Figure 5-20**).

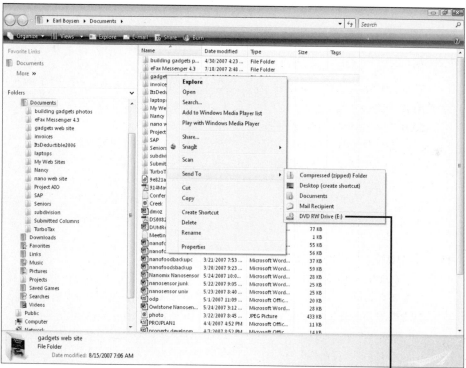

Figure 5-20

Choose your CD or DVD drive

5. In the Burn a Disc dialog box that appears, enter a disc title and choose whether you wish to change the file for-mat selection. Click Next.

6. In the window that appears (see **Figure** 5-21), click Burn to Disc. When the files have been copied, click the Close button to close the CD-R/RW-ROM or DVD-ROM window.

 If you want to back up the entire contents of a folder, such as the Document folder, you can just click the Documents folder itself in Step 2.

Click Burn to Disc

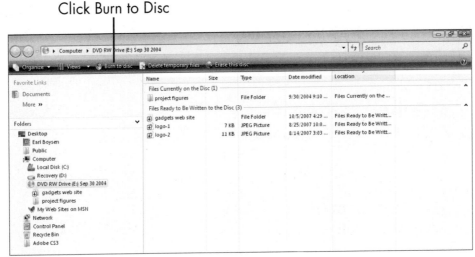

Figure 5-21

Working with Printers, Scanners, and Fax Machines

A computer is a great storehouse for data, images, and other digital information, but sometimes you need ways to turn printed documents into electronic files you can work with on your computer, or print *hard copies* (a fancy term for paper printouts) of electronic documents and images. Here are a few key ways to do just that:

➠ **Printers** allow you to create hard copies of your files on paper, transparencies, or whatever stock your printer can accommodate. To use a printer, you have to have software installed — a *print driver* — and use certain settings to tell your computer how to find the printer and what to print.

➠ You use a **scanner** to create electronic files — pictures, essentially — from hard copies of documents, pictures, or whatever will fit into/onto your scanner. You can then work with the files, fax or e-mail them, or print them. Scanners also require that you install a driver that comes with your machine.

➠ **Fax machines** let you send an electronic version of documents over your dial-up (phone line), broadband, or wireless Internet connection. The image received on the other end is an electronic version. There are fax machines that you can purchase where you insert a hard copy, enter a phone number, and send it on its way. However, if your computer is connected to the Internet, you can also fax an electronic document directly from your computer using a built-in feature in Windows Vista. Depending on the setup the person you're sending the fax to has, either a printed fax or electronic file will be received.

Install a Printer

1. A printer driver is the software your computer needs in order to communicate with your printer. After plugging your printer into your computer, read and follow the instructions that came with the printer. Some printers require that you install software before connecting them, but others can be connected right away.

2. Turn on your computer and then follow the option that fits your needs:

- If your printer is a Plug and Play device, Windows will be able to detect it and install the appropriate driver without you doing a thing. Connect the printer to your computer using the appropriate cable; Windows installs what it needs automatically, and you're done with this step list.

- Insert the CD or DVD that came with the device and follow the on-screen instructions. When you finish the instructions, your printer should be installed and ready to use, and you're done with this step list.

- If neither of the preceding bullets applies to you, choose Start⇨Control Panel⇨Printer; in the Printers window that appears, click Add a Printer to start the Add Printer

Wizard. If this is the option that you're following, proceed to the next step in this list.

3. If you choose the third option in Step 2, in the Add Printer Wizard, select the Add a Local Printer option (see **Figure 6-1**). Click Next.

4. In the resulting wizard screen (the Choose a Printer Port screen, as shown in **Figure 6-2**), you need to specify which slot (called a *port*) on your computer you plugged your printer into. Click the down arrow on the Use an Existing Port field and select a port. It's probably safe just to use the recommended port setting that Windows selects for you. Click Next.

5. In the next wizard screen (the Install the Printer Driver screen; see **Figure 6-3**), choose a manufacturer and then choose a printer. Click Next.

Click Add a Local Printer

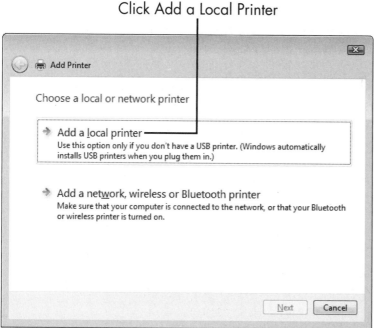

Figure 6-1

Select a printer port

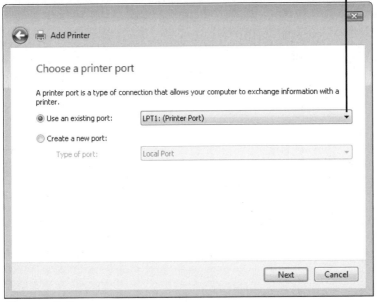

Figure 6-2

Choose a manufacturer

Then choose a printer

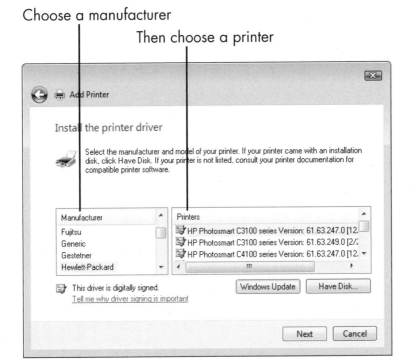

Figure 6-3

6. In the resulting Type a Printer Name screen (see **Figure 6-4**), enter a printer name. If you don't want this to be your default printer (the one your computer automatically selects to print), deselect the Set As the Default Printer option. Click Next.

7. In the resulting screen, click Finish to complete the Add Printer Wizard.

Enter a name for your printer

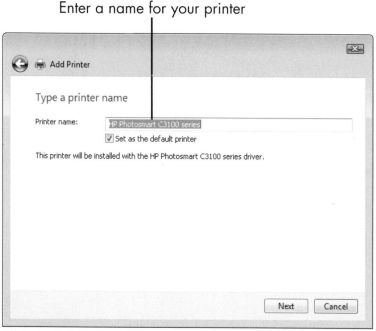

Figure 6-4

Set Printer Preferences

1. Your printer might have capabilities such as being able to print in color or black and white, or print in draft quality (which uses less ink) or high quality (which produces a darker, crisper image). To modify these settings for all documents you print, choose Start⇨Control Panel⇨ Printer (in the Hardware and Sound group).

2. In the resulting Printers window, any printers you have installed are listed. Click a printer to select it and then click the Select Printing Preferences link.

3. In the Properties dialog box that appears (as shown in **Figure 6-5**), click any of the tabs to display various settings, such as Color (see **Figure 6-6**). Note that different printers might display different choices and different tabs in this dialog box, but common settings include

- **Color/Grayscale:** If you have a color printer, you have the option of printing in color or not. The grayscale option uses only black ink. When printing a draft of a color document, you can save colored ink by printing in grayscale, for example.

- **Quality:** If you want, you can print in fast or draft quality (these settings might have different names depending on your manufacturer) to save ink, or you can print in a higher or best quality for your finished documents.

- **Paper Source:** If you have a printer with more than one paper tray, you can select which tray to use for printing. For example, you might have $8\frac{1}{2}$ x 11 paper in one tray and $8\frac{1}{2}$ x 14 in another.

- **Paper Size:** Choose the size of paper or envelope you're printing to. In many cases, this option displays a preview that shows you which way to insert the paper. A preview can be especially handy if you're printing to envelopes and need help figuring out how to insert them in your printer.

4. Click the OK button to close the dialog box and save settings and then click the Close button to close other open Control Panel windows.

Also, the settings in the Printing Preferences dialog box might differ slightly depending on your printer model; color printers offer different options from black and white ones, for example.

Whatever settings you make using the procedure in this task are your default settings for all printing you do. However, when you're printing a document from within a program such as Works word processor, the Print dialog box you display gives you the opportunity to change the printer settings for that document only. See the next task for more about this.

Click a tab to see different settings

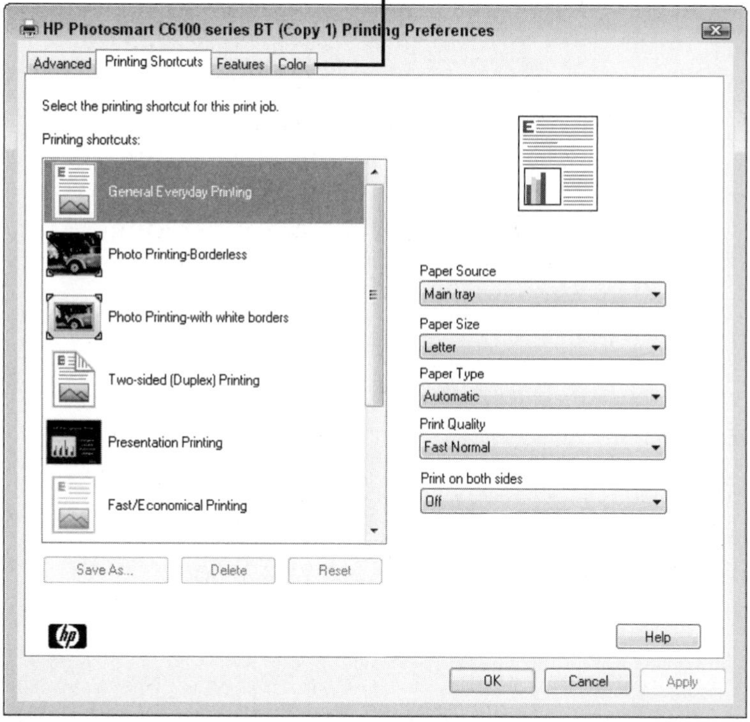

Figure 6-5

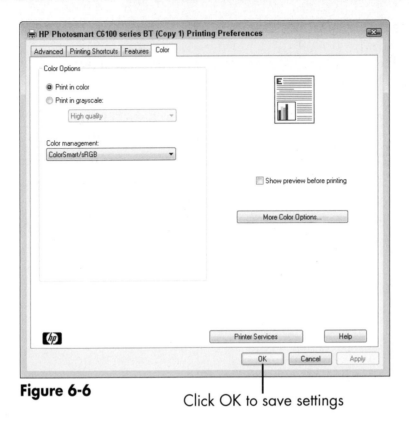

Figure 6-6

Click OK to save settings

Print a File

1. When you have your printer all set up and you're ready to print a file, first open the file in the application in which it was created. (You can find the steps for opening a file in Chapter 5.)

2. Choose File⇨Print. Note that if you're working with a Microsoft Office 2007 program the procedure to print involves clicking the Microsoft Office button and then choosing Print.

3. In the resulting Print dialog box (see **Figure 6-7**), select what to print from the Page Range section. The options in this dialog box might vary but generally include the following:

- **All** prints all pages in the document.

- **Current Page** prints whatever page your cursor is active in at the moment.

- **Selection** prints any text or objects that you have selected within the file when you choose the Print command. (Chapter 2 covers how to make selections using your mouse.)

- **Pages** prints a page range (two numbers separated by a hyphen) and/or series of pages (different page numbers separated by commas) that you enter in the field. For example, enter **3-11** to print pages 3 through 11; or enter **3, 7, 10-12** to print pages 3, 7, and 10 through 12.

4. In the Number of Copies field, click the up or down arrow to set the number of copies to make; if you want multiple copies *collated* (printed in page order), select the Collate check box.

5. Click OK to proceed with printing.

 You can use the Page Setup dialog box prior to printing to specify settings such as printing in landscape or portrait orientation (that is, with the long side of the paper across the top of your document or along the side); modify the document margins (how much white space to leave around the edge of the document); or print headers or footers (text you want to appear either on the top or bottom of every page, such as a page number or document title). To make these settings, choose File⇨Page Setup to display the Page Setup dialog box.

 Different applications might offer different options in the Print dialog box. For example, PowerPoint offers several options for what to print, including slides, handouts, and the presentation outline, and Outlook allows you to print e-mails in table or in memo style.

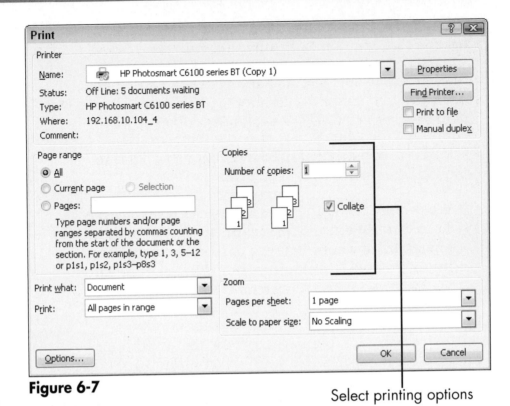

Figure 6-7

Select printing options

View Currently Installed Printers

1. Over time you might install multiple printers, in which case you might want to remind yourself of the capabilities of each or view the documents you have sent to be printed. To view the printers you have installed and view any documents currently in line for printing, choose Start⇨ Control Panel⇨Printer.

2. In the resulting Printers window (see **Figure 6-8**), a list of installed printers and fax machines appears. If a printer has documents in its print queue, the number of documents is listed under the printer name. If you want more detail about the documents or want to cancel a print job, select the printer and click the See What's Printing button. In the window that appears, click a document and choose

Document⇨Cancel to stop the printing, if you want. Click the Close button to return to the Printers window.

3. You can right-click any printer and then choose Properties (see **Figure 6-9**) to see details about it, such as which port it's plugged into or whether it can print color copies.

4. Click the Close button (the red X in the upper right) to close the window.

> When you click a printer in the list, a list of Printer Tasks appears to the left. You can use links in this list to view current print jobs for that printer, pause printing in progress, or set printer properties. See the earlier task, "Set Printer Preferences," for more about this last procedure.

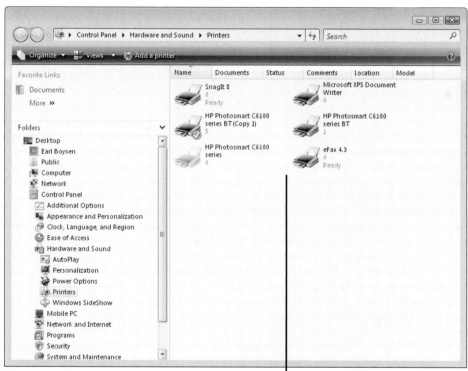

Figure 6-8

View all installed printers

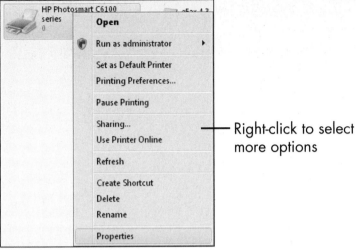

Figure 6-9

Right-click to select more options

Make a Printer the Default

1. If you install a new printer, you might want to make it the default printer so it's always used, unless you specify otherwise while printing a document. To make a printer the default, choose Start⇨Control Panel⇨Printer (in the Hardware and Sound group).

2. In the resulting Printers window (as shown in **Figure 6-10**), the current default printer is indicated by a check mark.

3. Right-click any printer that isn't set as the default and choose Set as Default Printer from the shortcut menu, as shown in **Figure 6-11**. (If you right-click the printer that is already set as the default, the Set as Default Printer command isn't available.)

4. Click the Close button in the Printers window to save the new settings and exit the window.

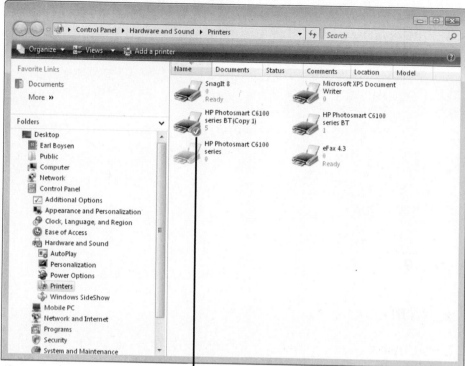

Figure 6-10

The default printer is checked

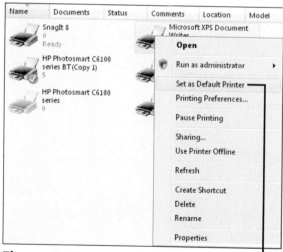

Figure 6-11

Choose Save As Default

Remove a Printer

1. Over time, you might upgrade to a new printer and chuck the old one. When you do, you might want to also remove the older printer driver from your computer so your Printers window isn't cluttered with printers you don't need anymore. To remove a printer, choose Start⇨Control Panel⇨Printer (in the Hardware and Sound group).

2. In the resulting Printers window (see **Figure 6-12**), click a printer to choose it.

3. Click the Delete This Printer button on the toolbar.

4. In the Printers dialog box that appears, click Yes; the Printers window closes, and your printer is removed from the printer list.

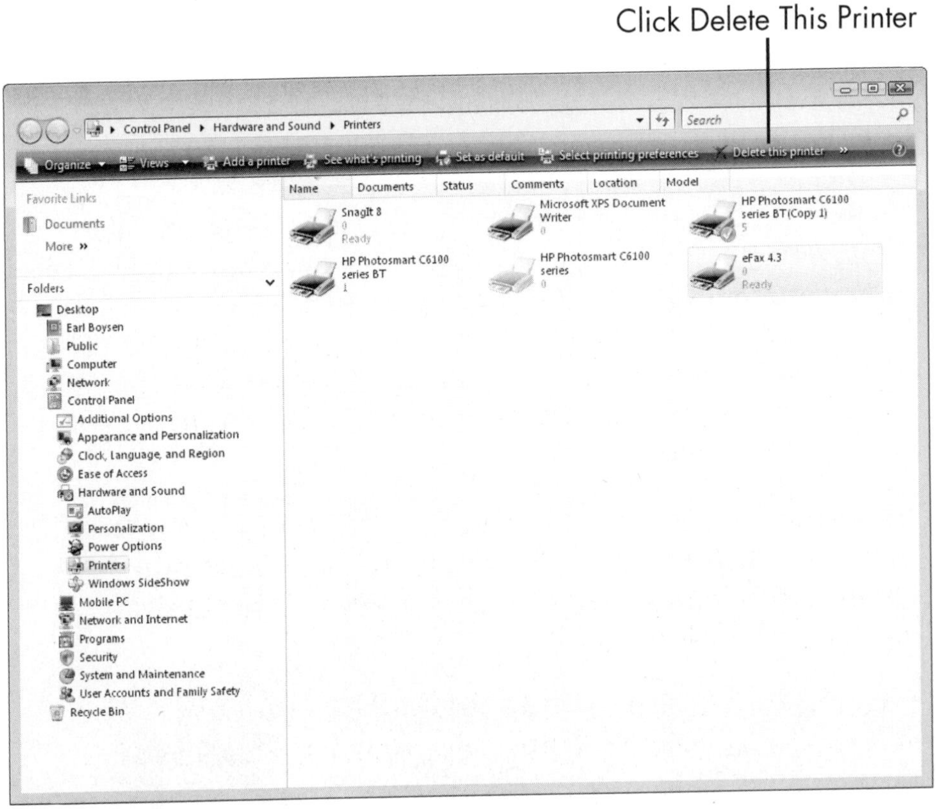

Click Delete This Printer

Figure 6-12

If you remove a printer, it's removed from the list of installed printers, and if it was the default printer, Windows makes another printer you have installed the default printer. You can no longer print to it unless you install it again. See the task, "Install a Printer," if you decide you want to print to that printer again.

Install a Scanner

1. Before you can scan documents into your computer with a scanner, you need to install the scanner driver so your scanner and computer can communicate. Start by connecting the scanner to your computer's USB or parallel port (a slot on your computer you plug a cable into), depending on your scanner connection (see your scanner manual for information about how it connects to your computer).

2. Some scanners use *Plug and Play*, a technology that Windows uses to recognize equipment and automatically install and set it up. If your scanner is Plug and Play enabled, Windows Vista shows a Found New Hardware message in the Task Bar notification area (in the lower-right corner). Most Plug and Play devices will then automatically install, the message changes to verify the installation is complete, and that's all you have to do. If that doesn't happen, you're not using a Plug and Play device, so you should click the Found New Hardware message to proceed.

3. In the resulting Found New Hardware Wizard (this starts only if you don't permit Windows Vista to automatically connect to Windows Update), click Yes, This Time Only and then click Next.

4. If you have a CD for the scanner, insert it in your CD drive and click Next. Windows Vista searches for your scanner driver software and installs it.

5. Choose Start⇨Control Panel⇨Hardware and Sound⇨ Scanners and Cameras.

6. In the resulting Scanners and Camera dialog box, click the Add Device button.

7. In the resulting Scanner and Camera Installation Wizard, click Next. In the next screen of the wizard (see **Figure 6-13**), click a Manufacturer in the list on the left and then click a model in the list on the right.

8. Follow the wizard directions based on the model of scanner you choose in Step 6 and whether you have a manufacturer's disc (a CD- or DVD-ROM). If you don't have a disc, Windows will help you download software from the Internet. When you reach the end of the wizard, click Finish to complete the installation.

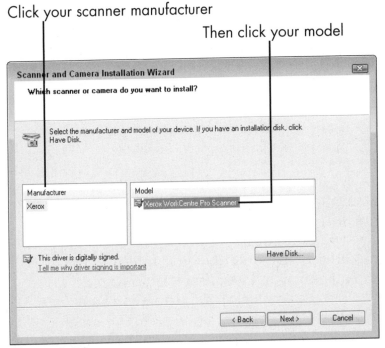

Click your scanner manufacturer

Then click your model

Figure 6-13

Modify Scanner Settings

1. After you install a scanner, you might want to take a look at or change its default settings. To do so, choose Start⇨Control Panel⇨Hardware and Sound.

2. In the resulting Hardware and Sound window, click Scanners and Cameras.

3. In the resulting Scanners and Cameras dialog box, a list of installed scanners appears (see **Figure 6-14**). Click any scanner in the Scanners and Cameras area, and then click the Scan Profiles button.

4. In the resulting Profiles dialog box, select a scanner and click Edit. In the Edit Default Profile dialog box (see **Figure 6-15**), review the settings, which might include (depending on your scanner model) color management for fine tuning the way colors are scanned and resolution settings that control how detailed a scan is performed (the higher the resolution, the crisper and cleaner your electronic document, but the more time it might take to scan).

5. Click Save Profile to return to the Properties dialog box and then click the Close button twice to close the Scan Profiles and Scanners and Cameras windows.

 When you're ready to run a scan, you place the item to be scanned in your scanner. Depending on your model, the item may be placed on a flat "bed" with a hinged cover or fed through a tray. Check you scanner manual for the specific procedure to initiate a scan (for example, pressing a Scan or Start button). After you begin the scan, your computer automatically detects it and displays a dialog box showing you the scan progress and allowing you to view and save the scanned item.

Click to select a scanner

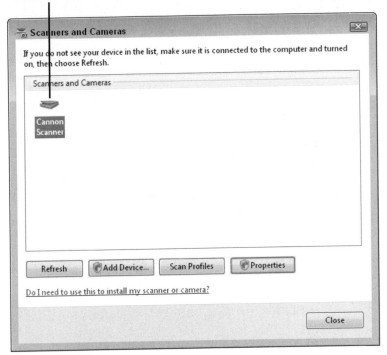

Figure 6-14

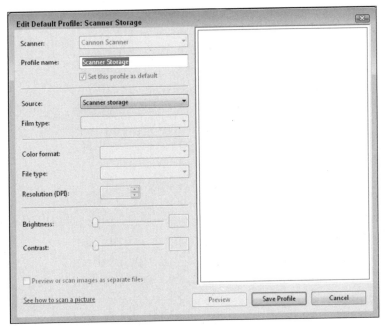

Figure 6-15

Set Up a Fax

1. You can make settings for your fax on the various tabs of the Properties dialog box, though most of the default settings are usually fine. These settings include whether to share the fax machine with others, what port it's connected to, the print driver to use for the fax, how documents are *spooled* (queued) to it, and whether colors are controlled automatically or manually. (Remember that setting up colors won't have much impact if the recipient of the fax doesn't have a color printer to print your fax with!)

After you've connected a fax machine to your computer, if you want to modify the machine's settings, choose Start⇨Control Panel⇨Printer (in the Hardware and Sound group).

2. In the resulting Printers window, as shown in **Figure 6-16**, click a fax in the list and then click the Select Printing Preferences button.

3. In the Fax Printing Preferences dialog box that appears (see **Figure 6-17**), make any of the following settings. *Note:* These settings might vary slightly, depending on your fax model.

- The default paper size is probably fine for more of your faxes, but if not, click the arrow for the Paper Size drop-down list and choose another paper size. Alternatively, type standard paper dimensions in the two fields below such as $8^{1}/_{2}$ x 14 for legal size paper.

- On the right, under the Click for Orientation label, you can click the image to change orientation between landscape and portrait. Landscape prints with the long side of the paper across the top, and portrait prints with the long side of the paper along the side.

- Make settings for image quality, if available, to specify how high quality a printing setting you want. (My fax, shown in Figure 6-17, doesn't have this setting.)

4. Click OK to close the dialog box and then click OK to close the Printers window.

Remember that a fax is treated like a printer by Windows Vista, and you can even follow the procedures given earlier for installing a printer to install your fax machine. You can rename a fax, set fax properties, delete a fax, and so on by following the same procedures outlined in printer tasks earlier in this chapter.

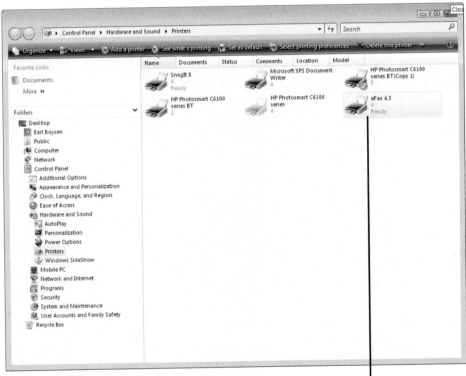

Figure 6-16

Click a fax

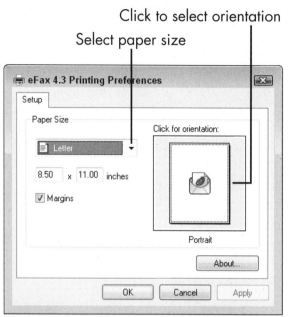

Click to select orientation

Select paper size

Figure 6-17

Send a Fax

1. To send a fax, you use the Print dialog box. With an application open, choose File (or the Microsoft Office button in Office 2007 products)⇨Print.

2. In the Print dialog box that appears (see **Figure 6-18**), click the arrow on the Name drop-down list and select your fax device or program.

If you chose not to change any default settings after installing your fax (as explained in the previous task), the Fax Setup Wizard might appear. Click the Connect to a Fax Modem link and then follow instructions to set up the connection.

3. When you finish the setup wizard, a new fax cover page form is displayed (see **Figure 6-19**).

4. Enter the recipient's information (this must be a contact you have saved with a fax number) and subject, as well as any message you want to include.

5. Click the Send button on the toolbar to send the fax.

If you have a scanner, you can scan images into your computer and then send them as attachments to e-mail, which is covered in Chapter 15. If the person you're trying to communicate with can't receive a fax, consider this alternative.

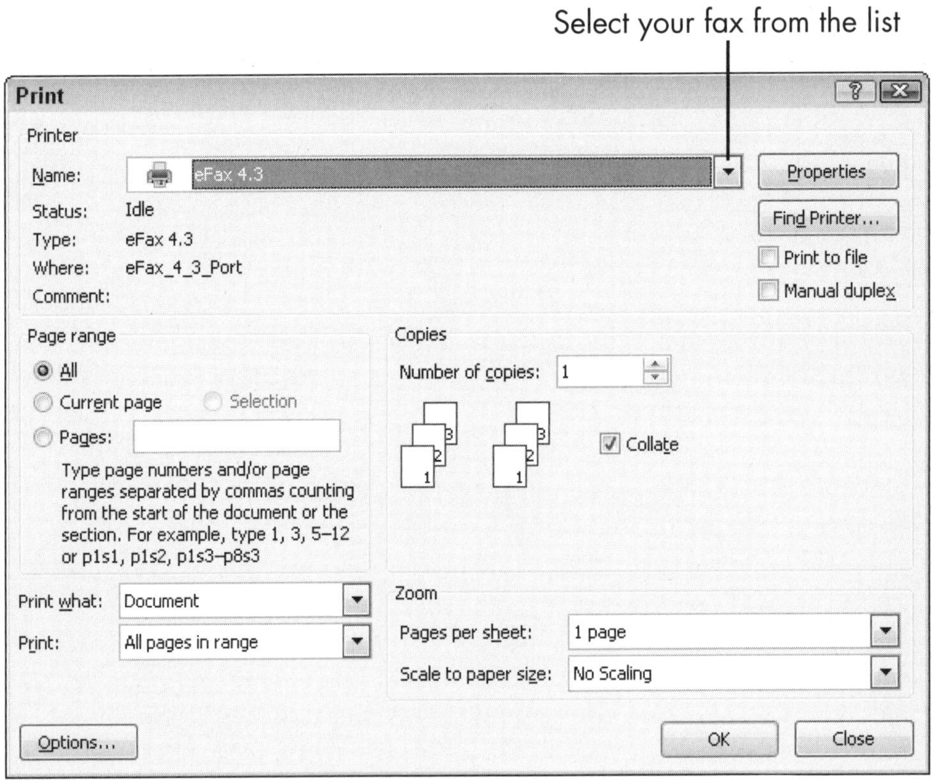

Select your fax from the list

Figure 6-18

Enter a contact that has a fax number

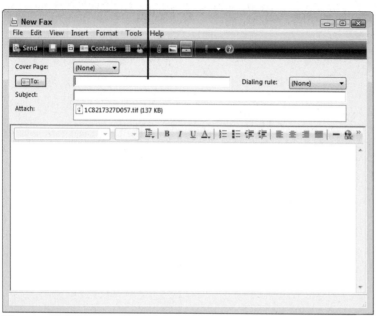

Figure 6-19

Getting Help

*W*indows Vista is a very robust program with lots of features. Now and then, you'll run into a feature that doesn't work right or isn't easy to figure out. That's when you need to call on the help resources that Microsoft provides.

Through the Help and Support Center, you can get help in various ways, including the following:

➠ **Access information that's stored in the Help system database.** Logically enough, a database contains data; in this case, it contains answers to questions that users have about Windows Vista organized by topics such as Printers or Using Your Mouse. You can drill down from one topic to another by clicking them one by one, or you can use a powerful search tool where you enter keywords such as *e-mail.* There's even a troubleshooting feature that helps you pin down your problem by going through a series of questions.

➠ **Get help from your fellow Windows users.** Tap into information exchanged by users in online Windows Communities. These are electronic discussion boards (similar to the community bulletin board at your local grocery store) where people post a question and others post answers. Though these folks aren't all experts, they can tell you about their experience with a feature or problem and how they solved it, which might just be what you need.

➠ **Ask for hands-on help with *Remote Assistance*,** which allows you to let another user view and even take over your computer from a distance (via the Internet) and figure out your problem for you. This feature is really useful if you have a friend or family member who is computer savvy, but who lives at a distance.

➠ **Access the Windows Help and How To or Windows Vista Solution Center for online help.** If you have an Internet connection, you can visit two online databases of information that might have more up-to-date information than the knowledge database that came with Windows Vista. From either of these sites, you can also get to paid tech support help (see the next bullet point).

➠ **Open your wallet and pay for it.** Microsoft offers some help for free (for example, help for installing its software that you paid good money for), but some help comes at a price. When you can't find help any-where else, you might want to consider forking over some money to pay for this kind of support. As of this writing, Microsoft offers 90 days of free support, after which time it will cost you about $60 per sup-port session (if you live in the United States).

Explore the Help Table of Contents

1. Your first stop in searching for help is likely to be the built-in help database. One of the simplest ways to find what you need here is to use the Table of Contents, which is similar to a book's Table of Contents. Choose Start⇨Help and Support to open the Windows Help and

Support window, as shown in **Figure 7-1**. Note: If your copy of Windows came built into your computer, some computer manufacturers (such as Hewlett-Packard) customize this center to add information that's specific to your computer system. Just a word of warning: In some cases, they customize the help system in ways that make it slightly different than my instructions here indicate.

Click Table of Contents

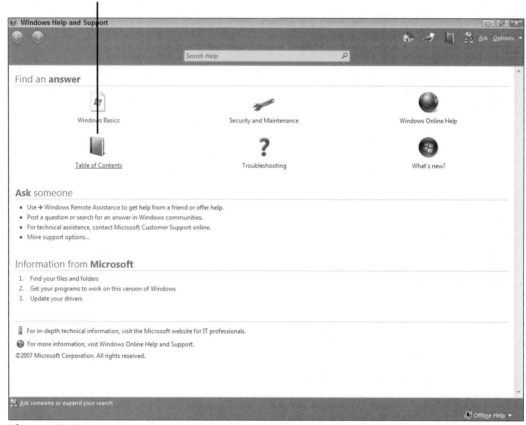

Figure 7-1

2. Click the Table of Contents link to display a list of topics.

3. In the new screen that appears, click any of the topics to see a list of subtopics. For example, you might click the Security and Privacy topic, then on Windows Firewall (the blue box to the left of that topic tells you there are additional subtopics here) and then click Using Windows Firewall. Eventually, you get down to the deepest level of detailed subtopics (in this example, a subtopic article would be Turn Windows Firewall On and Off); these have question mark icons next to them, as shown in **Figure** 7-2.

Click a help topic

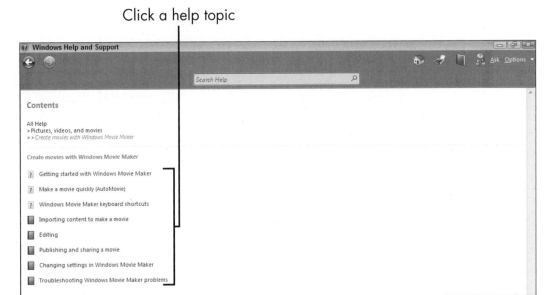

Figure 7-2

4. Click a subtopic to read its contents. Some subtopics contain blue links that lead to related topics. Links with a green arrow next to them perform an action when clicked, such as opening a dialog box so you can complete a task.

5. Click any word in green to view a definition of that term. Click outside the definition to close it.

6. When you finish reading a help topic, click the Close button to close the Help and Support window.

You can click the Print icon in the set of tools at the top-right corner of the Help and Support window to print any displayed topic. You can also click the Restore Down button in the title bar (it's the middle of the three tools in the top-right corner, and it looks like a little box) to reduce the size of the window and keep it available while you work in your computer.

 Having a connection to the Internet when you open Help and Support helps you to get the most up-to-date help information. If you aren't connected, you can still browse the database of help information installed with Windows Vista, but you'll see a message in the Help and Support window telling you that you aren't connected. See Chapter 13 for information about connecting to the Internet.

Search Help

1. If you don't find what you need by using the Table of Contents (for instance, say you wanted help using your mouse but didn't realize that's listed under the topic Getting Started), you might want to use the help search feature to find what you need by entering keywords such as *mouse* or *input.* Start by opening Help and Support. Choose Start⇨Help and Support to open the Help and Support window.

2. Enter a search term (such as *"input devices"*) in the Search Help text box and then click the Search Help button (the little magnifying glass icon on the right of the search box). The top search results, such as those shown in **Figure 7-3**, appear.

3. Click one of the numbered results to view a detailed article. Use the links listed under In This Article to jump to a section of the article that's of interest.

4. In some cases, these articles have links to other topics or subtopics (see **Figure 7-4**). Click any link under the See Also list at the bottom of the topic or a link within the article to go to related topics.

5. If the subtopic doesn't do the trick, click the Back arrow in the top-left corner to go back to the list of search results and click another one. If you still have no luck, try entering a different search term in the Search text box and clicking Start Help again.

 If you don't find what you need with Search, consider clicking the Browse Help button (the icon that looks like a little blue book) in the top-right corner of the Windows Help and Support window to display a list of major topics. The topics might also give you some ideas for good search terms to continue your search.

Click a search result   Search Help text box

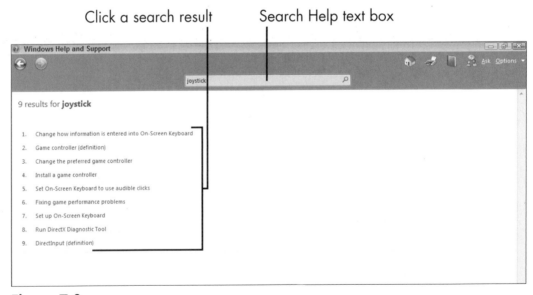

Figure 7-3

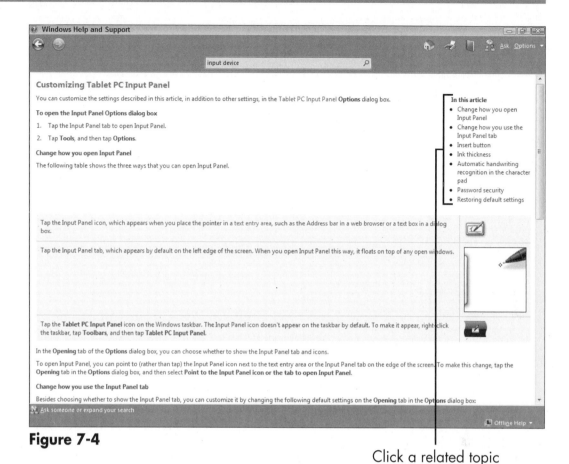

Figure 7-4

Click a related topic

Get Help in Windows Communities

1. If you want to see how other Windows users have solved a problem, you can visit Windows Communities and read posted messages, or even post one yourself and see if others can help you out. Choose Start➪Help and Support to open the Help and Support window. Then, in the Ask Someone section of the main help page, click the Windows Communities link.

2. In the Windows Vista Discussion Groups page that opens in your browser (see **Figure 7-5**), enter a keyword in the Search For field and click Go.

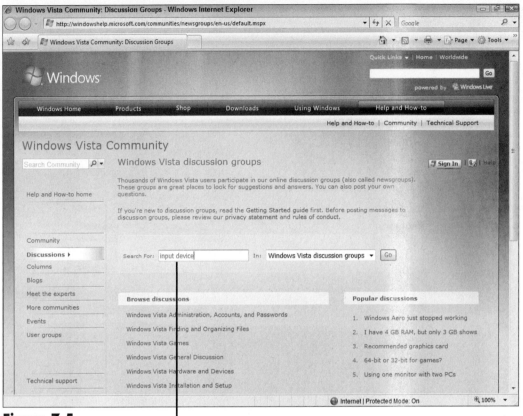

Figure 7-5

Type a keyword

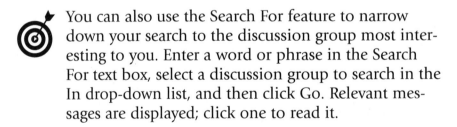 You can also use the Search For feature to narrow down your search to the discussion group most interesting to you. Enter a word or phrase in the Search For text box, select a discussion group to search in the In drop-down list, and then click Go. Relevant messages are displayed; click one to read it.

3. In the Search Results page that appears, click a discussion title to display the original message from a Windows user and a list of all replies from other users under it (each original posting and its replies are grouped under a discussion title). Click a reply to display it. (In **Figure 7-6**, you see a list of search results on the left and a reply to a message is displayed on the right.)

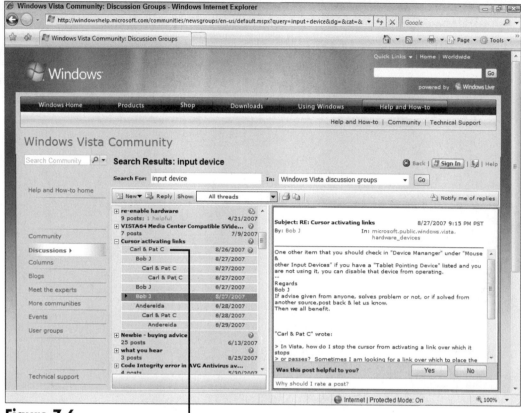

Figure 7-6

Click a discussion title

4. Perform any of the following actions to participate in the newsgroup. (Note: You have to click Sign In and enter your Microsoft Passport information to participate in the discussion. A *Microsoft Passport* is simple an automated way to sign into Web sites. If you don't have a Passport simply click the Sign Up Now link on the Sign In page.)

- **Update your profile.** Click the Manage Your Profile link at the bottom of the page to enter your display name and any other information about you that you want to appear when you post a message. If you don't want others to see personal information such as your full name or e-mail address, be sure to edit your profile accordingly.

- **Post a new message.** Choose New⇨Question, select a discussion group whose title seems to fit your question (such as Windows Vista Folders and Files if you're trying to organize your work) to participate in, and then enter the Subject and Message in their respective text boxes. Click Yes to accept the terms of use and then click the Post button to post your question.

- **Reply to a message in a discussion.** If you encounter a question somebody else has posted that you think you can help with, or if you get a reply from somebody else to your question and want to ask for further clarification or information, you can reply to another person's posting. With the list of postings and replies displayed, click the Reply button, fill in the message, and then click the Post button.

Access the Windows Help and How To Page

1. One of two online help sites that Microsoft offers Windows Vista users is the Help and How To site. This site is filled with step-by-step how to information (rather than help articles), so if you prefer this approach, it can be very — well, helpful! Choose Start⇨Help and Support to open the Help and Support window. Then click the Windows Online Help icon.

2. In the Windows Help and How-To window that appears (see **Figure 7-7**), you can use links and icons to access step-by-step procedures. Click an icon to find support in categories such as Printing, Pictures and Video, and Networking. (**Figure 7-8** shows the page that appears after you click Pictures and Video.)

3. Click one of the bullet item links, such as Print a Picture, to get to a procedure. If you want to return to the main page, just click the Back button in your browser or click the Help and How To link near the top of the page.

Click a category to find help

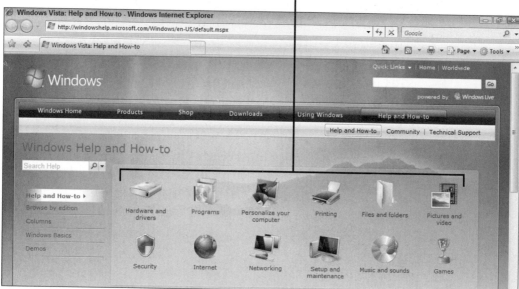

Figure 7-7

Click a topic link in the results list

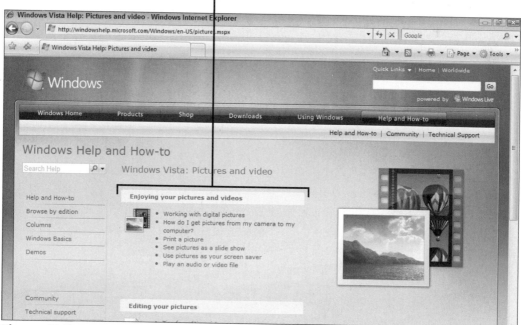

Figure 7-8

4. Click the Close button to close the online Windows Help and How To window and then click the Close button to close Windows Help and Support.

 You can set up Help and Support to always include Windows Online Help and Support when you search for help. To do so, click the arrow on the Offline Help button in the bottom-right corner of the Help and Support window, choose Settings, and select the check box labeled Include Windows Online Help and Support When You Search for Help. This setting changes the Offline Help button to the Online Help button.

Connect to Remote Assistance

1. Remote Assistance can be a wonderful feature for new computer users because it allows you to permit somebody else to view or take control of your computer from their own computer no matter where they are. You can contact that person by phone or e-mail, for example, and ask for help. Then, you send an invitation using Windows Vista Help. When that person accepts the invitation, you can give him or her permission to access your system. Be aware that by doing so you give the person access to all your files, so be sure this is somebody you trust. When that person is connected, he or she can either advise you about your problem or actually make changes to your computer to fix the problem for you. To use Remote Assistance, you and the other person have to have Windows Vista and an Internet connection.

2. First enable Remote Assistance by choosing Start⇨Control Panel⇨System and Maintenance⇨System⇨Remote Settings.

3. On the Remote tab of the resulting Systems Properties dialog box, as shown in **Figure** 7-9, select the Allow Remote Assistance Connections to this Computer check box and then click OK.

4. Choose Start⇨Help and Support to open the Help and Support window. Click the Windows Remote Assistance link in the Ask Someone area.

5. In the resulting Windows Remote Assistance dialog box, as shown in **Figure** 7-10, click the Invite Someone You Trust to Help You link.

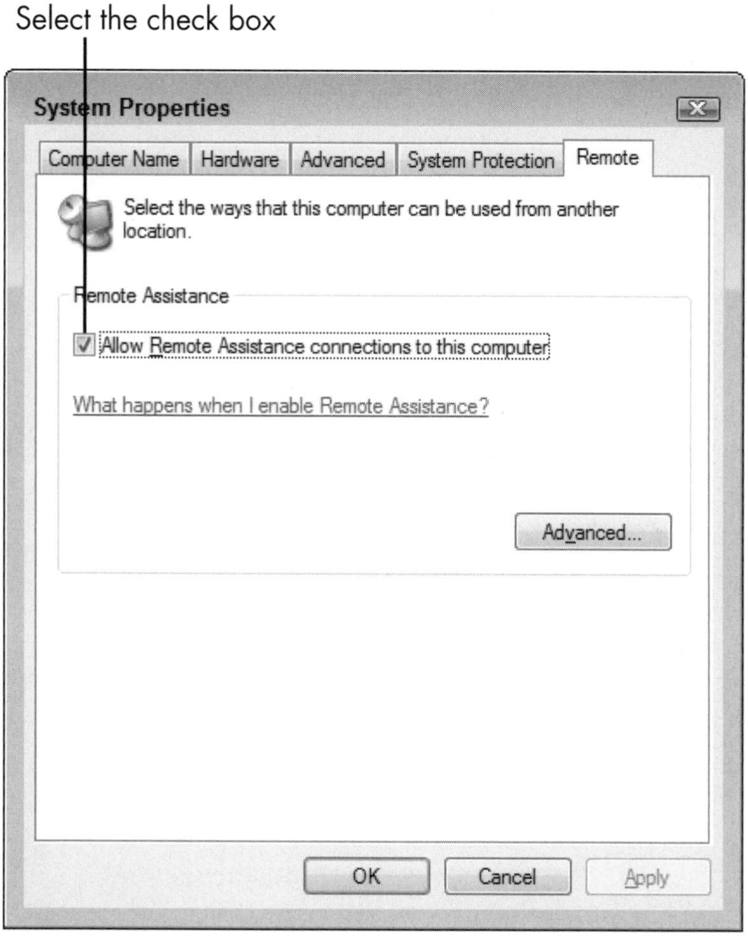

Select the check box

Figure 7-9

Click to invite a helper

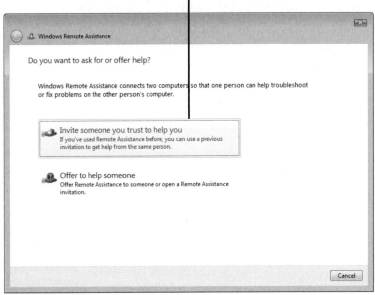

Figure 7-10

6. On the page that appears, choose a method to notify somebody that you want help. For example, you can use Windows Messenger or e-mail to invite somebody to help you. For these steps, click the Use E-Mail to Send an Invitation link. If you're new to e-mail, these steps will help you send the message, but you can find more details about using e-mail in Chapter 15.

7. Enter and retype a password, which your helper must enter to access your computer and click Next. (The password must be at least six characters long.)

8. Your default e-mail program opens with an invitation message prepared. Fill in your helper's e-mail address in the To field. (The address will look something like Chris@yahoo.com, with the @ sign and the period separating the different parts of the address.) If you like, add a personal message at the end of the automatically generated invitation. (For example, you might want to provide the password you assigned here if you don't want to call the person up to provide it.) Click Send.

9. The Windows Remote Assistance window, as shown in **Figure 7-11,** appears, and your remote helper now can view and navigate around your computer in a window on his or her own computer. When an incoming connection is made, you and your helper can use the tools here to do the following:

- **Chat:** Use this feature to enter messages and chat via text with your helper; if you prefer, you can just get on the phone with the person to have a live conversation.

- **Send a file:** You might want to send a file, for example, if you're having trouble opening a file and want your helper to see whether it's corrupted, or if you downloaded a help article that you think your helper should read.

- **Pause, cancel, or stop sharing:** At any time you can pause your sharing to take away access to your computer, cancel the session entirely, or just stop sharing with that individual.

10. When you're finished, click the Close button to close the Windows Remote Assistance window.

Figure 7-11

 People can't always set an appointment to help you, so you might have to allow access for a window of time, such as 3 hours. You can click the Advanced button in the System Properties dialog box you displayed in Step 2 (refer to Figure 7-9) to set a time limit by choosing a number and a time unit (minutes, hours, or days) from drop-down lists in the dialog box that appears. After all, you don't want somebody trying to log on to your computer unexpectedly two weeks from now when you've already solved the problem some other way.

 Remember that it's up to you to let the recipient know the password — it isn't included in your e-mail unless you add it. Although using a password used to be optional in Windows XP, it's mandatory in Windows Vista.

Get Help from the Windows Vista Solution Center

 1. The Windows Vista Solution Center is an online database of answers to common user questions and provides access to other help features such as Windows Communities. Choose Start⇨Help and Support to open the Help and Support window and then click the Ask button in the upper-right corner.

2. On the page that appears, as shown in **Figure** 7-12, click the Microsoft Customer Support link for help with issues that other users have encountered. The Windows Vista Solution Center page shown in **Figure** 7-13 appears.

Click the Windows Communities link   Ask button

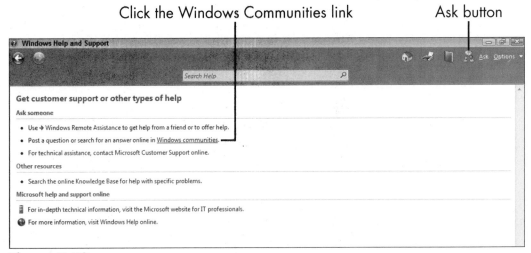

Figure 7-12

Click a topic

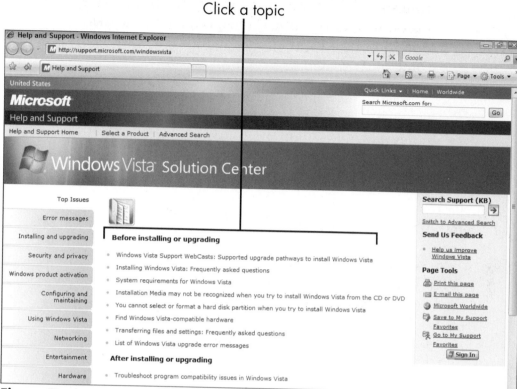

Figure 7-13

3. Click a topic in the list of links in the center of the page to read Microsoft's recommendations on how to resolve these problems.

4. If you don't find an answer and need help from Microsoft Support, click Contacts on the navigation bar on the left and then click the Contact a Support Professional by Chat, E-mail, or Phone link.

5. In the Select a Product window that appears, select the version of Vista you're using. In the following window, choose the type of support you want to use and follow the instructions.

The page where you access e-mail, chat, or phone support provides information about which services are free (sometimes for a limited period of time after you activate Vista) and which ones involve a fee. This information might change from time to time, so be sure to verify whether a cost is involved before accessing customer support using these features.

 Support might also be available from the manufacturer of your computer. In the Windows Vista Solution Center, click the Contacts button on the navigation bar on the left and then click the View Contact Information link for computer manufacturers. This link opens a window containing phone numbers or Web site addresses for several popular computer manufacturers.

Part II
Having Fun and Getting Things Done with Software

The 5th Wave

By Rich Tennant

The Levines Edit Their African Safari Photo Slideshow.

"Do you think the 'Hidden Rhino' photo should come before or after the 'Waving Hello' photo?"

Creating Documents with Works Word Processor

The two kinds of software programs that people use most often are word processors (for working with words) and spreadsheets (for working with numbers). In this chapter, you get to see the basic tools of the word processor built into Microsoft Works.

Works or a trial version of the product comes preinstalled on some computers. If not, the program is relatively inexpensive (anywhere from US $25 to $35 depending on where you shop), so it's a good entry-level program you might want to have on your computer.

With a word processor, you can create anything from simple letters to posters or brochures. You can use both text and graphics to add style to your documents. You can even use a word processor to print envelopes or labels so you can send those holiday newsletters or brochures for the local food co-op on their way.

In this chapter, you explore the following:

⟹ Enter text and format it by applying different fonts, colors, and effects.

⟹ Insert tables for organizing information.

⟹ Insert graphics and arrange them on the page.

⟹ Prepare your document for printing by using spelling and grammar checking tools, modifying the page setup, and finally, printing it!

Open a New Document and Enter and Edit Text

1. Your first step in creating any document is to open your word processor and enter and edit some text. Choose Start➪All Programs➪Microsoft Works and then select the Microsoft Works Word Processor. The program opens, and a blank document is displayed (see **Figure 8-1**).

2. Begin typing your text. Works (like all word processing programs) *wraps* the text, which means it automatically moves to the next line within a paragraph as you type. Press Enter on your keyboard only when you want to start a new paragraph.

3. To edit text you have entered, perform any of the following actions:

• Click anywhere within the text and press Backspace on the keyboard to delete text to the *left* of the mouse cursor.

• Click anywhere within the text and press the Delete key to delete text to the *right* of the mouse cursor.

• Click and drag your cursor over text to select it and press Delete or Backspace to delete the selected text.

• Click anywhere within the text and type additional text.

Begin typing in a blank document

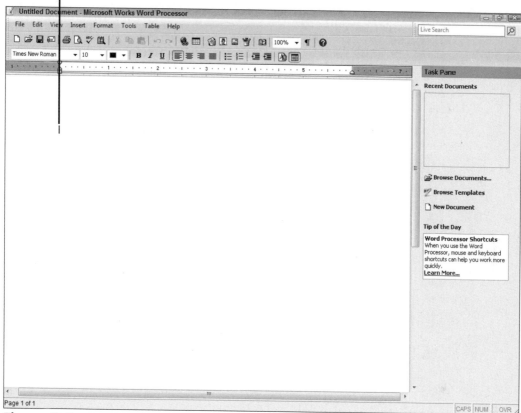

Figure 8-1

Save a Document

1. To save a document for the first time, choose File⇨Save.

2. In the resulting Save dialog box (see **Figure 8-2**), click the arrow on the right of the Save In field and click a different folder. Alternatively, click a folder icon (such as Documents) along the left side of the Save As dialog box if you want to choose a different location to save the file to.

3. Type a name for the document in the File Name text box.

4. Click Save.

If you want to save the document in another format (for example, you can save a Works document as plain text so any word processor can open it), click the arrow on the Save As Type field in the Save As dialog box and choose a different format before you click the Save button.

Type a name for your document

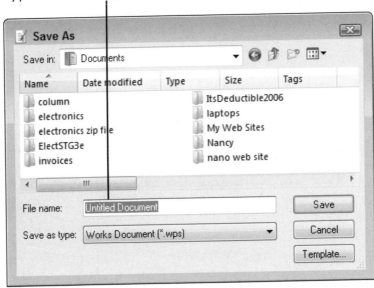

Figure 8-2

Open an Existing Document

1. After you create a file and save it, you can open it to add to or edit the contents, or you can to print it. To open a file after you save it, with the Works word processor open, choose File⇨Open.

2. In the Open dialog box that appears (see **Figure 8-3**), locate the file on your computer or storage disc by clicking the arrow on the Look In field and clicking the disc or folder where your file is located.

3. When you locate the file, click it and then click the Open button. The file opens, ready for you to edit or print it.

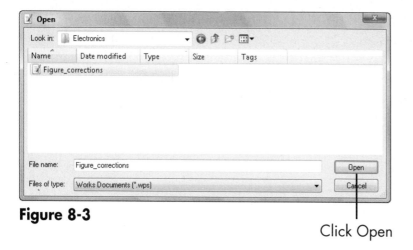

Figure 8-3

Click Open

Cut, Copy, and Paste Text

1. You can cut and paste or copy and paste selected text to move or duplicate it in another location in your document. With a document open in Works word processor, click and drag over text to select it; the text is highlighted (see **Figure** 8-4).

2. Perform either of the following two steps, depending on whether you want to *cut* the text (remove it) or *copy* it (leave the existing text and make a copy of it):

• Click the Cut button on the toolbar to cut the text.

• Click the Copy button on the toolbar to make a copy of the text.

3. Windows places the cut or copied text on its *Clipboard,* a temporary holding place for cut or copied text or objects. To paste the cut or copied text to another location within the document, click where you want the text to appear and click the Paste button on the toolbar. The text appears in the new location.

Click Cut

Click Copy

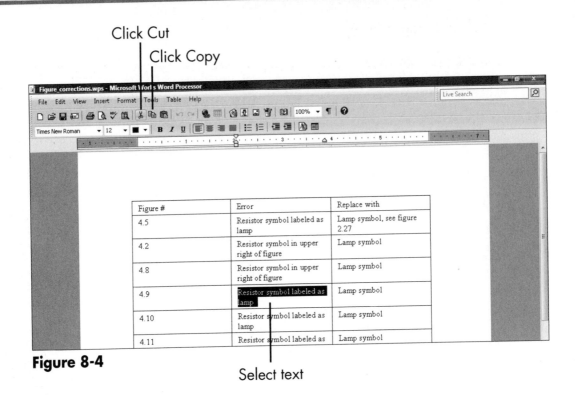

Figure 8-4

Select text

 After you place text or an object on the Windows Clipboard, you can paste it anywhere. For example, you can open another document and paste it there or paste it in an e-mail message. However, it won't stay on the Clipboard forever. If you cut or copy other text or objects, your earlier item will soon be removed from the Clipboard, which holds only a few items at a time.

Format Text

1. To format text means to change its size, apply effects such as bold or italic to it, or change the font (that is, a family of typeface with a certain look and feel to it). You start by selecting the text you want to format. Click and drag your mouse over the text you want to format to select it. (**Figure 8-5** shows how the selected text is highlighted in black.)

Click and drag to select text

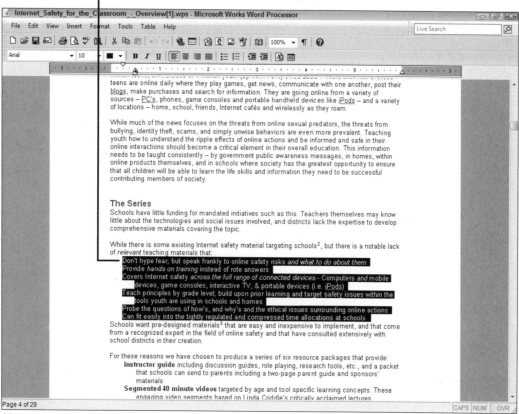

Figure 8-5

2. Choose Format⇨Font. In the resulting Font dialog box (see **Figure 8-6**), make any of the following formatting choices:

- Select a font from the list of available fonts. Use the scroll bar in this list to see more choices and click the one you want to select it. The font is previewed in the large box near the bottom of the dialog box.

- Select a font style such as Bold or Italic from the Font Style list. Font styles are useful for emphasis.

- Choose a different text size by selecting a point size setting from the Size list. The higher the point size, the larger the text.

- If you want to underline the selected text, choose a style from the Underline drop-down list.

- Click the arrow on the Color drop-down list and select a different color for the text.

- Click any of the Effects check boxes to apply effects to the text.

Click the arrow to see options

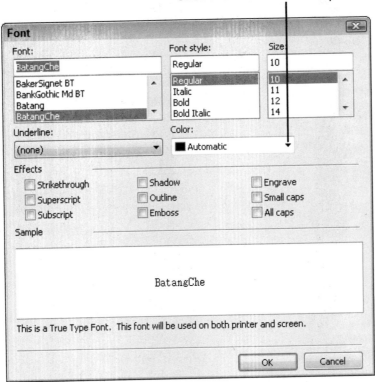

Figure 8-6

3. Click OK to apply the formatting options you have selected.

 You can also use the Formatting toolbar to apply individual formatting settings to selected text. For example, you can click the Bold button or choose a different font from the Font drop-down list. If you

don't see the Formatting toolbar, choose
View⇨Toolbars⇨Formatting.

 Try not to use too many formatting bells and whistles
in a single document, as the formatting might become
distracting or make the document difficult to read. A
good guideline is to use only two fonts on a single
page and use effects such as bold or shadowed text
for emphasis only.

Insert a Table

1. A table is a handy way to organize information with
   headings, rows, and columns. You can easily insert tables
   in word processors and then fill in the data you want to
   organize. With a document opened, choose Table⇨Insert
   Table.

2. In the Insert Table dialog box that appears (see **Figure
   8-7**), click a predesigned format for the table in the Select
   a Format list box. A sample of the format is displayed.

3. Use the arrows on the other four fields to set the number
   of rows and columns in the table and to specify row
   height and column width. If you don't change the height
   and width settings, rows and columns will adjust automatically to the text you enter in each table cell.

4. Click OK to insert the table. In the blank table that
   appears (see **Figure 8-8**), the cursor is ready and waiting
   for you in the top-left cell, and if that's where you want
   your first entry, you can simply begin typing your table
   contents.

5. Press Tab to move to the next cell in the table. If you
   reach the last cell in the last row and press Tab, a new row
   is inserted. Alternatively, you can click in any cell where
   you want to add text.

Select a table style

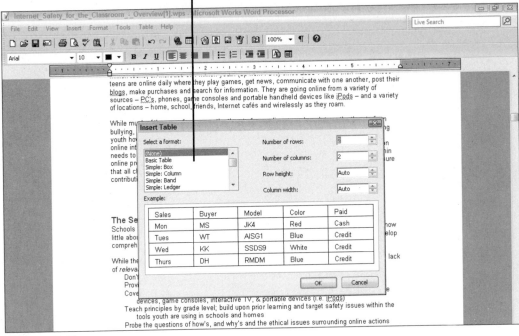

Figure 8-7

 You can format text you enter in a table just as you do any other text in your document. Just click and drag to select the cells you want to format and then follow the steps in the preceding task, "Format Text."

 To insert additional columns after you've created your table, click in the column next to which you want to insert a column and choose Table➪Insert Column. Then choose either the Before or After Current Column option, depending on whether you want the new column to appear to the left or right of the current column.

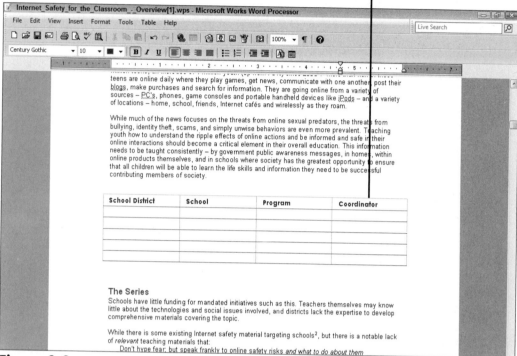

Type text in the table cells

Figure 8-8

Add Graphics

1. If you have files that contain a drawing or photo, you can insert them in your document to spruce it up or help you make a point. With a document open, choose Insert⇨Picture⇨From File.

2. In the resulting Insert Picture dialog box (see **Figure 8-9**), click the file in your Pictures folder to select it. If the picture file is in a subfolder within the Pictures folder, double-click the folder to display those files. If you want to use a picture file located elsewhere, click the arrow on the Look In field and choose another location.

3. Click the Insert button. The picture is inserted in your document.

You can also insert built-in drawings and photos called *Clip Art* by choosing Insert⇨Picture⇨Clip Art. In the dialog box that appears, select a category and subcategory to display picture previews. Then click a picture and click the Insert button to place it in your document.

Click the picture

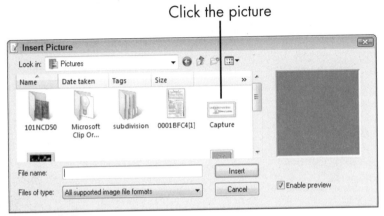

Figure 8-9

Resize Objects

1. After you insert a picture or piece of art, you may want to resize it. Click the object (such as a photo or Clip Art) to select it. Small boxes called *handles* appear around its edges. See **Figure 8-10**.

2. Do any of the following to resize the object:

- Click the center handles on the left or right side of the object and drag outward to make the object wider, or drag inward to make object narrower. This distorts the original proportions.

- Click the center handles on the top or bottom of the object and drag up or down to make the object higher or shorter. This action also distorts the proportions.

- Click a handle in any corner and drag outward to enlarge the object and keep it in proportion, or drag inward to shrink the object, again keeping it in proportion to its original size.

 You can use another method to resize objects. Select the object and choose Format➪Object to display the Format Object dialog box. Click the Size tab and enter new Height and Width settings. Click OK to accept the new settings. Depending on the dimensions you enter, the resulting object might be out of proportion.

Figure 8-10

Click a handle and drag

Check Spelling

1. If you never won spelling bees in school, you'll be glad to hear that Works has a tool that helps you check and correct your spelling. Although the tool won't catch every error (if you typed *sore* instead of *soar*, the tool won't catch it), it can catch many spelling mistakes. With the document you want to check open, choose Tools⇨Spelling and Grammar. If you didn't make any discernable errors, a message appears that the spelling check is complete, but if you did, a dialog box appears.

2. In the resulting Spelling and Grammar dialog box (see **Figure 8-11**), take any of the following actions:

- Click Ignore Once to ignore the current instance of the word not found in the dictionary.

- Click Ignore All to ignore all instances of this word.

- Click Add to add the word to the dictionary so it is no longer questioned in a Spelling and Grammar check.

- Click a suggested spelling and then click Change to change just this instance of the word.

- Click a suggested spelling and click Change All to change all instances of the word.

3. The Spell Checker moves to the next suspect word, if any, and you can use any of the options in the preceding list to fix mistakes. This continues until the Spell Checker tells you the Spell Check is complete.

4. Click Close to close the dialog box.

If you would also like to have Works check your grammar, you can select the Check Grammar check box in the Spelling and Grammar dialog box. When you next run the Spelling and Grammar check, Works displays sentences with possible grammatical problems and suggestions for how to fix them.

 It's a good idea to use the Add feature to put unusual words or acronyms you use often in the dictionary. For example, you might add unrecognized names of people or companies, scientific terms, or acronyms such as IBM or MTV. By adding such words to the dictionary, you save yourself the time it takes to tell Works over and over again that those words are correct.

Click to select an alternate spelling

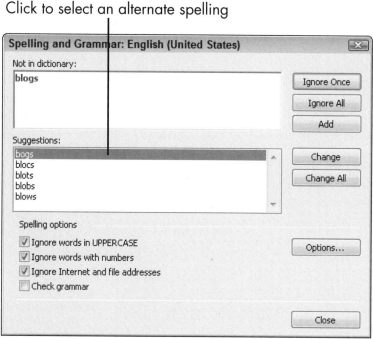

Figure 8-11

Change Page Setup

1. Word processors use default page setup, that is settings such as margins and orientation of your contents on the document page. If you want to change those settings, you can do that when you first create the document, or you may wait until you're ready to print the document onto paper. With the document whose setup you want to change displayed, choose File⇨Page Setup.

2. In the Page Setup dialog box that appears (see **Figure 8-12**), click the Margins tab. Use the up and down arrows (called *spinner arrows*) to increase or decrease margin settings, or type a new measurement in any of the Margins boxes.

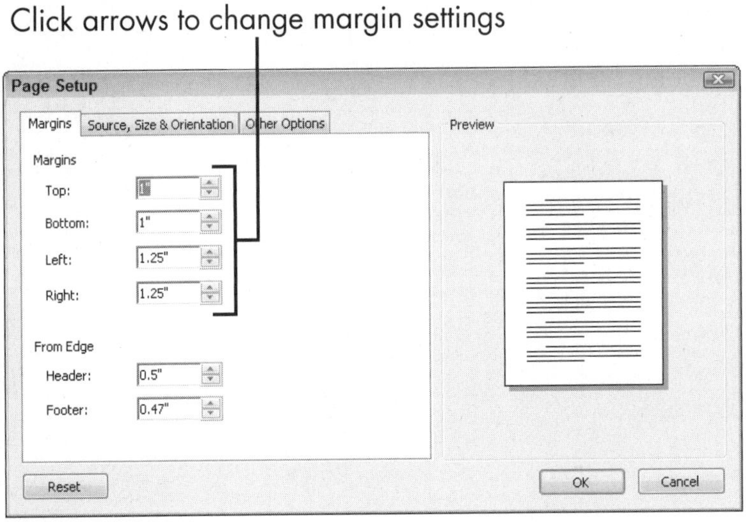

Click arrows to change margin settings

Figure 8-12

3. Click the Source, Size & Orientation tab (see **Figure 8-13**). Select a radio button for either Portrait orientation (with the longer edges of the paper on the sides) or Landscape (with the shorter edges of the paper on the sides).

4. Also on the Source, Size & Orientation tab, you can use the Paper settings to specify the size of paper you will print to, and if you have multiple paper trays, select the source for the paper.

5. Click OK to save the new settings.

   If you're inserting a header or footer (for example, a page number or the name of the document that you want to appear on every page on either the top or bottom), you should check some settings in this dialog box. On the Margins tab, you can specify how far from the edge of the paper the header or footer should appear. On the Other Options tab, you can control what page number you start with and whether the header or footer should appear on the first page of the document. (To insert headers or footers in your document, use the Header and Footer command on the View menu.)

Choose an orientation

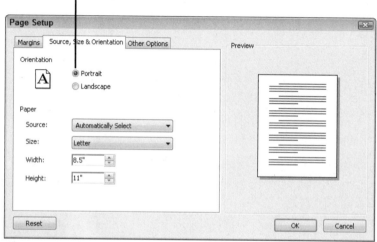

Figure 8-13

Print a Document

In Chapter 6, I cover printing files. All Windows software uses a similar procedure to print files, and Works is no different. The variables you have to consider when printing are

→ **How many copies of the document you want to print:** Be sure there's enough paper in your printer to handle them all!

→ **Whether to collate the copies:** Collating assembles sets of documents in the correct page order rather than printing, say, five page 1s, then five page 2s, and so on. This can save you effort assembling your documents yourself.

➠ **What pages to print:** The Print dialog box you see in Windows software allows you to print the current page, text you select before giving the Print command, the entire document, or a specified page or range of pages.

➠ **Which printer to print to and preferences for that printer:** You can determine preferences such as the print quality and whether to print in color or grayscale.

Always remember before you print to proofread your document and run a Spell Check to make sure it's letter perfect.

Work with Numbers and Finances

A spreadsheet program allows you to automate both simple and complex calculations. You enter numbers and then perform actions on them such as calculating an average or generating a sum for a range of numbers. You can format the data in a spreadsheet and also generate charts based on the numbers your enter.

Microsoft Works includes a spreadsheet program that provides some pretty sophisticated tools for working with numbers and charts. You can also use this and other spreadsheet programs to create tables of data, such as your home inventory or investments.

In addition to working with a spreadsheet program, there are several ways you can get information about your investments and perform financial transactions online. Together, a spreadsheet program and the financial tools you can use on the Internet can make managing your financial life much easier.

Explore the Structure of a Spreadsheet

Spreadsheet software, such as Microsoft Works Spreadsheet and Microsoft Excel, uses a grid-like structure for entering data. The individual cells of the grid are formed by the intersection of a row with a column, and so a cell is identified by a column letter followed by a row number. For example, B3 identifies the cell located at the intersection of the second column over and third row down.

Here are some additional facts you should know about spreadsheets:

➡ You can enter text or numbers in spreadsheets.

➡ When you click in a cell, the Formula bar becomes active. You can enter contents and edit those contents in the Formula bar (see **Figure 9-1**).

➡ Use the two scrollbars, the one to the right and the one at the bottom, to move horizontally or vertically through a large spreadsheet. (Though Works Spreadsheet contains only 85 rows, some spreadsheet programs contain hundreds of rows and columns.)

➡ You can perform calculations on numbers that you've entered in a spreadsheet, such as adding up numbers or calculating an average of several numbers.

➡ You can format the contents of cells or use an AutoFormat feature to apply predesigned styles to selected cells. Note that in some predesigned formats, the grid lines are neither displayed nor printed.

➡ After you've entered some data into your spreadsheet, you can easily generate a chart representing that data graphically.

Enter data in the Formula bar

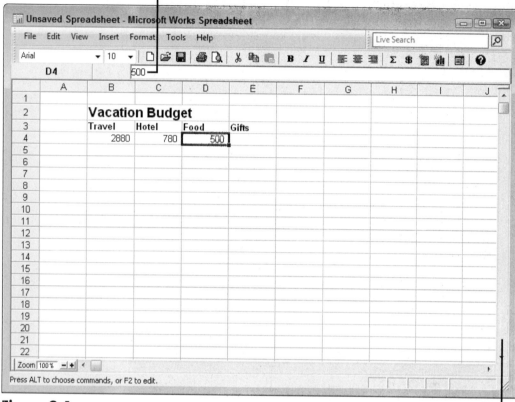

Figure 9-1

Scroll bar

Open Works Spreadsheet and Enter Text

1. To start a new spreadsheet and begin filling it with information, first choose Start⇨All Programs⇨ Microsoft Works⇨Spreadsheet.

2. In the blank spreadsheet that appears, click in a cell to make it active (see **Figure 9-2**).

3. Begin typing; notice that what you type appears in both the cell and Formula bar.

4. Press Tab to complete the entry and move to the next cell. Note that you can also click the Enter button (see **Figure 9-3**), which looks like a check mark, to complete your entry and keep the current cell active.

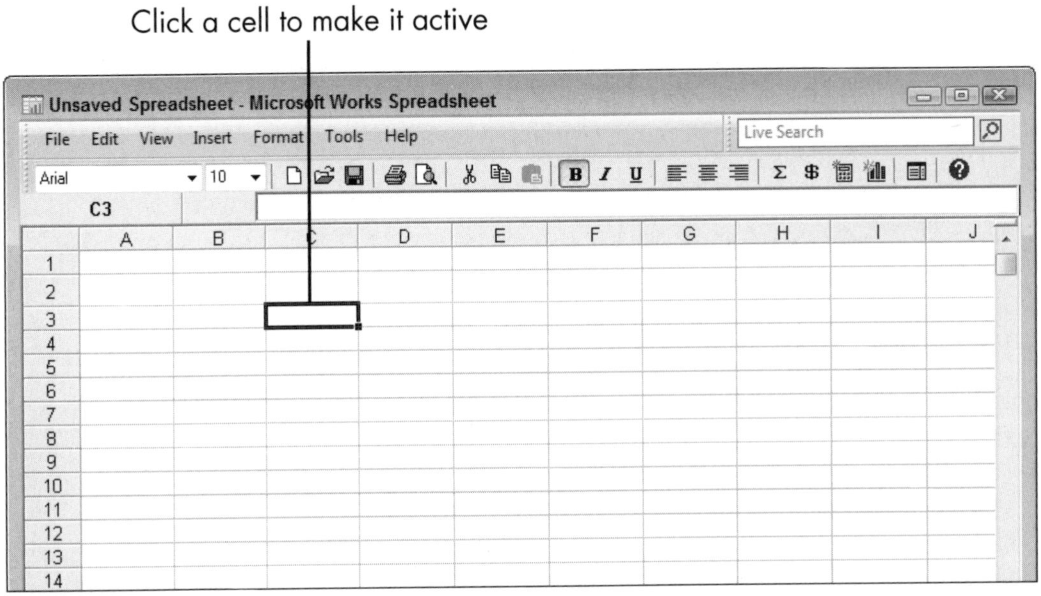

Click a cell to make it active

Figure 9-2

The Enter button

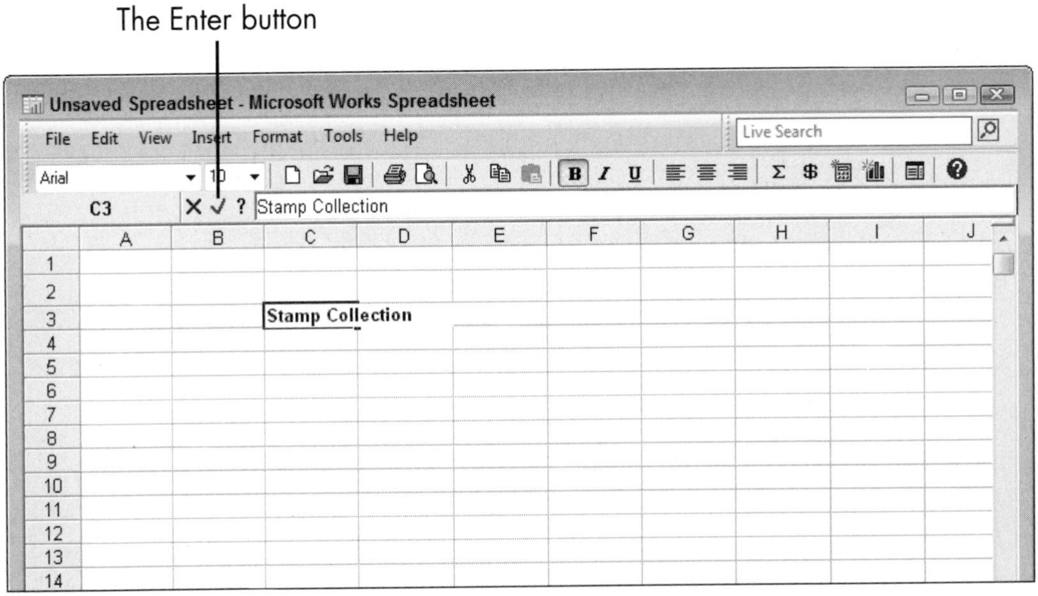

Figure 9-3

You can open a new, blank spreadsheet at any time by choosing File⇨New. To open an existing, saved file, choose File⇨Open to locate and open it.

 Remember to save your work often to avoid losing anything. See Chapter 8 for information about saving.

Format Numbers

1. You can format text in the cells of a spreadsheet by applying effects or changing the text font or color, just as you do for text in a word processor (see Chapter 8). However, formatting numbers in a spreadsheet is a bit different. In this procedure, you format the number to fit a category such as currency or to include a certain number of decimal points. To begin formatting numbers, first click the cell containing the numbers you want to format. To select multiple cells, click a cell and drag up, down, right, or left to select a range of cells.

2. Choose Format⇨Number.

3. In the Format Cells dialog box that appears with the Number tab displayed (see **Figure 9-4**), click an option in the Select Format Type list, such as Currency or Percent.

4. Click the up or down arrow on the Set Decimal Places field to specify how many decimal places the number should have; for example, 22.10 (two decimals), 22.1 (one decimal), or 22 (no decimals). Your settings appear in the Preview box.

5. Click OK to apply your formatting selections and close the dialog box.

 Currency and General are common options for formatting numbers in lists or budgets, but they aren't the only ones. You can even format numbers to display as dates, times, or fractions. If you want any zero to appear as False (in other words no value) and any number (that is any value at all) to appear as True, choose the True/False number type.

Click a number format

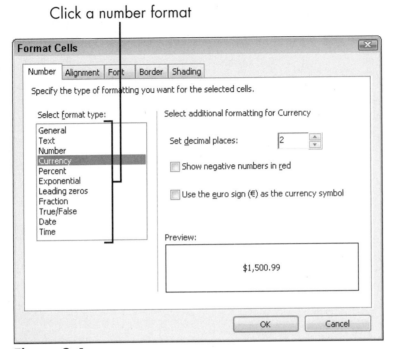

Figure 9-4

Apply AutoFormats to Cells

1. You can also format sets of cells by using the AutoFormats, which are predesigned sets of formatting choices such as cell shading or borders. Click and drag to select a range of cells.

2. Choose Format⇨AutoFormat.

3. In the AutoFormat dialog box that appears (see **Figure 9-5**), select a format from the list provided. You see a preview of the design.

4. If you like, you can modify the settings for including column and row headings and totals by selecting or deselecting any of the four check boxes on the right of the dialog box.

5. Click OK to apply the selected formatting to the cell range.

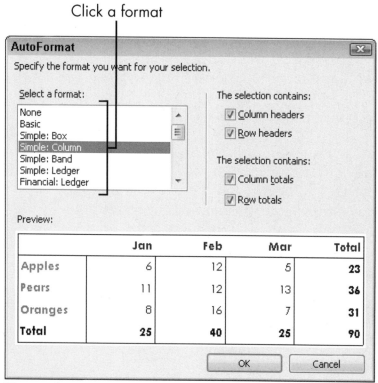

Figure 9-5

Perform Simple Calculations

1. A spreadsheet program is way more than just a place to list numbers and text. After you've entered some numbers in your spreadsheet, you can use powerful spreadsheet tools to perform simple or complex calculations, from averaging a set of numbers to complex statistical analysis. Click in a cell where you would like calculation results to appear.

2. Choose Tools⇨Easy Calc or press the Easy Calc button on the toolbar.

3. In the Easy Calc dialog box that appears (see **Figure 9-6**), click a function in the Common Functions list box and then click Next.

4. In the following dialog box (see **Figure 9-7**) enter a range of cells, such as A1:C4, in the Range field. Or click the button on the right of the Range field; the dialog box is hidden allowing you to click and drag on your spreadsheet to select the cells you want to calculate. After you make the selection, the dialog box appears again.

5. Click Next. In the Final Result dialog box, you can enter a different cell location, such as G5, in the Result At text box, and the result will be saved in the cell you indicate. Click Finish to complete the calculation. The result of the calculation now appears in the designated cell.

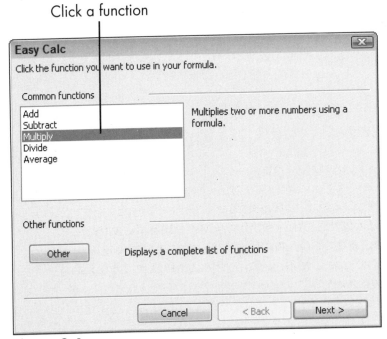

Figure 9-6

To quickly add numbers, you can simply click in the cell where you want to place the results and then click the AutoSum button on the toolbar (which looks kind of like a capital *M* turned sideways). Spreadsheet suggests cells you might want to include in the calculation, but you can click and drag to select more or different cells. Click or press Enter to complete the sum.

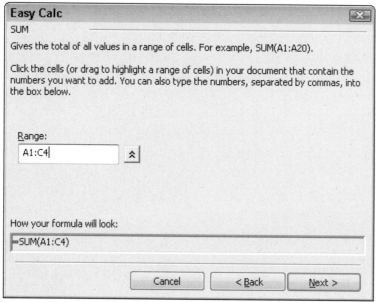

Figure 9-7

Complete a Series with Fill

1. Life consists of patterns, and spreadsheets make entering items with patterns quick and easy. For example, if you are entering a series of odd numbers (1, 3, 5, and so on), you can use tools to complete the series automatically. Enter some data in sequential cells that constitutes the beginning of a series, such as 1, 2, 3 or January, February, March (see **Figure 9-8**).

2. Click and drag over the data; a small handle appears at the end of the series (in the bottom-right corner for items in a column or at the far right for items in a row).

3. Click and drag the handle to add items to your series (see **Figure 9-9**). For a series in a column, drag down, but for a series in a row, drag to the right. For example, if you entered January, February, and March, you might drag over nine blank cells to add the rest of the months of the year. Works Spreadsheet completes the series.

 Items in a series don't have to be sequential. Works Spreadsheet can detect patterns as well. For example, if you enter 11, 22, and 33 and fill out the series, you get 44, 55, 66, and so on. However, if selected data has no discernable pattern, when you drag to fill, the data will simply be repeated again and again.

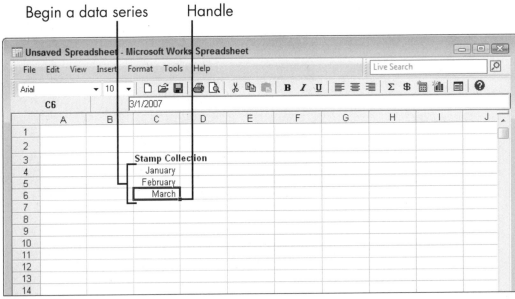

Figure 9-8

Drag the handle to fill out the series

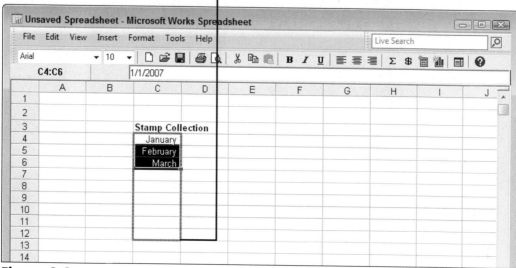

Figure 9-9

Insert a Chart

1. If you want to see your data represented visually, the Works spreadsheet can create attractive charts from your data. To start, you have to first enter the data you want your chart to be based on.

2. Click and drag over the data to select it and then click the New Chart button on the toolbar.

3. In the resulting New Chart dialog box (see **Figure 9-10**), click a Chart Type image to select it.

4. Enter a title for the chart in the Chart Title text box. Click the Show Border or Show Grid check boxes to apply those effects.

5. Click OK to display the chart (see **Figure 9-11**). To go back to the spreadsheet, you can choose View⇨Spreadsheet.

Click a chart type

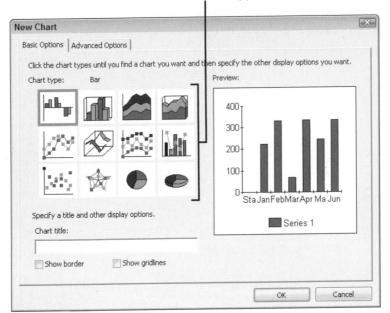

Figure 9-10

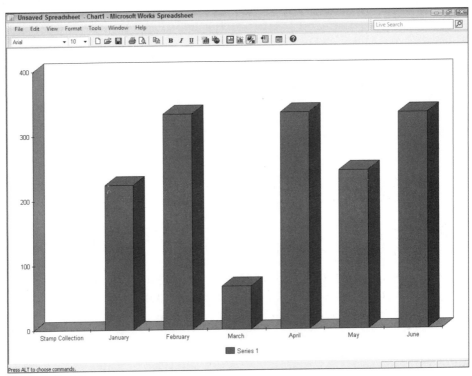

Figure 9-11

After you insert a chart, you can use tools on the Format menu or on the Chart toolbar such as the Chart Type button or Borders button to make changes to chart type, borders used around the chart, or font style or size.

Get Advice about Finances Online

You can use the Internet to access a wealth of financial information online. You can read current news stories, get advice about how to invest, and connect with others to share information. Keep in mind that the quality of information online can vary drastically, and you can't always believe everything you read. Try to find sites of reputable financial companies you might know from your offline financial dealings, such as Merrill Lynch or Forbes Magazine. Also, never give out financial account numbers to anybody via e-mail, even if they claim to be with a reputable company.

Here are some of the resources available to you for planning and monitoring your finances (see Chapter 14 for details about how to go to any Web site):

➡ Visit sites such as `www.money.cnn.com/magazines/moneymag/money101` for simple financial lessons about topics such as setting a budget and planning your retirement from CNNMoney.

➡ Visit `www.financialplan.about.com` for financial planning advice by age.

➡ Search for online publications such as The Wall Street Journal (`www.wallstreetjournal.com`), Forbes (`www.forbes.com`) as shown in **Figure 9-12**, or Kiplinger's (`www.kiplinger.com`) for articles about the latest financial and investing trends.

➠ Check out online chat rooms such as www.money.MSN.com to connect with others who are interested in learning more about finances. However, be very careful not to reveal too much personal information to anybody you meet online, especially about your specific finances and accounts.

In the U.S., you're entitled to order a free credit report from major credit report organizations every year, and you can order those reports online. Visit www.annualcreditreport.com to get started.

Windows Vista Sidebar lets you display *gadgets* (little programs that do handy things like a calculator) on your desktop. Add the Stocks gadget to check stock quotes at a glance. See Chapter 3 for details on adding gadgets.

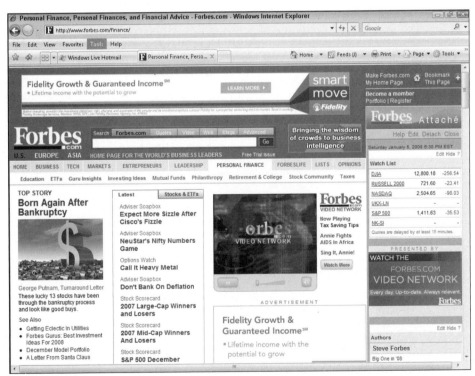

Figure 9-12

Bank Online

Many people today are banking online because it's convenient. You can typically make account transfers, check your balance, and even download your account activity to a program such as Quicken to manage your financial records or work with your taxes.

Consider this information when banking online:

➡ Most online banks such as Barclay's in the United Kingdom (see **Figure 9-13**) have very strong security measures in place; however, you should be sure that you're using a secure Internet connection to go online. If you use a wireless home network that isn't protected, for example, it's possible for someone to tap into your online transactions, so you should have whoever sets up your network enable security and a firewall. (See Chapter 17 for an introduction to basic security.) Also, if you use a public wireless network such as those in airports or hotels, unless you can ask somebody in authority if it is secure, don't log on to any financial accounts.

➡ You might need to set things up with your bank so that you can access your account online and make transfers among your different accounts. Talk to your bank about what they require.

➡ Be careful to choose strong passwords (random combinations of letters, numbers, and punctuation are best) for accessing your bank accounts. If you write the passwords down, put them someplace safe. See Chapter 2 for advice about strong passwords.

➡ Be aware of your financial rights, such as how credit cards and bank accounts are protected by law. The FDIC Web site offers lots of information about your banking and financial life at www.fdic.gov. It's specific to the U.S., but some of the advice about online financial dangers is pertinent no matter where you live.

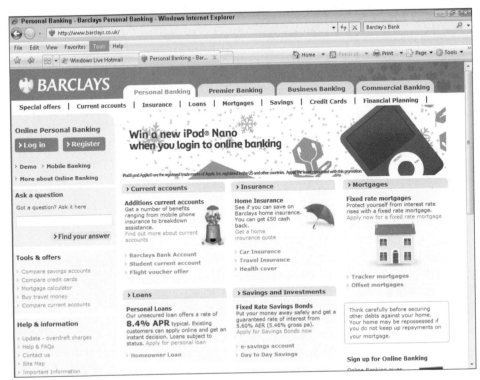

Figure 9-13

Invest Online

Every major broker has an online presence. Investing online is convenient, and online brokers enable you to place buy or sell orders very quickly and inexpensively. In addition, you can manage investment accounts online.

Here are some tips for online investing:

→ **Understand the fees.** Online brokerage fees are typically lower than working with a full-service broker. However, online broker fees can vary widely. Shop around for a broker you trust with reasonable fees.

→ **Buyer beware.** Though online banking is protected by most federal governments including the United States, online investment accounts don't always share similar protections, depending on what country you live in. Consider asking your investment counselor for advice about how protections work in your country.

→ **Handle various types of investments.** Beyond buying and selling stocks, you can invest in bonds, deposit to your IRA or other retirement accounts, and more. Companies such as Fidelity (`www.fidelity.com`) give you lots of investment choices.

→ **Retain offline access to your account.** Remember that one downside to online investing is that if your computer connection is down or your broker's server is down, you can't get to your online brokerage to invest. Keep a phone number handy so you can reach your broker by an alternative method in the case of technical glitches.

→ **Check what others have to say.** Visit sites such as MotleyFool.com (see **Figure 9-14**) for articles and advice on investing.

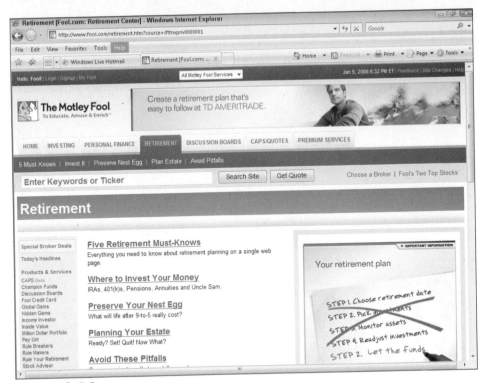

Figure 9-14

Get the Most from Movies and Digital Photos

Camcorders and digital cameras have become as ubiquitous as popcorn at your local movie theater. Your PC gives you the tools to play and edit movies to your heart's content and to manipulate digital images. Microsoft has built tools into Windows Vista to make this possible, including

➠ Media Player to play movies

➠ Movie Maker for editing and organizing movies

➠ Windows Photo Gallery for viewing and editing photos

You can use sample movie clips included with Windows Vista in the My Videos folder or photos in the My Pictures folder to get you started. (See Chapter 5 for an introduction to the existing folders set up in Vista.) You can also upload video files from your camcorder and photos from your digital camera, or you can download movies or photos from the Internet. (See Chapter 14 for information about how to download files.)

When you have movies and photos to play with, here's what you can do:

➡ Play back your movies using features to play, pause, stop, fast-forward, or rewind.

➡ Open movies in Movie Maker and play with video effects.

➡ Upload, view, edit, and print photos.

➡ Organize images and play slide shows.

Work with Media Software

Your computer is a doorway into a media-rich world full of music, digital photos, and movies. Your computer provides you with all kinds of possibilities for working with media. Windows Vista has three useful media programs built right into it: Windows Media Player, Windows Photo Gallery, and Windows Movie Maker. In combination, they give you the ability to play music and set up libraries of music tracks; view, organize, and edit photos; and edit and play your own home movies.

Here's what you can do with each of these programs:

➡ **Windows Media Player** (see **Figure 10-1**) is just what its name suggests: a program you can use to play music, watch movies, or view photos. It also offers handy tools to create *playlists* (customized lists of music you can build and play) and set up libraries of media to keep things organized. You can even burn media to a DVD so you can play it on your DVD player or another computer.

➡ **Windows Photo Gallery** (see **Figure 10-2**) enables you to work with both photos and movie files. This program offers tools to edit your photos, adjusting brightness or color saturation, for example. You can also open and play movies and add captions (though you can't adjust the image quality as you can with photos). Just as with Windows Media Player, Photo Gallery provides you with tools to organize your photos and videos into categories by the date created, by using a rating system, or by adding keyword *tags* (such as "Vacation") to each file. These lists of files are organized in a Navigation pane on the left of the Photo Gallery window. You can also burn media to a disc or e-mail it from within Photo Gallery. If you click the Make a Movie button in Photo Gallery, Windows automatically opens Windows Movie Maker (see next bullet).

Organize music into libraries

The Library tab

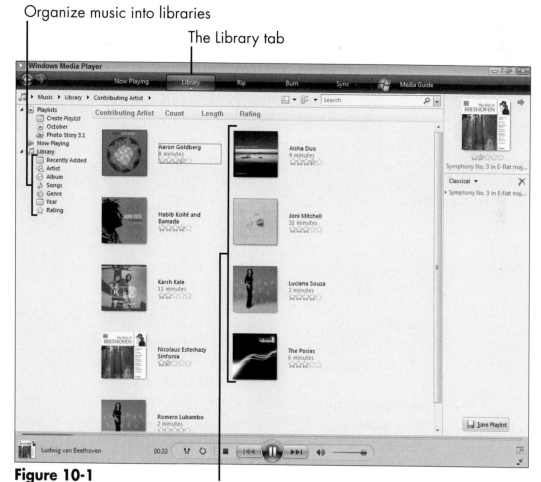

Figure 10-1

Songs and albums in the library

Organize movies and photos   Browse photo files

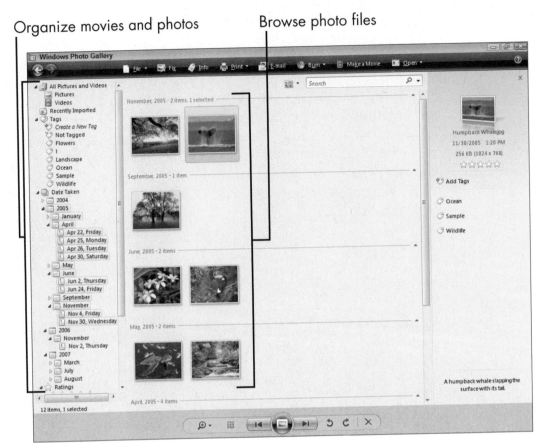

Figure 10-2

➠ **Windows Movie Maker** (see **Figure 10-3**) is for people who've always wanted to make their own movies. You can import movies from your camcorder, import pictures and put them together as a movie, and even add audio to your movie. If you like, you can edit your movie by rearranging or deleting some content. There are a few sample videos included in Windows' Sample Videos folder (which you can access easily from Movie Maker) for you to practice with. Unfortunately, going into detail about using Windows Movie Maker is beyond the scope of this book, but as you get more comfortable and experienced using your computer, you might want to check out this easy-to-use program.

Import movie clips   Preview your movie

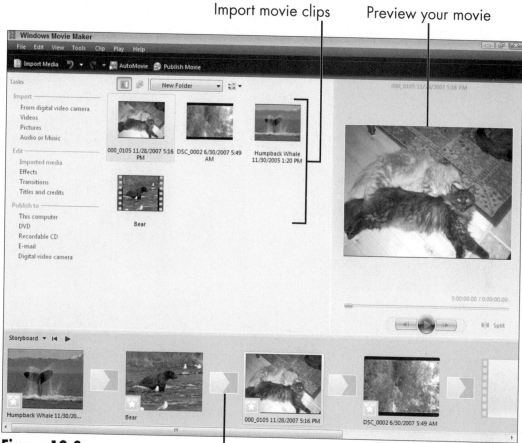

Figure 10-3

Edit them into a story

Play Movies with Windows Media Player

1. To open Windows Media Player and begin working with music and movie files, choose Start⇨All Programs⇨ Windows Media Player.

2. Click the Maximize button in the resulting Media Player window. (Maximize is in the upper-right corner of the window, next to the X-shaped Close button, and has two square icons.)

3. Click the arrow on the bottom of the Library button at the top and click Video.

4. In the window listing video files that appears, click the Library folder that contains the movie you want to play (as shown in **Figure 10-4**).

Click a Library folder   Movie files

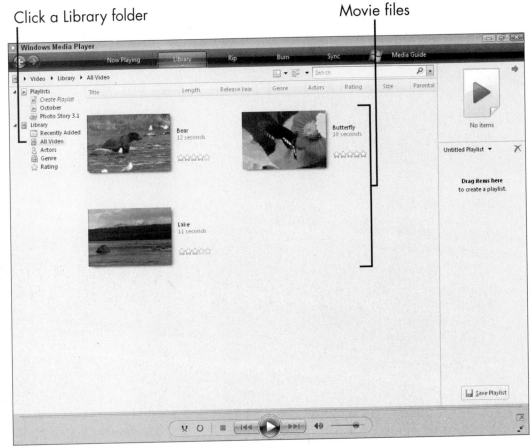

Figure 10-4

5. Double-click a file to begin the playback (see **Figure 10-5**). Use tools at the bottom of the screen to do the following:

- Adjust the volume of any sound track by clicking and dragging the slider left (to make it softer) or right (to make it louder). Click the megaphone-shaped volume icon to mute the sound (and click it again to turn the sound back on).

- Pause the playback by clicking the round Pause button in the center of the toolbar.

- Stop the playback by clicking the square-shaped Stop button toward the left.

- Skip to the next or previous movie by clicking the arrow buttons to the left or right of the Pause button.

6. Click the Close button to close Media Player.

To stop the movie before it finishes, click the Stop button. Note that the Previous and Next tools aren't available for single movie clips — they jump you from one track to another when playing sound files.

Figure 10-5

Adjust volume or mute sound

Upload Photos from Your Digital Camera

Uploading photos from a camera to your computer is a very simple process, but it helps to understand what's involved. (This is similar to the process you can use to upload movies from a camcorder — in both cases, check your manual for details.) Here are some highlights:

➡ **Making the connection:** To upload photos from a digital camera to a computer requires that you connect the camera to a USB port on your computer using a USB cable that typically comes with the camera.

➡ **Installing software:** Digital cameras also typically come with software that makes uploading photos to your computer easy. Install the software and then follow the easy-to-use interface to upload photos. If you're missing such software, you can simply connect your camera to your computer and use Windows Explorer to locate the camera device on your computer and copy and paste photo files into a folder on your hard drive. (Chapter 5 tells you how to use Windows Explorer.)

➡ **Printing straight from the camera:** Some cameras save photos onto a memory card, and many printers include a slot where you can insert the memory card from the camera and print directly from it without having to first upload pictures. Some cameras also connect directly to printers. However, if you want to keep a copy of the photo and clear up space in your camera's memory, you should upload even if you can print without uploading.

View a Digital Image in Windows Photo Gallery

1. After you upload your photos to your computer, you can view them onscreen. To begin, choose Start➪All Programs➪Windows Photo Gallery.

2. In the resulting Windows Photo Gallery window, as shown in **Figure 10-6**, click any of the items in the Navigation pane on the left to choose which images to display (such as those taken in a certain year or saved in a certain folder).

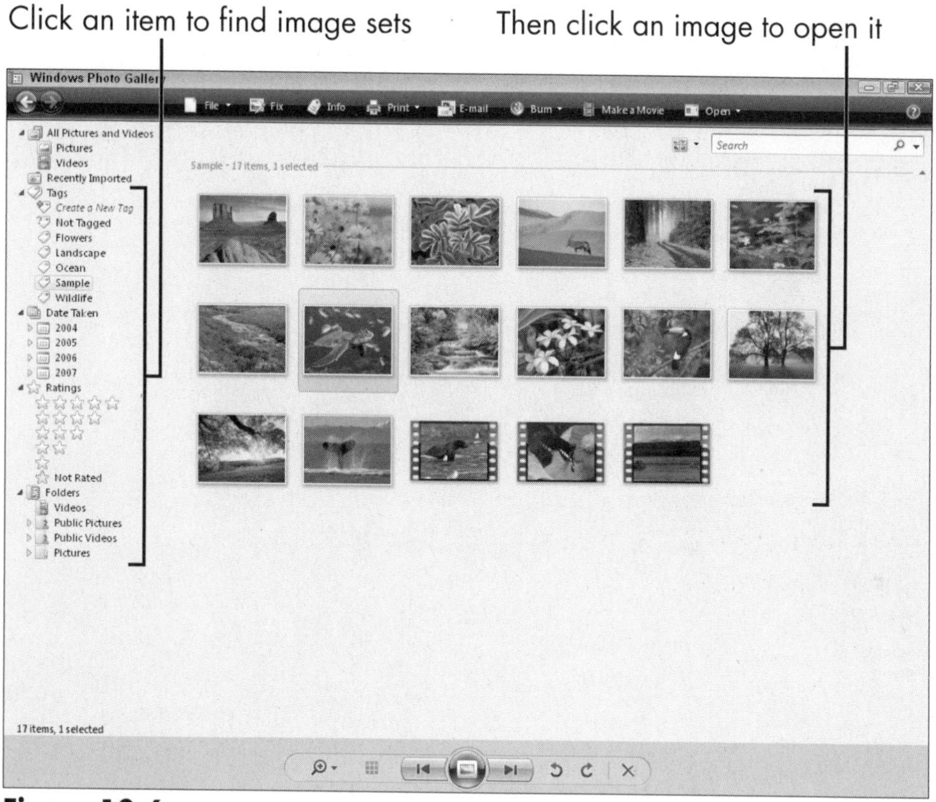

Click an item to find image sets   Then click an image to open it

Figure 10-6

3. In the main area of the window, double-click an image to display it. Then you can use the tools at the bottom of the window that appears (see **Figure 10-7**) to do any of the following:

- The large rectangular icon in the middle is the **Play Slide Show** button. Click it to begin a slide show of your photos, played one after the other.

- The **Display Size** icon displays a slider you can click and drag to change the size of the image thumbnails.

- The **Next** and **Previous** icons move to a previous or following image in the same folder.

- The **Rotate Clockwise** and **Rotate Counterclockwise** icons spin the image 90 degrees at a time.

- The **Delete** button deletes the selected image.

4. When you finish viewing images, click the Close button in the top-right corner to close the Photo Gallery.

Figure 10-7

Use tools to modify photos

Add a Tag to a Photo

1. A *tag* is simply a keyword that you attach to a photo file so you can easily search for categories of files. For example, attach the tag "grandchildren" to all photos of your grandchildren so you can display them all together or even create a slide show of them. To create a new tag in Windows Photo Gallery, click the Create a New Tag item in the Navigation pane on the left. The box opens for editing. Type a tag name and then click anywhere outside it.

2. Right-click the photo and choose Add Tags. Begin to type a tag name, and choose it from the drop-down list that appears (see **Figure 10-8**). Press Enter to add the tag, which then appears in the list of tags associated with that photo.

3. Hover your mouse pointer over a photo. Information about the photo, including tags associated with it, appears in a pop-up window (see **Figure 10-9**).

4. To see all photos associated with a certain tag, click the tag in the Tags list in the Navigation pane.

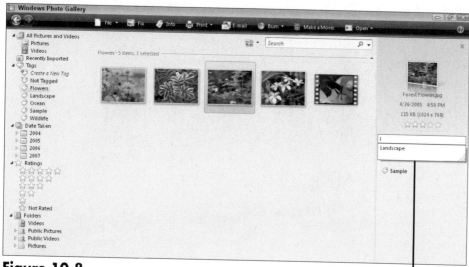

Figure 10-8

Choose a tag from the list

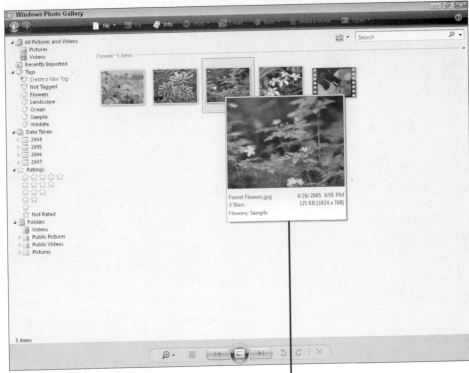

Figure 10-9   Click the pop-up info to see the task pane on the left

> To delete a tag, right-click the tag in the Navigation pane and choose Delete. To rename a tag, right-click it and choose Rename.

> To see a list of all photos in the Photo Gallery organized by tags, click the Tags item in the Navigation pane. Categories for each tag appear in the Photo Gallery window with a note of the total items having that associated tag.

Organize Photos by Date

1. Photo files automatically have a date taken associated with them and appear in the Date Taken list of Photo Gallery by that year and month. If you want to use the Date Taken category to organize photos, you might sometimes want to change a photo's date. For example, if you design a brochure for your local homeless shelter and want to use pictures from 2007 in the 2008 brochure, you might change the date of a photo so you can find it in the 2008 folder. With Windows Photo Gallery open, click a month or date in the Date Taken section of Navigation pane on the left. (You might have to scroll down to locate this section.) Photos taken in that timeframe are displayed (see **Figure 10-10**).

2. Right-click a photo and choose Properties to access and change the Date Taken field.

3. On the Details tab of the Properties dialog box that appears (see **Figure 10-11**), click the Date Taken field and adjust the date by typing a new one, or click the calendar icon and choose a new date from the pop-up calendar.

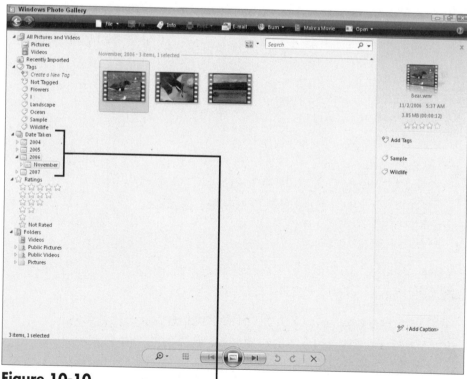

Figure 10-10

Click a month or date

Adjust the date

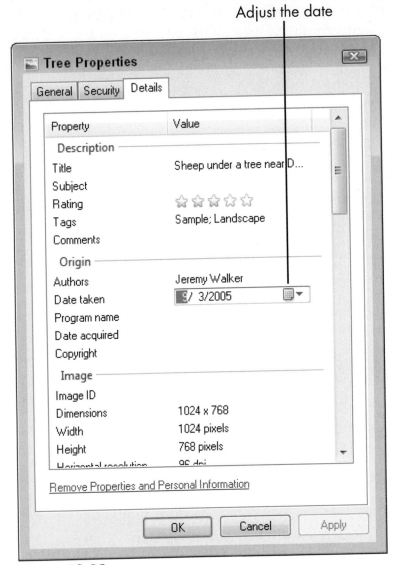

Figure 10-11

4. Click OK. The photo is now in the newly selected date's folder.

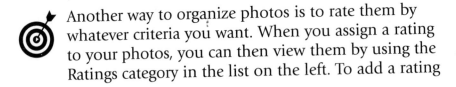 Another way to organize photos is to rate them by whatever criteria you want. When you assign a rating to your photos, you can then view them by using the Ratings category in the list on the left. To add a rating

to a photo, select it and then click the Info button at the top of the window. Click the chosen star for the rating number; that is, if you want to rate a photo a 3, click the third star from the left.

 You can also change other properties of a photo or video in the Properties dialog box. For example, you can change the title, subject, rating, author, date acquired, and copyright. If you're serious about your photography, you can even add information about camera make, model, lenses, and aperture settings here.

Play a Slide Show

1. You can instantly turn a group of photos into a slide show so they're shown one after the other in sequence. You might first want to create a folder containing these photos. So, with Windows Photo Gallery open, click the set of photos you'd like to use for the slide show from the Navigation pane.

2. Click the Play Slide Show button (the big round button in the center with a rectangle in it), as shown in **Figure 10-12**. The slide show begins to play. Note that the Play Slide Show button has changed; it now is the Pause button, and it shows two vertical lines. Click this button to pause the show and the button changes to an arrow; click the arrow to continue playing the show.

3. Slides proceed at a preset speed. You can change this speed by right-clicking the screen and choosing Slide Show Speed Slow, Medium, or Fast (see **Figure 10-13**).

4. To move manually to the next or previous slide, press the right- or left-arrow key.

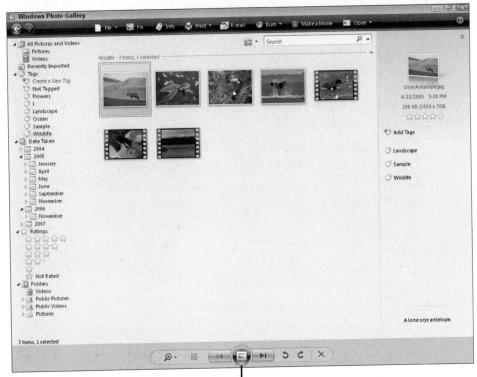

Figure 10-12

Click Play Slide Show

5. To pause the show, click the Pause button.

6. To end the show, press the Esc key.

 If you want to create a custom show, you can create a new tag, assign it to the photos you want to be in the show, and then choose that tag in the Navigation pane before running the show. See the earlier task, "Add a Tag to a Photo," for more about how to do this.

Figure 10-13

Right-click to change the speed

Fix a Photo

1. Photo Gallery has tools for editing a photo, adjusting settings such as the photo brightness, and cropping to a portion of the image. You can use these tools and use the Undo and Redo tools at the bottom of the Fix pane if you change your mind. However, after you close the Fix pane, any changes you made and haven't undone are saved permanently. With the Photo Gallery open, display a photo by locating it with the Navigation pane. (See the task "View a Digital Image in Windows Photo Gallery" earlier in this chapter for detailed steps if you need them.) Then click the thumbnail to select it.

2. Click the Fix button at the top of the Photo Gallery Window. The Fix window appears, as shown in **Figure 10-14**.

3. Click **Auto Adjust** to let Photo Gallery fix the photo or use any of the following tools. Click the tool name once to display options (see **Figure 10-15**) and click it again to close that tool.

- Click **Adjust Exposure** and use the sliders to adjust brightness and contrast.

- Click **Adjust Color** and use the sliders to adjust temperature, tint, and saturation.

- Click **Crop Picture** and use the handles on the rectangle that appears to enlarge or shrink the area on the photo to be cropped. Alternatively, click the rectangle and drag it around your picture to crop to another location on it. Click the Apply button to apply the cropping.

Fix automatically with Auto Adjust

Figure 10-14

- If your picture contains a face with red, glowing eyes, click the **Fix Red Eye** tool and then click and drag around the eye you want to fix in your image to adjust it.

4. You can use the navigation tools at the bottom to zoom in or out, fit the image to the window, move to the next image, undo or redo actions, or delete the picture. When you're finished, click the Back to Gallery button. All changes are saved permanently.

The Undo feature in this window allows you to pick the action you want to undo, unlike many Undo features that force you to undo all the actions leading back to the action you want to undo. Click the arrow on the Undo button under the tools, rather than on the set of buttons along the bottom, to use this feature.

Click to access the Adjust Color settings

Figure 10-15

Burn Photos to a CD or DVD

1. Insert a writable CD or DVD into your disc drive. (Discs come in read and write versions; you need a writable disc to save data to it and not just read data from it. See Chapter 5 for more about disc formats.)

2. With the Photo Gallery open, display a photo by locating it with the Navigation pane and then click the thumbnail to select it. To select additional images, hold down the Ctrl key while clicking the images.

3. Click the Burn button at the top of the Photo Gallery window, and then choose Video DVD from the menu that appears.

4. In the resulting Windows DVD Maker dialog box (see **Figure 10-16**), click the image and then click then Next.

Figure 10-16

Click Next

5. In the Ready to Burn Disc window that appears (see **Figure 10-17**), click the Burn button to proceed.

6. The Burn a Disc window appears. If you want, modify the disc title or adjust the recording speed and then click Next. A progress bar appears.

7. When the files have been burned to the disc, a confirming dialog box appears, and your disc drawer opens. Click Finish to complete the process and close the wizard.

In the confirmation dialog box that appears in Step 7, you can select the Yes, Burn These Files to Another Disc check box if you want to make another copy of the same files.

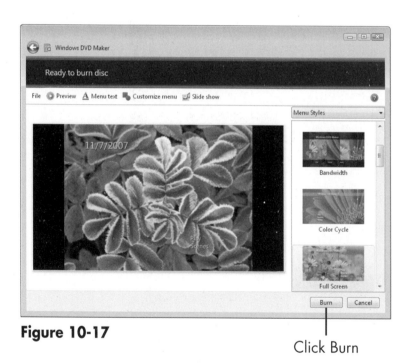

Figure 10-17

Click Burn

Listening to Music

Chapter 11

usic is the universal language, and your computer opens up many opportunities for appreciating it. Your computer makes it possible for you to listen to your favorite music, download music from the Internet, play audio CDs and DVDs, and organize your music by creating playlists. You can also save (or *burn* in computer lingo) music tracks to a CD/DVD or portable music device such as the hugely popular iPod.

You discover a variety of music-related tasks in this chapter, including

➡ Getting your computer ready for listening by setting up your speakers and adjusting the volume

➡ Downloading music from the Internet or a CD/DVD and playing it

➡ Managing your music by creating playlists of tracks you download

➡ Burning tracks to CD/DVD or downloading music to portable devices so that you and your music can hit the road

Set Up Speakers

1. Attach speakers to your computer by plugging them into the appropriate connection (often labeled with a little megaphone or speaker symbol) on your central processing unit (CPU), laptop, or monitor.

2. Choose Start⇨Control Panel⇨Hardware and Sound; in the Hardware and Sound window that appears, click the Manage Audio Devices link (under Sound).

3. In the resulting Sound dialog box (see **Figure 11-1**), double-click the Speakers item.

Double-click the Speakers item

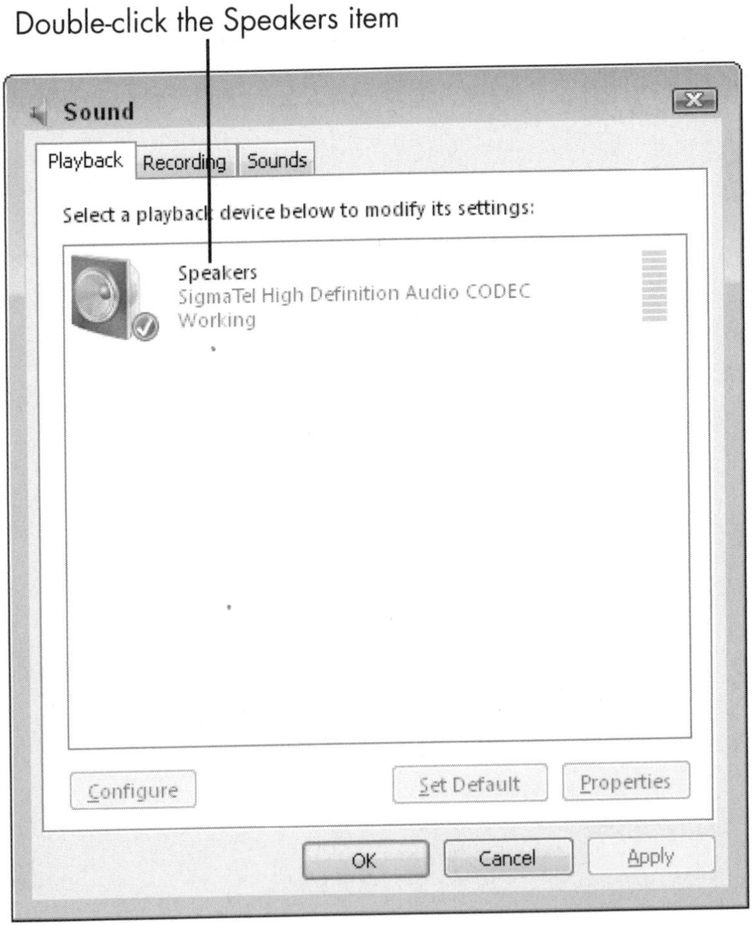

Figure 11-1

4. In the resulting Speakers Properties dialog box, click the Levels tab, as shown in **Figure 11-2**, and then click and drag the Speakers slider to adjust the speaker volume. Dragging the slider to the left lowers the volume; dragging to the right raises the volume. *Note:* If there's a small red *x* on the speaker button, click it to activate the speakers.

5. Click the Balance button. In the resulting Balance dialog box, use the L(eft) and R(ight) sliders to adjust the balance of sounds between the two speakers.

6. Click OK three times to close all the open dialog boxes and save the new settings.

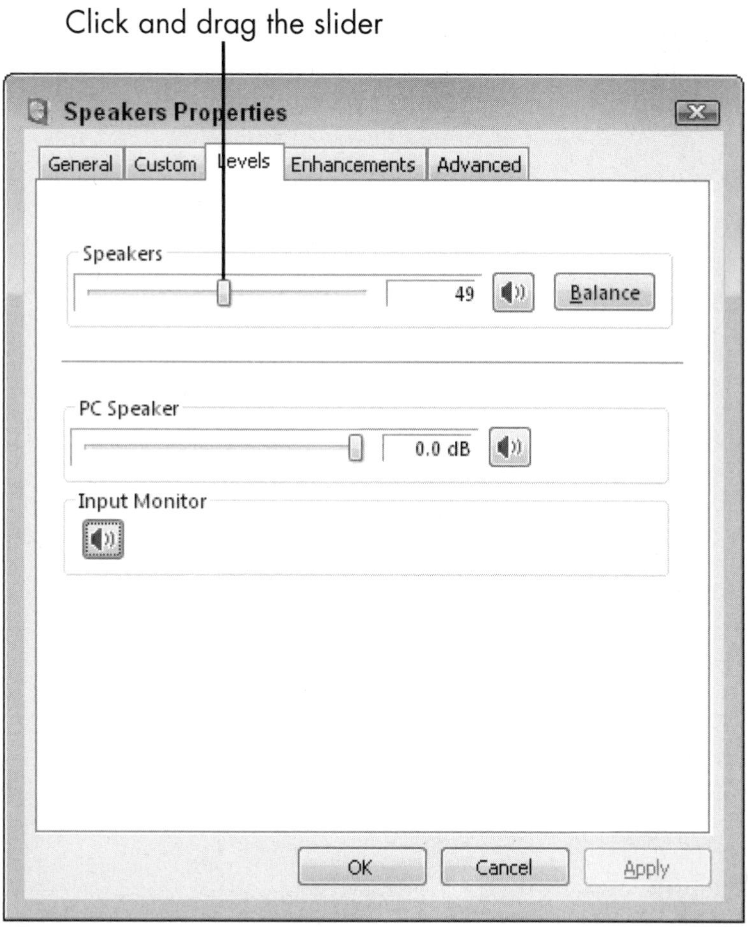

Click and drag the slider

Figure 11-2

You can easily test your speakers. On the Advanced tab of the Speakers Properties dialog box, choose your speaker configuration and then click the Test button. This feature tests first one speaker and then the other to help you pinpoint whether one of your speakers is having problems or whether you should adjust the balance between the speakers for better sound.

Control the System Volume

1. Choose Start➪Control Panel➪Hardware and Sound.

2. In the resulting Hardware and Sound window, click the Adjust System Volume link under Sound to display the Volume Mixer dialog box (as shown in **Figure 11-3**).

3. Make any of the following changes to the settings:

- Click and drag the Device volume slider up or down to adjust the main system volume.

- For sounds played by Windows, adjust the volume by clicking and dragging the Applications slider.

- To mute the main system or application volume, click the speaker icon beneath either slider. When the volume is muted, a red symbol appears. To turn sound back on, click the icon again.

4. Click the Close button twice.

 Here's a handy shortcut for quickly adjusting the volume of your default sound device. Click the Volume button (which looks like a little gray speaker) in the Windows System Tray located in the bottom-right corner of your screen. To adjust the volume, use the slider on the Volume pop-up that appears or select the Mute check box to turn off sounds. (To turn sound on again, deselect the check box.)

Click and drag the slider

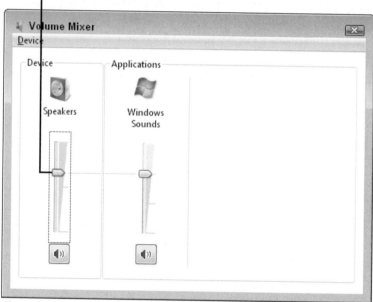

Figure 11-3

Add (Rip) a CD/DVD to Media Player

1. You can use Windows Media Player to play music from a CD/DVD in your computer hard drive, and if you want to copy the music from a disc into a Windows Media Player library, you can. Just remember that the music is only for your personal use. If you e-mail the music files or in some other way share them with others, you could be violating copyright laws. To get started copying music from a disc to Windows Media Player, insert a disc into your computer's CD/DVD-RW drive. The CD/DVD should contain songs or video you want to add to your computer.

2. Open the Windows Media Player (choose Start⇨All Programs⇨Windows Media Player), click the Library tab, and then click an album or playlist to open it.

3. Click the Rip tab at the top of the window. The Rip window lists the titles on the currently open disc with check boxes to the left of each. Ripping begins automatically;

but if the list includes a track you don't want to copy, quickly deselect its check box in the Rip window (see **Figure 11-4**).

4. Click the Start Rip button if ripping doesn't begin automatically. When the rip is complete, the titles appear in the playlist in the Library window.

Click to deselect check boxes for tracks you don't want to copy

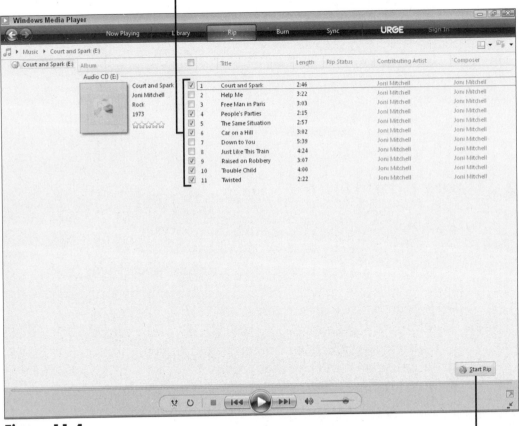

Figure 11-4

Click Start Rip

Windows Media Player offers a few different formats for ripping. For example, Windows Media Audio offers you a smaller file size and good audio quality. Windows Media Audio Lossless provides better quality at the cost of a larger file size. Other choices include MP3 and WAV. If you have a personal music player, choosing the MP3 format is often helpful because this format plays on just about any player. To change this setting, click the arrow under the Rip tab at the top, choose Format, and click an option in the menu that appears.

Play Music in Media Player

1. One of the major uses of Windows Media Player is to play music that is stored on your hard drive or on an audio CD or DVD you insert into your computer disc drive. Choose Start➪All Programs➪Windows Media Player.

2. In the resulting Windows Media Player window, click the Library tab to display the library, as shown in **Figure 11-5**. Click an album or playlist to open it; the titles of the songs are displayed in the right pane.

3. Use the buttons on the bottom of the Player window (as shown in **Figure 11-6**) to do the following:

- Click a track, and then click the Play button to play it.

- Click the Stop button to stop playback.

- Click the Next or Previous button to move to the next or previous track in an album or playlist.

- Use the Mute and Volume controls to pump up the sound or tone it down without having to modify the Windows volume settings.

Tired of the order in which your tracks play? You can use the Turn Shuffle On button on the far left of the playback controls to have Windows Media Player play the tracks on your album randomly. Click this button again to turn off the shuffle feature.

Rather than using the Next and Previous buttons to jump to another track, you can click a track in the track list in the Media Player window. This can be much quicker if you want to jump several tracks ahead or behind of the currently playing track.

Click a playlist

Click an album   Click the library tab

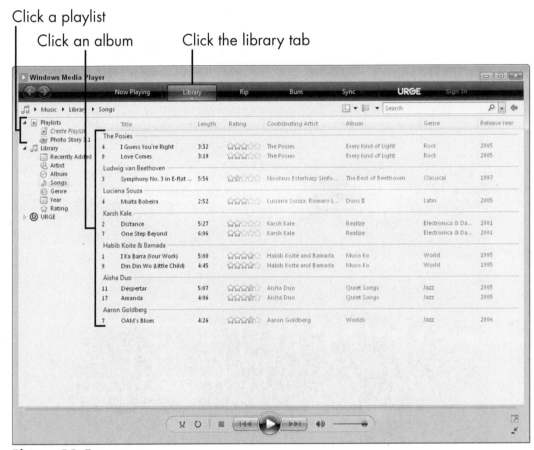

Figure 11-5

Play

Turn shuffle on   Previous   Next   Volume slider

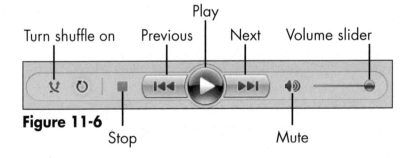

Figure 11-6

Stop   Mute

Create a Windows Media Player Playlist

1. Windows Media Player (see Chapter 10 for more about this handy program) helps you play and organize your music files. One way it does that is by allowing you to create *playlists*, which are custom collections of music you can put together, kind of like mixing your own album with whatever music you choose. You can further organize playlists and individual tracks into libraries to help you catalog certain types of music. To build a playlist, choose Start⇨All Programs⇨Windows Media Player.

2. In the Windows Media Player window that appears, click the Library tab and then click the Create Playlist link at the left under the Playlists item.

3. The Create Playlist label disappears, and a text box opens in its place; type a playlist title there and then click outside the title. An empty playlist with that name appears in the List pane on the right.

4. Click a library in the left pane of the Media Library, and the library contents appear (see **Figure 11-7**). Click an item and then drag it to the new playlist in the right pane. Repeat this step to add additional titles to the playlist.

5. When you finish adding titles, click the Save Playlist button in the bottom-right corner of the window. To play a playlist, click it in the Library pane and then click the Play button (the circular button at the bottom of Media Player, with the triangle-shaped icon).

6. You can manage the playlist by right-clicking it and choosing Edit in List Pane. Click the arrow next to the playlist title and use the drop-down menu commands to do the following tasks:

   • Choose Clear List to remove all tracks from the playlist.

- Choose Skipped Items to indicate how to deal with tracks you have skipped. For example, if you skip over tracks while playing back your music, you can choose to have Windows Media Player prompt you to remove those tracks next time you save, or it can skip those tracks every time you listen to the playlist.

- Choose Shuffle List Now to randomly reorganize the titles to play in a different order.

- Choose Sort to sort the playlist by title, artist, release date, and so on.

- Choose Rename Playlist to give it a different name.

- Choose Save Playlist As to save the playlist with a new name.

Click a library   Drag items to the new playlist

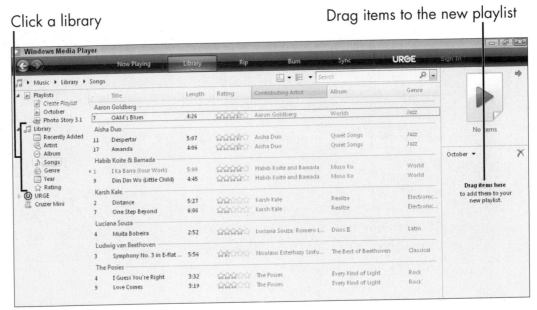

Figure 11-7

Create (Burn) a Music CD/DVD

1. If you have music tracks or playlists in Windows Media Player libraries that you want to save to a disc, you can do so. (Just keep in mind the copyright issues that prohibit you from sharing such a disc.) Insert a blank CD or DVD suitable for storing audio files into your computer's CD/DVD drive. (See Chapter 5 for more about CD/DVD formats.)

2. Open Windows Media Player and click the Burn button.

3. Click the albums or playlists that you want to put on the disc and drag them to the Burn List pane (see **Figure 11-8**).

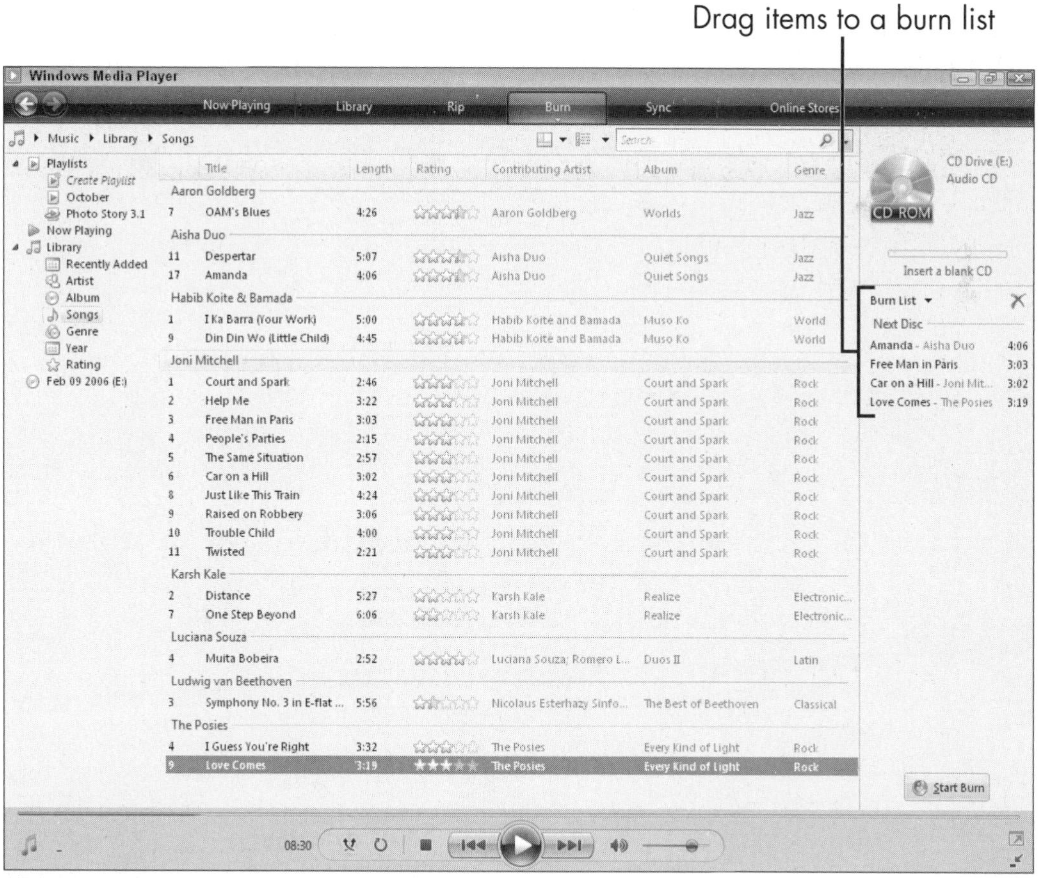

Drag items to a burn list

Figure 11-8

4. Click the Start Burn button in the bottom-right corner. Windows Media Player begins to burn the items to the disc. The Status column for the first song title reads Writing to Disc, which changes to Complete when the track is copied.

5. When the burn is complete, your disc is ejected (although you can change this option by clicking the arrow under the Burn tab and choosing Eject Disc After Burning to deselect it).

 If you send and receive (or *swap*) music online through various music-sharing services, copy them to CD/DVD, and then pass them around to your friends, always do a virus check on the files before handing them off. Also, be sure you have the legal right to download and swap music with others.

Buy Music Online

1. There is a world of music on the Internet, and you can buy it and download it to your computer or portable music device using Windows Media Player tools. Choose Start⇨All Programs⇨Windows Media Player.

2. In the resulting Windows Media Player window, choose Online Stores⇨Browse All Online Stores. *Note:* If you've set up a default online store, the Online Stores button displays that store's name.

3. In the resulting window displaying a choice of online stores (see **Figure 11-9**), click a category in the Categories list on the left and then click a store icon on the right.

4. A message appears, confirming that you want to go to this store. Click Yes. (The store is now your default store in this category, and its name is displayed on the Online Stores button.)

5. In the resulting store's Web site, follow that site's procedure to browse or make purchases. Most sites have a search feature where you can enter information such as the artist or CD name. You might also click categories of music such as Jazz or Classical to locate the music you want.

6. When you finish shopping, click any of the tabs in Media Player to close the online store and return to using Media Player.

If you've set up a store in more than one category, whichever store you visited last is displayed on the Online Stores button. To easily switch to another store, click the arrow on the Online Stores button and choose Add Current Service to Menu. Now you can quickly go to that store by choosing it from the menu.

Click a category   Then click a store

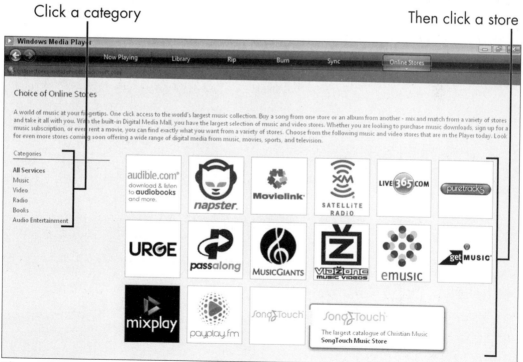

Figure 11-9

Play Online Radio Stations

1. Today, many radio stations are *streaming* on the Net, which simply means that their programs are available for you to listen to on your computer. To start listening, choose Start⇨All Programs⇨Windows Media Player.

2. In the resulting Windows Media Player window, click the arrow on the Online Stores button and choose Media Guide. *Remember:* If you've set up a default online store, the Online Stores button displays that store's name.

3. Click the Radio option in the list of media across the top (see **Figure 11-10**).

4. Click a category of music in the list on the right. A list of radio stations and programs appears (see **Figure 11-11**).

5. Click the Listen to Station link for an item to launch the radio station.

Click Radio

Figure 11-10

Figure 11-11   Click to listen to a station

Clicking some links takes you to another Web site from which your music is played. These sites have their own security and privacy settings. Don't go to a site that you don't recognize if you have concerns about security.

You can click the logo for any radio station to play it. To play a different station, just click its logo. To turn off the radio feature, click the Close button in the top-right corner of the window to exit Media Player, choose another feature such as TV/Celebs, or play a song from your music library.

Playing Games in Windows Vista

All work and no play is just wrong no matter what your age. So, Microsoft has built plenty of games into Windows Vista to keep you amused.

Many computer games are essentially virtual versions of games that you already know, such as Solitaire and Chess. But Windows Vista has added some interesting treats to the mix — several that depend to a great extent on some neat on-screen animation.

Altogether, you can access several built-in games through Windows, and this chapter gives you a sampling of the best of them, as well as an overview of how you play games online. Here's what you can expect:

➠ Traditional card games, such as Solitaire and Hearts

➠ Games of dexterity, such as Minesweeper, where the goal is to be the fastest, smartest clicker in the West

➠ The traditional game of strategy, Chess, played on a virtual board

⟶ An entire world of online gaming where you can interact with other players from around the world

Play Solitaire

Solitaire is the great single-player card game that many of us while away too many hours on. Now you can play Solitaire and let your computer do all the shuffling and dealing — you simply move cards around the piles to try to win the game.

1. To begin playing Solitaire on your computer, choose Start⇨Games. In the resulting Games window, (see **Figure 12-1**), double-click Solitaire.

2. In the resulting Solitaire window, click a card that's facing up in the row of seven cards (see **Figure 12-2**). Then click a card in another deck that you want to move it on top of or click and drag it to the other card. The first card moves on top of the second.

Figure 12-1

Double-click Solitaire

Figure 12-2

Click a card

3. When playing the game, you have the following options:

- If no moves are available, click the stack of cards in the upper-left corner to deal another round of cards.

- If you move the last card from one of the six laid-out stacks, leaving only a facedown card, click the facedown card to flip it up. You can also move a King onto any empty stack.

- When you reach the end of the stack of cards in the upper-left corner, click them again to redeal the cards that you didn't use the first time.

- You can play a card in one of two places: either building a stack from King to Ace on the bottom row, alternating suits; or starting from Ace in any of the top four slots, placing cards from Ace to King in a single suit.

- When you complete a set of cards (Ace to King) in the six card slots across the middle of the screen, click the top card and then click one of the four blank deck spots at the top-right of the window. If you complete all four sets, you win.

4. To deal a new game, choose Game⇨New Game. Unlike life, it's easy to start over with Solitaire!

5. To close Solitaire, click the Close button.

Play FreeCell

Freecell is kind of a variation on Solitaire, where you assemble sets of cards, but you get a bit more latitude about setting cards aside until you find the right match for them.

1. Choose Start⇨Games; in the Games window, double-click FreeCell.

2. In the resulting FreeCell window, as shown in **Figure 12-3**, a game is ready to play. If you want a fresh game, you can always choose Game⇨New Game; a new game is dealt and ready to play.

 The goal is to move all the cards, grouped by the four suits, to the *home cells* (the four cells in the upper-right corner) stacked in order from Ace at the bottom to King at the top. The trick here is that you get four free cells (the four cells in the upper-left corner) where you can manually move a card out of the way to free up a move. You can also use those four slots to allow you to move up to five cards in a stack at once. (For example, you can move a Jack, 10, 9, and 8 all together onto a Queen.) You can move only as many cards as there are free cells available plus one. Free spaces in the rows of card stacks also act as free cells.

You win when you have four stacks of cards for each of the four suits placed on the home cells.

3. To move a card, click it and then click a free cell or another card at the bottom of a column. **Figure** 12-4 shows a game where two free cells are already occupied.

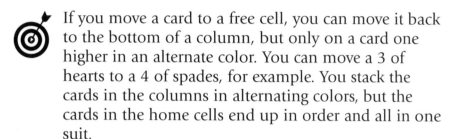

If you move a card to a free cell, you can move it back to the bottom of a column, but only on a card one higher in an alternate color. You can move a 3 of hearts to a 4 of spades, for example. You stack the cards in the columns in alternating colors, but the cards in the home cells end up in order and all in one suit.

If you get hooked on this game, try going to www.freecell.com, a Web site devoted to FreeCell. Here you can engage in live games with other players, read more about the rules and strategies, and even buy FreeCell merchandise. Don't say I didn't warn you about the possibility of addiction.

Stack cards in the home cells

Figure 12-3

Two free cells are occupied

Figure 12-4

Play Minesweeper

If you like your games a little more explosive, try Minesweeper. The object is to click cells on the game board without clicking on hidden mines.

1. Choose Start➪Games; in the Games window, double-click Minesweeper. In the window that appears, you can click the level of difficulty you prefer.

2. The Minesweeper game board opens (see **Figure 12-5**). Click a square on the board, and a timer starts counting the seconds of your game.

- If you click a square and a number appears, the number tells you how many mines are within the eight squares surrounding that square; if the square remains blank, there are no mines within the eight squares surrounding it.

- If you click a square and a bomb appears, all the hidden bombs are exposed (see **Figure 12-6**), and the game is over.

- Right-click a square once to place a flag on it, marking it as a mine. Right-click a square twice to place a question mark on it if you think it might contain a bomb. The question mark acts as a warning to you to stay away for now.

Click a square to start the same

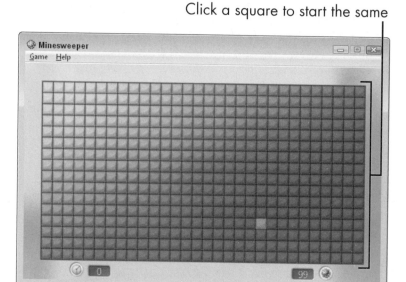

Figure 12-5

Clicking a bomb ends the game

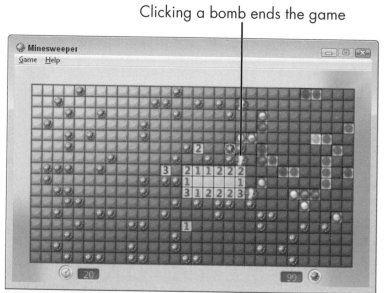

Figure 12-6

3. To begin a new game, choose Game⇨New Game. In the New Game dialog box, click Quit and Start a New Game. If you want to play a game with the same settings as the previous one, click Restart This Game.

4. You can set several game options through the Game menu:

- To change the expertise required, choose Game⇨Options and then choose Beginner, Intermediate, or Advanced. Higher level games throw more squares at you with more potential bombs.

- To change the color of the playing board, choose Game⇨Change Appearance.

- If you want to see how many games you've won, your longest winning or losing streak and more, choose Game⇨Statistics.

5. To end the game, click the Close button.

 If you want a bigger game board (more squares, more bombs, more fun) choose Game⇨Options and then click Custom and specify the number of squares across and down as well as the number of bombs hidden within them.

Play Hearts

Hearts is a trick-taking card game, similar to euchre or bridge.

1. To begin playing this popular card game, choose Start⇨Games and double-click Hearts. If you've never played before, you see a Microsoft Hearts Network dialog box; enter your name and click OK.

2. In the resulting Hearts window, as shown in **Figure 12-7**, your hand is displayed, but the computers' hands are hidden. Begin play by clicking three cards to pass to your opponent and then clicking the Pass Left button. (If you need help figuring out which cards to pass, review the rules of the game by pressing F1 to view game Help.)

3. Each computer player, moving clockwise around the window, plays a card of the same suit; when it's your turn, make your play with a card by clicking it. The one who plays the highest card of the suit in play wins the trick. (A *trick* is the cards you collect when you play the highest card of the suit.) The object generally is to avoid being forced to play a card that wins the trick (though there are some bonuses for winning some tricks).

4. Choose Game⇨Options to change the settings shown in **Figure 12-8**. You can rename the other three players, play sounds, show tips, or specify how to save a game.

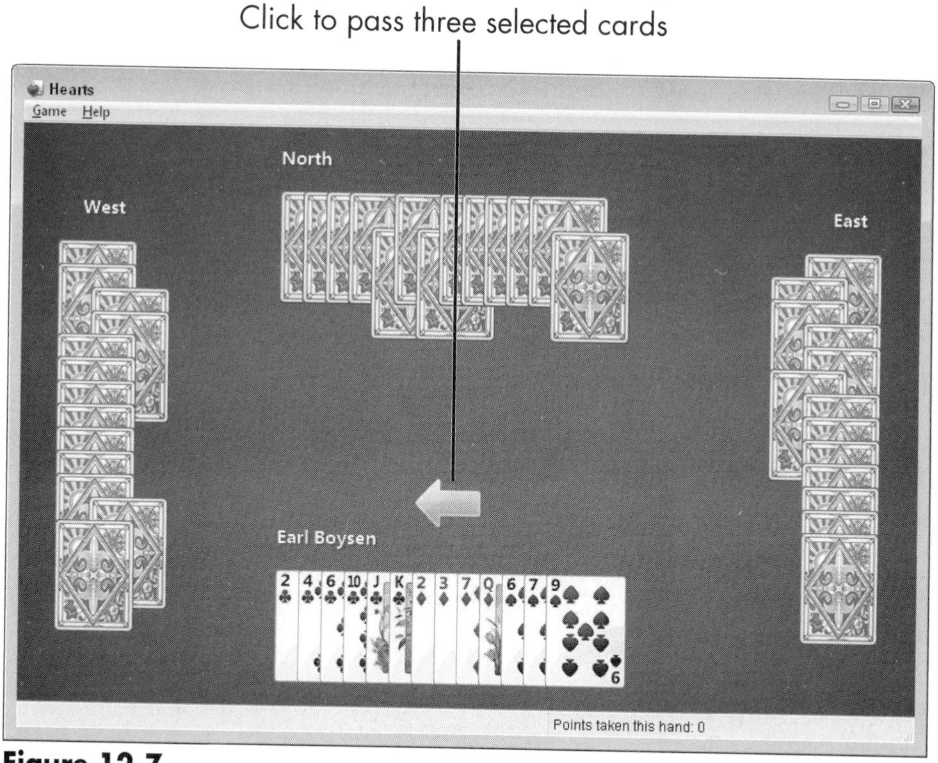

Click to pass three selected cards

Figure 12-7

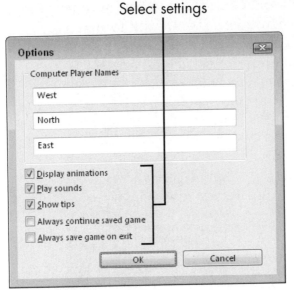

Select settings

Figure 12-8

5. To end the game, choose Game⇨Exit or click the Close button.

Check out the menus in the Games window for organizing and customizing the various games that Windows Vista makes available.

Play Chess Titans

Chess is an ancient game of strategy. If you're a chess buff, you'll enjoy playing a computer opponent in the Windows version, Chess Titans. If you're new to the game, which is rather complex, try visiting www.chess.com for beginner instructions and strategies.

1. To begin playing chess, choose Start⇨Games; in the Games window, double-click Chess Titans. The first time you play the game, the Select Difficulty window appears. Click a skill level to start a game.

2. In the resulting Chess Titans window, a new game is ready to play. By default a new game will be played against the computer, but you can choose to play another person when you start a new game. If you want to start a new game at any time, you can always choose Game⇨ New Game Against Computer or New Game Against Human; a new game is ready to play.

3. Click a piece; all possible moves are highlighted. To move the piece, click the space where you want to move it. Once you make a play, your opponent (either the computer or another human) moves a piece. **Figure 12-9** shows a game in progress with possible moves highlighted.

This knight has a bishop in a tight spot

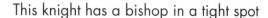

Figure 12-9

 You can change the game options so that possible moves are not highlighted. Choose Game⇨Options. In the resulting Options window, deselect the Show Valid Moves check box and then click OK. The

Options dialog box also lets you control a variety of other settings, including whether you're playing as black or white, whether to show tips or play sounds, and the quality of graphics.

 Don't like the look of your chess board? You can modify it to look like a different material, such as wood. Choose Game➪Change Appearance. In the Change Appearance window, click a style of chess piece and a style of chess board. Click OK to save your settings.

Play Online Games

There are thousands of gaming sites online that let you interact with other players from around the world. Search in your browser using keywords such as "card games" or "Chess" to find them. Some are simple games like Poker or Chess. Others are part of sophisticated virtual worlds where you take on a personality, called an avatar, and can even acquire virtual money and goods.

Here are some tips for getting involved in online gaming and some advice for staying safe:

➡ Safety first! You're playing games with strangers, so avoid giving out personal information or choosing a revealing username. If somebody gets inappropriately emotional or abusive while playing the game, leave the game immediately and report the player to the site owner.

➡ In some cases, you can play a computer; in others, you're playing against other people the game site matches you up with. You can usually request a level of play, so if you're a beginner, you can feel comfortable that you'll be matched with other beginners.

➡ To play some games, you might need additional software, such as Adobe Shockwave Player or software to enable your computer to play animations. If you see such a message on a game site, be sure you're downloading software from a reputable source that has a good privacy policy for users and credentials like a Better Business Bureau seal so you don't download a virus or spyware.

➡ Many games are free, though some require that you enter information about yourself to become a member. Read the fine print carefully when signing up.

➡ Many game sites offer tutorials or practice games to help you learn and improve. **Figure 12-10** shows the Tutorial page for Legends of Norrath, an multiplayer online role playing game.

Tutorials explain game strategies

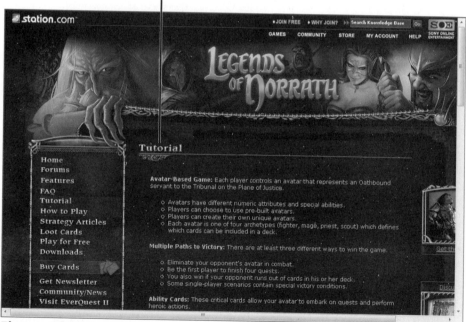

Figure 12-10

➡ Some games allow several players to participate at once, so you might have to be on your toes! In addition to manipulating pieces or characters, you might also be able to communicate with other players using text messaging or even voice messages. Chapter 16 explains how text messaging (also called instant messaging) works.

➥ Online gaming can be addictive, so be as moderate in your playing online as you are offline. Remember that these games are just for fun.

Part III
Exploring the Internet

The 5th Wave
By Rich Tennant

"Awww, cool – a Web Cam! You should point it at something interesting to watch. The fish bowl! The fish bowl!"

Understanding Internet Basics

*F*or many people, going online might be the major reason to buy a computer. You can use the Internet to check stock quotes, play interactive games with others, and file your taxes, for example. For seniors especially, the Internet can provide wonderful ways to keep in touch with family and friends located around the country or on the other side of the world via e-mail or instant messaging. You can share photos of your grandchildren or connect with others who share your hobbies or interests.

But before you begin all those wonderful activities, it helps to understand some basics about the Internet and how it works and to master the art of getting around the online environment.

This chapter helps you to understand what the Internet and World Wide Web are, as well as some basics about Internet connections. You also find out how to browse the Web and keep yourself safe while doing so.

Chapter 13

Get ready to . . .

Understand What the Internet Is

The Internet, cyberspace, the Web . . . people and the media bounce around many online-related terms these days, and folks sometimes use them incorrectly. Your first step in getting familiar with the Internet is to understand what some of these terms mean.

Here's a list of common Internet-related terms:

⟹ The **Internet** is a large network of computers that contain information and technology tools that can be accessed by anybody with an Internet connection. (See the next task for information about Internet connections.)

⟹ Residing on that network of computers is a huge set of documents, which form the **World Wide Web**, usually referred to as just **the Web**.

⟹ The Web includes **Web sites**, which are made up of collections of **Web pages** just as a book is made up of individual pages. Web sites can be informational, host communication tools such as **chats** or **discussion boards** that allow people to "talk" via text messages, or enable you to buy or bid for a wide variety of items in an entire online marketplace referred to as the world of **e-commerce**.

⟹ To get around online, you use a software program called a **browser**. There are many browsers available, and they're free. Internet Explorer is Microsoft's browser; others include Mozilla Firefox and Opera. Browsers offer tools to help you navigate from Web site to Web site and from one Web page to another.

⟹ When you open a Web site, you might see colored text or graphics that represent **hyperlinks**, also referred to as **links**. You can click links to move from place to place within a Web page, on a Web site, or around the Internet. **Figure 13-1** shows some hyperlinks indicated by highlighted text or graphics.

 A link can be an graphic or text. A text link is identifiable by colored text, and it's usually underlined. After you click a link, it usually changes color to show that you've followed the link.

Click a text hyperlink   Click a graphical hyperlink

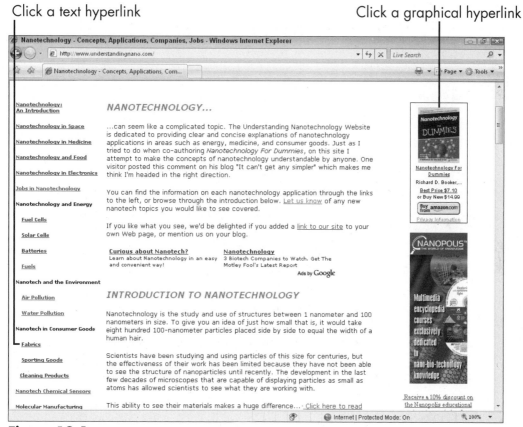

Figure 13-1

Explore Different Types of Internet Connections

Before you can connect to the Internet for the first time, you have to have certain hardware in place and choose your Internet service provider (also referred to as ISP or simply a provider). An ISP is a company that owns dedicated computers (called *servers*) that you use to access the Internet. ISPs charge a monthly fee for this service.

In the past, you could sign up with an ISP such as Microsoft's MSN to get dial-up access (that is, access via your regular phone line) to the Internet. Today many people pay to access the Internet through their telephone or cable television provider, whose connections are much faster than a dial-up connection. Companies such as AOL still offer dial-up connections, but today their main attraction is the content they provide such as news, human interest stories, horoscopes, and games.

You can choose a type of connection to go online. Depending on the type of connection you want, you will go to a different company for the service. For example, a DSL connection might come through your phone company, whereas a cable connection is available through your cable-TV company. Not every type of connection is necessarily available in every area, so check with phone, cable, and small Internet providers in your town to find out your options and costs.

Here are the most common types of connections:

➡ **Dial-up connections:** With a dial-up connection, you use a phone line to connect to the Internet, entering a phone number that's provided by your ISP. This is the slowest connection method, but it's relatively inexpensive. Your dial-up Internet provider will give you *local access numbers,* which you use to go online. Using these local access numbers, you won't incur long distance charges for your connection. However, with this type of connection, you can't use a phone line for phone calls while you're connected to the Internet.

➡ **Digital Subscriber Line:** DSL also uses a phone line, but your phone is available to you to make calls even when you're connected to the Internet. DSL is a form of broadband communication, which may use phone lines and fiber-optic cables for transmission. You have to subscribe to a broadband service (check with your phone company) and pay a monthly fee for access.

→ **Cable:** You may also go through your local cable company to get your Internet service via the cable that brings your TV programming rather than your phone line. This is another type of broadband service and is also faster than a dial-up connection. Check with your cable company for monthly fees.

→ **Wireless hotspots:** If you take a wireless-enabled laptop computer with you on a trip, you can piggyback on a connection somebody else has made. You will find wireless hotspots in many public places, such as airports, cafes, and hotels. If you're in range of such a hotspot, your computer usually finds the connection automatically, making Internet service available to you for free.

Internet connections have different speeds that depend partially on your computer's capabilities and partially on the connection you get from your provider. Before you choose a provider, it's important to understand how faster connection speeds can benefit you:

→ Faster speeds allow you to send data faster. In addition, Web pages and images display faster.

→ Dial-up connection speeds run at the low end about 56 kilobits per second, or Kbps. Most broadband connections today are around 500 to 600 Kbps. If you have a slower connection, a file might take minutes to upload (for example a file you're attaching to an e-mail). This same operation might take only seconds at a higher speed.

Depending on your type of connection, you'll need different hardware:

➡ A broadband connection uses an Ethernet cable and a modem, which your provider should make available, as well as a connection to your phone or cable line.

➡ Most desktop and laptop computers come with a built-in modem for dial-up connections and are enabled for wireless. If you choose a broadband connection, your phone or cable company will provide you with an external modem (usually for a price).

➡ If you have a laptop that doesn't have a built-in wireless modem, you can add this hardware by buying a wireless CardBus adapter PC card at any office supply or computer store. This card enables a laptop to pick up wireless signals.

Set Up Your Internet Connection

1. Today it makes sense to use a broadband connection if you're planning on connecting to the Internet on a regular basis and can afford the monthly fee. To set up your computer for broadband access, you can start by choosing Start⇨Network.

2. In the resulting window, click Network and Sharing Center.

3. In the resulting Network and Sharing Center window (see **Figure 13-2**), click the Set Up a Connection or Network link.

4. In the Choose a Connection dialog box, accept the default option Connect to the Internet by clicking Next.

5. In the resulting dialog box, click your connection type. (These steps follow the selection of Broadband.) If you have a current connection, a window appears and asks whether you want to use a current connection. Click Next to accept the default option of creating a new connection.

6. In the resulting dialog box, as shown in **Figure 13-3**, enter the username and password your ISP provided, and a connection name of your choosing (if you want to assign one) and then click Connect. Windows automatically detects the connection, and the Network and Sharing Center appears with your connection listed.

7. Click the Close button to close the dialog box.

In many cases, if you have a CD from your ISP, you don't need to follow the preceding steps. Just pop that CD into your CD-ROM drive, and instructions for setting up your account appear.

Click Set Up a Connection or Network

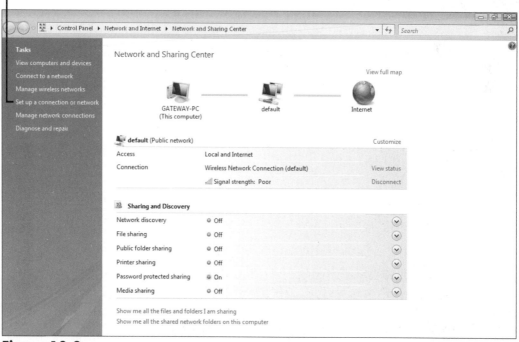

Figure 13-2

Enter a user name and password

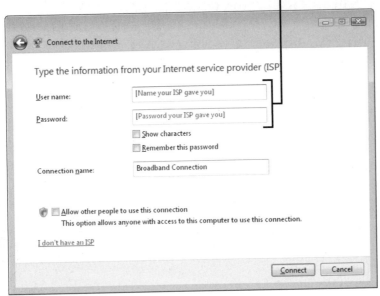

Figure 13-3

Navigate the Web

1. After you've connected to the Internet, you're ready to step foot into the virtual world. The first thing you should know is how to navigate the Web by using a browser. Internet Explorer (also called simply IE) from Microsoft is probably built into your Windows-based computer so it's a good place to start. Open Internet Explorer by clicking its icon on the Quick Launch bar located on the Windows Vista taskbar.

2. Enter a Web site address in the Address bar, as shown in **Figure 13-4**, and then press Enter. If you don't know any URLs, just type **www.understandingnano.com** to visit one of my Web sites.

3. On the resulting Web site, you'll notice different areas of content on the page, including a navigation bar, which includes text or graphics you can click to visit various pages on the site, as well as content in the form of text and graphics. Usually, the browser window doesn't display a whole page. To display the rest of the page, click the arrow at the bottom of the scroll bar on the right side of the window to see more. Or press the Page Down key on your keyboard.

Enter a Web address

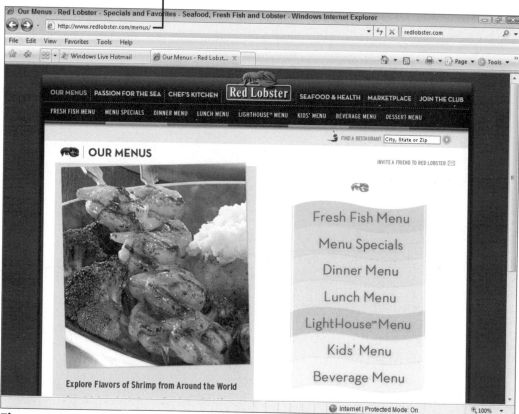

Figure 13-4

4. When you want to go somewhere else, either click a link (which might jump you to another page on the current site or to another site) or enter another address in the Address bar to jump to a different site.

5. Click the Back button to move back to the first page that you visited. Click the Forward button to go forward to the second page that you visited.

6. Click the down-pointing arrow at the far right of the Address bar to display a list of sites that you visited recently, as shown in **Figure 13-5**. Click a site in this list to go there.

Click the arrow

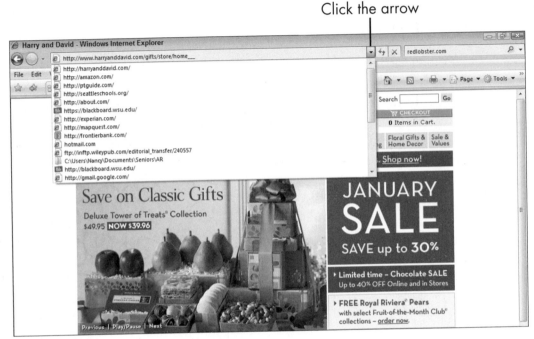

Figure 13-5

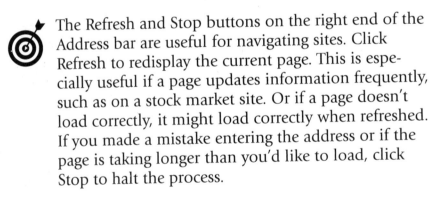 The Refresh and Stop buttons on the right end of the Address bar are useful for navigating sites. Click Refresh to redisplay the current page. This is especially useful if a page updates information frequently, such as on a stock market site. Or if a page doesn't load correctly, it might load correctly when refreshed. If you made a mistake entering the address or if the page is taking longer than you'd like to load, click Stop to halt the process.

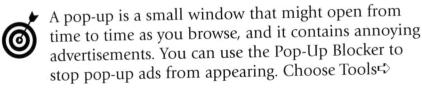 A pop-up is a small window that might open from time to time as you browse, and it contains annoying advertisements. You can use the Pop-Up Blocker to stop pop-up ads from appearing. Choose Tools⇨

Pop-up Blocker⇨Turn On Pop-up Blocker to activate this feature. You can also use the Pop-up Blocker Settings command on this menu to specify sites on which you want to allow pop-ups. For details, see Chapter 14, which explains how you set privacy settings.

Use Tabs in Browsers

Internet Explorer (IE) and several other browsing programs, such as Opera, offer a feature called tabbed browsing. In addition to opening multiple home pages on tabs, you can open new tabs as you browse the Web (see **Figure 13-6**). You can then click tabs to jump to other sites you have displayed on those tabs without having to navigate backwards or forwards in a single window to sites you've previously visited.

Click the New Tab button

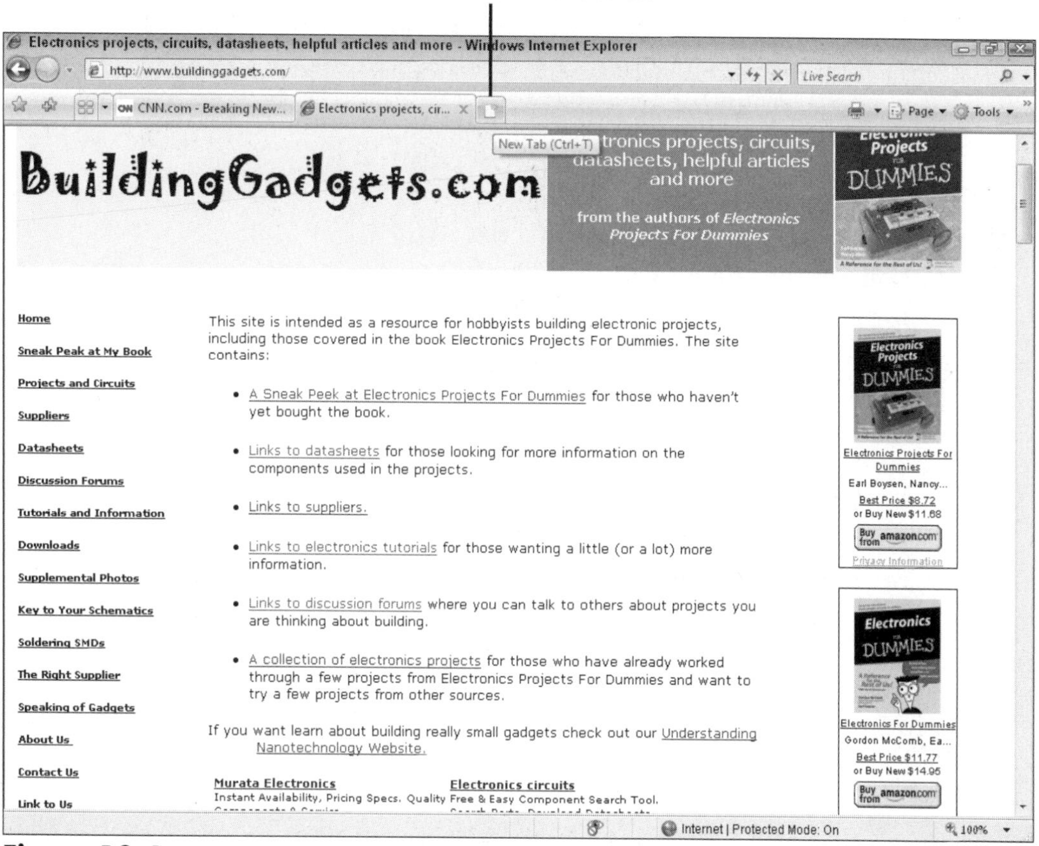

Figure 13-6

Here's how to use tabbed browsing for maximum efficiency in Internet Explorer:

⟹ Click the New Tab button to open a new, blank tab. The new tab now appears above the body of the tab area to the right of any other open tabs.

⟹ Enter an address in the Address bar and press Enter; the site appears in your newly displayed tab.

⟹ Click another tab to jump to another site.

⟹ Click the New Tab button again to add another tab for browsing.

⟹ Click the Close button on any active tab to close it.

 You can open a linked page in a new tab quickly by right-clicking the link and choosing Open in New Tab. A new tab opens with the page displayed.

Set Up a Home Page

1. If you find yourself going to one page often, for example your e-mail page or the local weather, you can set one or more home pages. Whenever you open your browser, home pages display on tabs automatically. Open IE and choose Tools➪Internet Options.

2. In the resulting Internet Options dialog box, on the General tab, enter a Web site address to use as your home page, as shown in **Figure 13-7**. Note that you can enter multiple home pages that will appear on different tabs every time you open IE. Alternatively, click one of the following preset option buttons, as shown in Figure 13-7:

• **Use Current:** Sets whatever page is currently displayed in the browser window as your home page.

- **Use Default:** This setting makes the MSN Web page your home page.

- **Use Blank:** If you're a minimalist, this setting is for you. No Web page displays; you just see a blank area.

3. Click OK to save your setting and close the dialog box.

4. Back in Internet Explorer, click the Home icon (it looks like a house) to go to your home page.

Type the address for your desired home page

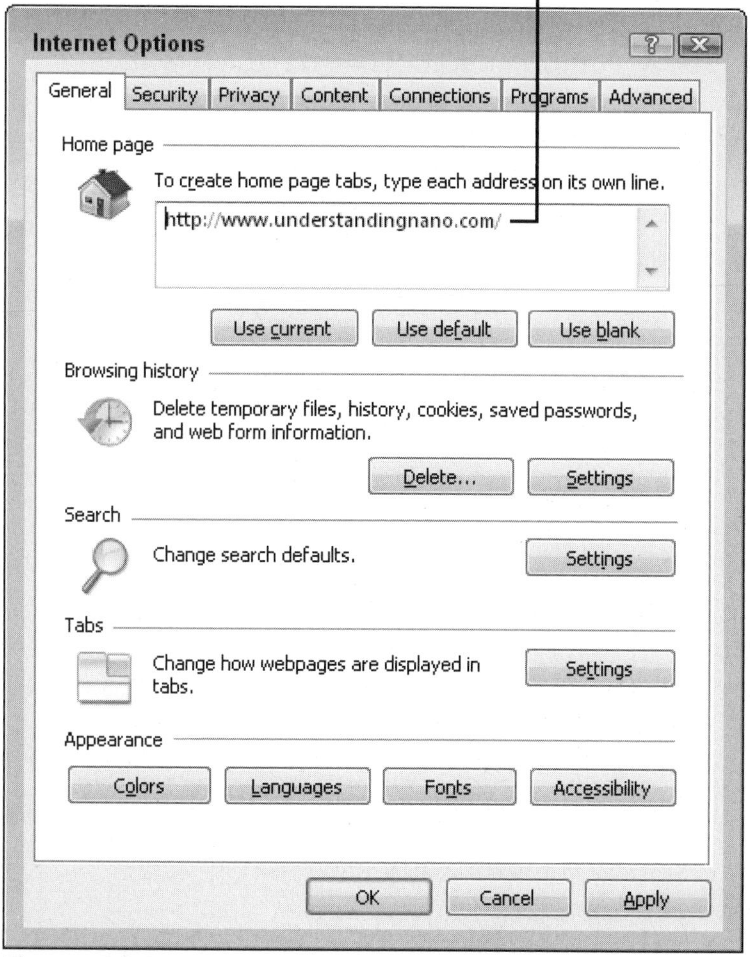

Internet Options

General | Security | Privacy | Content | Connections | Programs | Advanced

Home page

To create home page tabs, type each address on its own line.

http://www.understandingnano.com/

Use current | Use default | Use blank

Browsing history

Delete temporary files, history, cookies, saved passwords, and web form information.

Delete... | Settings

Search

Change search defaults.

Settings

Tabs

Change how webpages are displayed in tabs.

Settings

Appearance

Colors | Languages | Fonts | Accessibility

OK | Cancel | Apply

Figure 13-7

If you want to have more than one home page, you can create multiple home page tabs that will display when you click the Home icon. Click the arrow next to the Home icon and choose Add or Change Home Page. In the Add or Change Home Page dialog box that appears, select Add This Webpage to Your Home Page Tabs radio button and then click Yes. Display other sites and repeat this procedure for all the home page tabs you want.

 To remove a home page you have set up, click the arrow next to the Home icon and choose Remove. In the submenu that appears, choose a particular home page or choose Remove All.

Stay Safe Online

The Internet provides wonderful opportunities to both you and criminals. Information that you place online can be secure or not secure, depending on where it's posted and who you're dealing with. Online predators and scam artists might try to make you a victim, but by understanding how your actions can make you vulnerable, you can stay safe just as you stay safe in the real world by using a little common sense.

To stay safe online, follow these guidelines:

→ **Be careful with whom and what you share online:** Be aware of who has access to information you post online. Deal only with online businesses you trust and who have secure technology (you can spot these from the https at the front of their URL rather than http) and strong privacy policies in place. (Look for a Privacy Policy link to see the policy.) If you post your own information in a blog or on a social site, restrict access to that information to those you know. Or, if you make the information available to the general public, do not reveal any personal information or information that could be used to steal your identity, such as your mother's maiden name.

➡ **Share photos carefully as well:** If you post pictures of you or your family or friends online that are accessible to the general population, make sure they don't reveal anything that could put you or them at risk, such as your street address, car license plate number, or organization (for example, a school or business name on a sweatshirt).

 Be aware that information about you online is cumulative. A criminal might not be able to hurt you from one item you put online, but by trolling the Internet, looking at your friends' blogs, your genealogy files, your alumni newsletter, government site information about your property and property tax, and online phone directories, a criminal might get a good picture of your life that can be used to scam or otherwise harm you. Also remember that information you or others post might stay online for a very long time. Ask friends not to expose you online, and don't expose them.

➡ **Never give out account information:** No reputable business, from ISPs to banks to department stores, will contact you to ask for your account information or password. If you get an e-mail from your bank or stock broker asking for this information, report the message as a scam (called *phishing* and pronounced *fishing*). There's usually a button in your e-mail program you can click with the message displayed to report the problem. If you're concerned about the message, contact the company by phone immediately, using a phone number from your account statement or the company's Web site (which you visit by entering a URL in your address bar, rather than by clicking any link in the e-mail).

➠ **Use technology to defend yourself:** Use both anti-spyware and antivirus software to protect your computer. See Chapter 17 for more information.

➠ **Be suspicious of junk e-mail:** If possible, simply do not open e-mails from people you don't know. If you get an e-mail from somebody you know with an attachment you aren't expecting, contact that person before opening the attachment to be sure it's from that person. Attached files with an .exe extension at the end (such as freeoffer.exe) are particularly dangerous. If you must open e-mails from people you don't know (perhaps because you run a small home business and are sometimes approached by new customers), avoid clicking links in those e-mails, which can take you to sites you'd rather not visit.

➠ **Use junk mail filters:** Use junk mail filters in your e-mail program (see **Figure 13-8**) to isolate and get rid of unwanted messages. These filters identify certain words that are often associated with phony or disreputable offers (such as *Viagra* or *sex*) and phony sounding names of senders, and place suspect e-mails into a Junk folder. You can still retrieve them, but they have been flagged as potentially dangerous so you will be more cautious in handling them. You can also create your own rules that tell your e-mail program how to handle e-mails with certain words in subject lines or from certain senders. See Chapter 15 for more about rules.

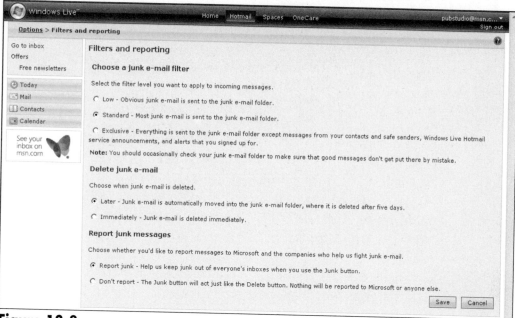

Figure 13-8

Browsing the Web with Internet Explorer

A *browser* is a program that you can use to get around the Internet, but you can also use it to perform searches for information and images. Most browsers, such as Internet Explorer, Opera, and Netscape Navigator, are also available for free. Macintosh computers come with a browser called Safari.

Chapter 13 introduces browser basics, such as how to go directly to a site when you know its Web address, how to use the Back and Forward buttons to move among sites you've visited, and how to view your browsing history. In this chapter, you find out about other features of Internet Explorer, including searching the Internet, saving favorite sites to easily return to them, and accessing more advanced history tools. With your browser, you can do the following tasks:

➠ **Search for information and Web sites you need.** One of the most powerful features of the Internet is how easy it is to search for information, entertainment, images, and more. You can use keywords to find just about anything, but successful searching involves a few procedures that I cover here.

➠ **Saving your favorites.** If a site is interesting or useful, you might want to visit it often. For example, if you're a writer like me, you probably want a dictionary site and a good research site at your fingertips. You can make these sites part of your Favorites list, so you can easily find them and go to them at any time.

➠ **Go back to places you've been via the History feature.** When you browse the Internet, you sometimes come across sites and don't realize till days or weeks later that you might like to return. If you do, you might need a reminder of the site URL. To find sites you've visited by the dates you visited them or other criteria, use the History feature. This displays a pane with sites you've visited organized by day.

➠ **Download files to your computer or print.** When you find what you want online, such as a graphic image or free software program, you might want to save it to your computer for future use (called *downloading*). Do you need a hard copy of what you've found? Just use the Print feature of IE. You can even download and play *podcasts*, which are prerecorded audio programs on a variety of topics.

➠ **Protect yourself.** The Internet is a bit dangerous — a place where some people try to get at your private information and make nefarious use of it. IE provides privacy settings and special features to control the use of *cookies* (small files that folks who run Web sites insert on your hard drive to help them track your online activities). You can use the Content Advisor to alert you to the types of online locations that you want to avoid visiting.

This chapter focuses on the functionality of Internet Explorer that you can use to find what you need on the Internet, explains ways to download and print files, and shows you how to use built-in tools for a safer experience.

Search the Web

1. Simple-to-use programs called search engines make it easy to find information on the Internet — probably more information than you ever wanted! To use Internet Explorer's search feature, open IE and click in the Search text box in the top-right corner on the toolbar. The default search engine is Windows Live Search.

2. Enter a search term in the text box and then click Search. A search term is simply a word or phrase that relates to the results you seek. For example, if you want information about arthritis, enter the word **arthritis** or the phrase **joint pain**.

3. In the resulting list of links (see **Figure 14-1**), click a link to go that Web page.

Note that browsers often return sponsored links at the top or side of the search results page. These are sites that pay to have their information included. You can click them, but remember that they are paid advertisers, and there's a greater risk of downloading dangerous software to your computer if you click a sponsored link.

4. If you don't see the link that you need, click and drag the scrollbar to view more results. (You can find out more about links in Chapter 13.)

Knowing how search engines work can save you time. For example, if you search by entering *golden retriever*, you typically get sites that contain both words or either word. If you put a plus sign between these two keywords, *golden+retriever*, you get only sites that contain both words.

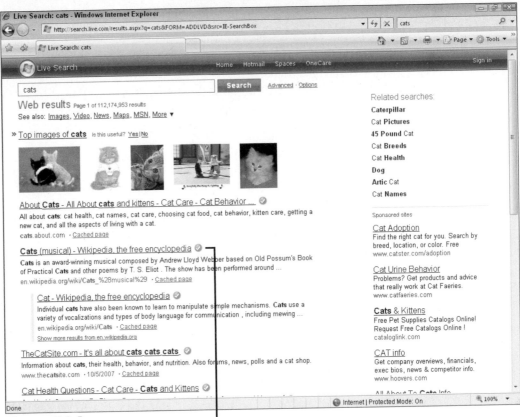

Figure 14-1

Click a link in the results list

Find Content on a Web Page

1. In addition to locating information anywhere on the World Wide Web, after you display a Web page, you can search within it for particular words or phrases. This saves you having to scroll through the page and read every word to find what you need. With IE open and the Web page that you want to search displayed, click the arrow on the Search text box in the top-right corner and choose Find on This Page.

2. In the resulting Find dialog box, as shown in **Figure 14-2**, enter the word that you want to search for. Use the following options to narrow your results:

- **Match Whole Word Only:** Select this option if you want to find only the whole word (for example, if you enter *elect* and want to find only *elect* and not electron or electronics).

- **Match Case**: Select this option if you want to match the case (for example, if you enter *Catholic* and want to find only the always-capitalized religion and not the adjective *catholic*).

3. Click the Next button. The first instance of the word is highlighted on the page (see **Figure 14-3**). If you want to find the next instance, click the Next button again. Click the Previous button to move back to the last match.

4. When you're done searching, click the Close button in the Find dialog box.

Many Web sites, such as www.amazon.com, have a Search This Site feature that allows you to search not only the displayed Web page but all Web pages on a Web site. Look for a Search This Site text box to make sure that it searches the site — and not the entire Internet.

Type the word you want to find

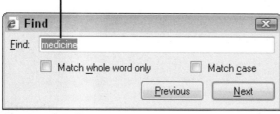

Figure 14-2

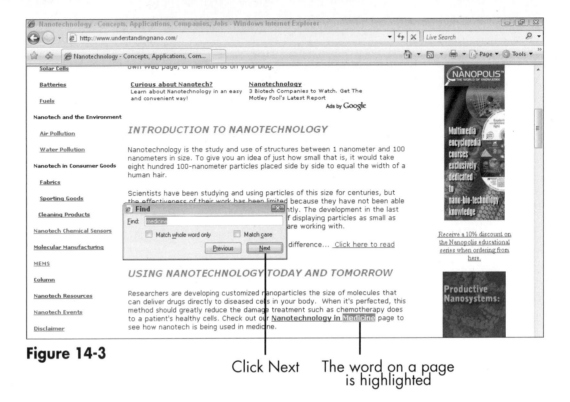

Figure 14-3

Click Next   The word on a page
is highlighted

Add a Web Site to Favorites

1. Open IE, enter the URL of a Web site that you want to add to your Favorites list, and then press Enter.

2. Click the Add to Favorites button and then choose Add to Favorites.

3. In the resulting Add a Favorite dialog box, as shown in **Figure 14-4**, modify the name of the Favorite listing to something easily recognizable.

4. If you want, choose another folder to store the favorite in by clicking the arrow on the Create In field. You can also create a folder to store the favorite in by clicking the New

Folder button, entering the folder name in the Create a Folder dialog box that appears, and clicking the Create button. Placing favorites in different folders (such as a Finances folder and a Hobbies folder) helps you organize them and find the favorite you need faster.

5. Click Add to add the site to your favorites.

6. When you want to return to the site you've saved as a favorite, click the Favorites Center button and then click the name of the site from the list that's displayed (see **Figure 14-5**).

Regularly cleaning out your Favorites list is a good idea — after all, do you really need the sites that you used to plan last year's vacation? With the Favorites Center displayed, right-click any item and then choose Delete or Rename to modify the favorite listing.

You can keep the Favorites Center as a side pane in Internet Explorer by displaying it and then clicking the Pin the Favorites Center button (which has a left-facing green arrow on it and is located to the right of the button labeled History).

Change the favorite name

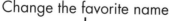

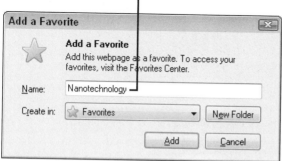

Figure 14-4

Click the Favorites button

Figure 14-5

Organize Favorites

1. As you add favorites, they can become jumbled, and it's
helpful to tidy them up into folders or otherwise organize
them. With Internet Explorer open, click the Add to
Favorites button and then choose Organize Favorites.

2. In the resulting Organize Favorites dialog box (see **Figure
14-6**), click on a favorite, and then click the New Folder,
Move, Rename, or Delete buttons to organize your
favorites.

3. When you finish organizing your Favorites, click Close.

If you create new folders in the preceding steps, you have to manually transfer files into those folders. To do this, just display the Favorites Center and click and drag files listed there on top of folders.

Click a favorite

Figure 14-6

Then click an action

View Your Browsing History

1. Sometimes you need to find a site you visited but didn't save as a favorite. To do that, you can review your browsing history. Click the Favorites Center button and then click History to display the History pane.

2. Click the down arrow on the History button (see **Figure 14-7**) and select a sort method:

- **By Date:** Sort favorites by date visited.

- **By Site:** Sort alphabetically by site name.

- **By Most Visited:** Sort with the sites visited most on top and those visited least at the bottom of the list.

- **By Order Visited Today:** Sort by the order in which you visited sites today.

3. In the History pane, you can click a site to go to it. The History pane closes.

Select a sort option

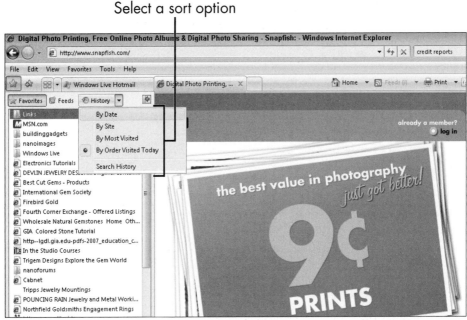

Figure 14-7

You can also choose the arrow on the right of the Address bar to display sites you've visited during your current online session.

 With the Favorites Center open, choose Search History from the History menu to display a search box you can use to search for sites you've visited.

Customize the Internet Explorer Toolbar

1. The tools to the right of the tabs in Internet Explorer help you do common tasks with a click, such as Print to print the currently displayed page and Home to go to your home page. However, you might want to change the tools that are available; for example, if you never use RSS Feeds (a technology that allows you to sign up to a *feed* and get information on a certain topic delivered to you) but always use your e-mail, you might remove the RSS Feeds button (the one with little orange stripes) and add the Read Mail button (a little envelope-shaped button). Open IE.

2. Choose Tools⇨Toolbars⇨Customize. The Customize Toolbar dialog box appears, as shown in **Figure 14-8**.

3. Click a tool in the left box and then click the Add button to add it to the toolbar.

 If you want to add some space between tools on the toolbar so they're easier to see, click the Separator item in the Available Toolbar Buttons list and add it before or after a tool button.

4. Click a tool in the right box and then click the Remove button to remove it from the toolbar.

 You can use the Move Up and Move Down buttons in the Customize Toolbar dialog box to rearrange the order in which tools appear on the toolbar. To reset the toolbar to defaults, click the Reset button in that same dialog box.

5. When you're finished, click Close to save your new tool-bar settings. The new tools appear (see **Figure 14-9**); click the double-arrow button on the right of the toolbar to display any tools that IE can't fit on-screen.

Select a tool   Then click Add

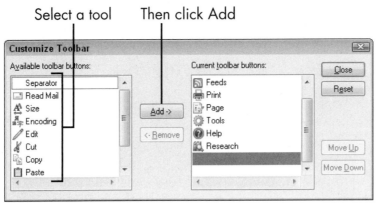

Figure 14-8

Find new tools here

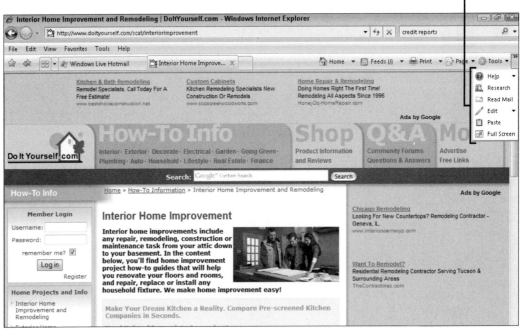

Figure 14-9

Download Files

1. As you browse the Web, you might find files you want to download, such as music files or movie files you buy from an online store or which are free. Open a Web site that offers files you want to download. Typically Web sites offer a Download button or link that initiates a file download.

2. Click the appropriate link to proceed. Windows Vista might display a dialog box asking your permission to proceed with the download; click Yes.

3. In the resulting File Download dialog box, as shown in **Figure 14-10**, choose either option:

- **Click Open to download to a temporary folder.** You can run an installation program for software, for example. However, beware: If you run a program directly from the Internet, you might be introducing dangerous viruses to your system. You should buy and follow the software manufacturer's instructions to install and set up an antivirus program such as McAfee or Norton Antivirus to scan files before downloading them.

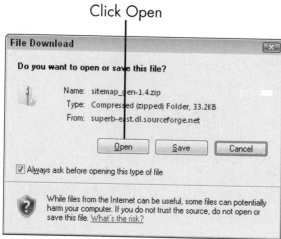

Figure 14-10

- **Click Save to save the file to your hard drive.** In the Save As dialog box, select the folder on your computer or removable storage media (a CD-ROM, for example) where you want to save the file. If you're downloading software, you need to locate the downloaded file and click it to run the installation.

 If a particular file will take a long time to download (I've had some big ones take over 20 hours!), you might have to babysit it. If your computer goes into standby, it might pause the download. Check in periodically to keep things moving along.

Print a Web Page

1. If a Web page includes a link or button to print or display a print version of a page, click that and follow the instructions.

2. If the page doesn't include a link for printing, click the Print button on the IE toolbar.

3. In the resulting Print dialog box, if you want to print only text you selected on the page, choose selection or leave the setting at All to print the entire Web page, and then select one of the options in the Page Range area, as shown in **Figure 14-11**. (You can find out more about printing and the Page Range area in Chapter 6.)

 Note that choosing Current Page or entering page numbers in the Pages text box of the Print dialog box doesn't mean much when printing a Web page — the whole document might print because Web pages aren't divided into pages the way word processing documents are.

4. Click the up-arrow in the Number of Copies text box to print multiple copies. If you want multiple copies collated, select the Collate check box.

5. When you adjust all settings you need, click Print.

 To see what your Web page will look like printed, use the Print Preview feature before you print. Click the arrow on the right side of the Print button and choose Print Preview. Use the Next and Previous arrows at the bottom of the page to scroll through the pages. Click the Close button to close Print Preview.

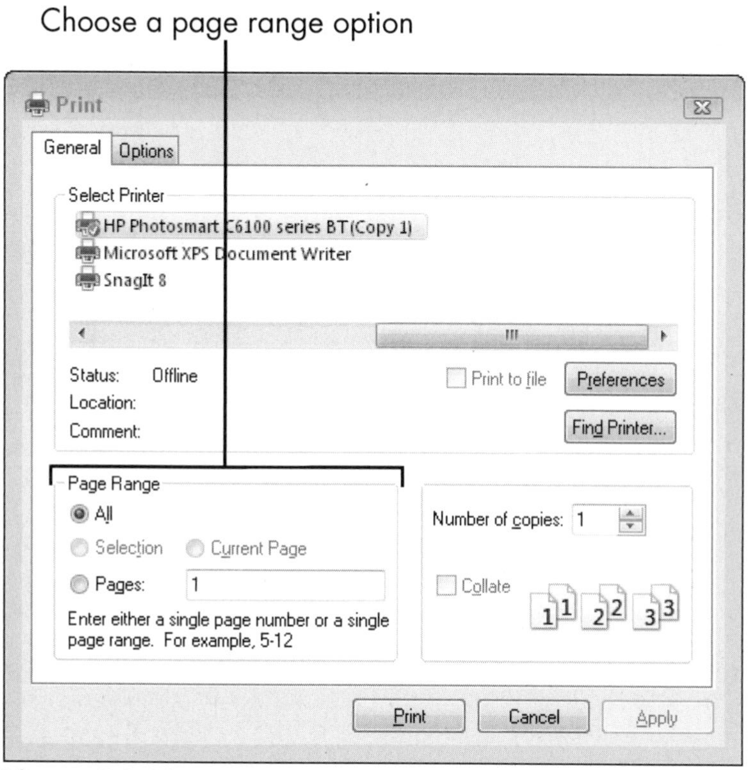

Choose a page range option

Figure 14-11

Play a Podcast

A *podcast* is a prerecorded program in the form of a digital file that you can access online. Podcasts are typically free and can be found on a wide variety of topics from a wide range of sources.

Here are the key points to understand about podcasts:

➡ When you encounter a podcast link, as shown in **Figure 14-12**, click it. When you click the link, your default media player opens, and the podcast begins to play.

Click a podcast link

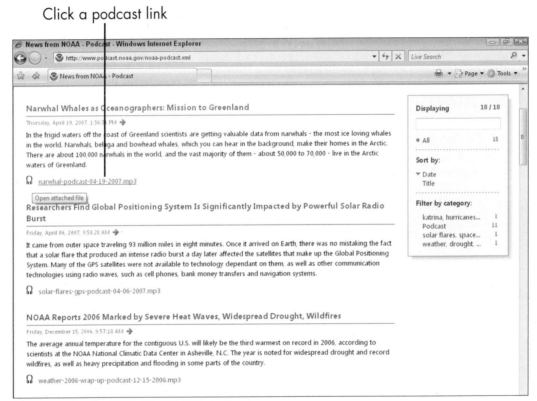

Figure 14-12

➡ You can also download podcasts and play them from your computer or a portable device such as an iPod. On your computer, simply double-click such a down-loaded file to play it.

➡ Podcasts can be syndicated to a variety of sites. You can subscribe to series of podcasts using something called a feed reader, such as an RSS feed reader. These readers essentially aggregate specified programs from the Web and deliver them to you to read or listen to.

⇒ Some popular podcast sites include www.usa.gov/
Topics/Reference_Shelf/Libraries/
Podcasts.shtml for United States government
podcasts; http://podcast.net, a directory of
podcasts on various topics; and Apple's iTunes (www.
apple.com/itunes/store/podcasts.html),
where you can subscribe to any number of podcasts
to be delivered to you through the iTunes software.

Change Privacy Settings

1. Cookies, small files that Web sites place on your computer with information about your browsing habits, can
be harmless (allowing a site to say Welcome Nancy! every
time I go there), or they can be an invasion of your privacy. For that reason, you might want to modify your privacy settings in your browser to prohibit use of cookies.
With IE open, choose Tools⇨Internet Options and click
the Privacy tab, as shown in **Figure 14-13**.

2. Click the Settings slider and drag it up or down to make
different levels of security settings. The information to the
right of the slider changes depending on your setting.

3. Read the choices and select a setting that suits you.

The default setting, Medium, is probably a good bet
for most people. If you set a higher or lower level of
security and want to restore the default setting at any
point, click the Default button in the Internet
Options dialog box Privacy tab or use the slider to
move back to Medium.

4. To specify sites to always or never allow the use of cookies, click the Sites button. For example, you might want
pop-ups on the mortgage application site so you can
complete the application process, but perhaps you
don't want them when you visit an online store. In the
resulting Per Site Privacy Actions dialog box (as shown in

Figure 14-14), enter a site in the Address of Website box and click either Block or Allow.

5. Click OK twice to save your new settings.

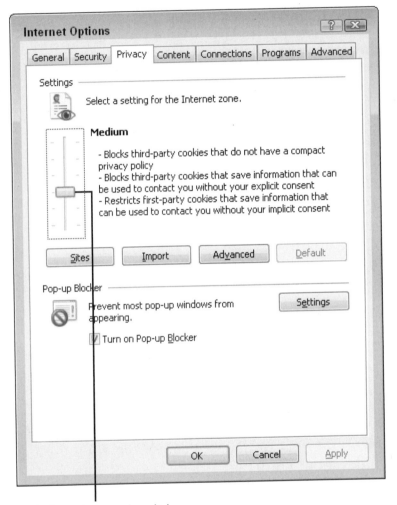

Click and drag the slider

Figure 14-13

 Pop-ups can be in the form of annoying advertisements or they could be pop-up windows that allow you perform an action in a site, such as calculating estimated payments on a mortgage site. You can also use pop-up blocker settings on the Privacy tab to specify which pop-up windows to allow or block. Just click the Settings button, enter a Web site name, and then click Add to allow pop-ups.

Enter a Web address here

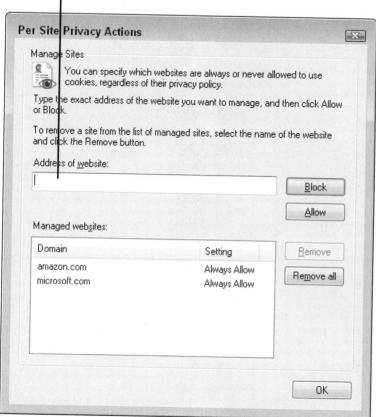

Figure 14-14

Enable the Content Advisor

1. Not everything that's online appeals to everybody. If you find some types of content objectionable, you might use Content Advisor in Internet Explorer to filter out that content. If you have several user accounts on your Windows Vista computer, your settings will apply to them all. With IE open, choose Tools⇨Internet Options.

2. In the resulting Internet Options dialog box, click the Content tab to display it.

3. Click the Enable button. (*Note:* If there is no Enable button but Disable and Settings buttons instead, Content Advisor is already enabled. Click the Settings button to see the options and make changes if you want.)

4. On the Ratings tab of the resulting Content Advisor dialog box (see **Figure 14-15**), click one of the categories in the list box (such as Depiction of Drug Use) and then move the slider below it to use one of three site-screening settings: None, Limited, or Unrestricted.

5. Repeat Step 4 for each of the categories.

6. Click the Approved Sites tab (see **Figure 14-16**) and enter the name of a specific site that you want to control access to. Then click Always or Never.

- **Always** allows users to view the site, even if it's included in the Content Advisor screening level you've set.

- **Never** means that nobody can visit the site even if it's acceptable to Content Advisor.

7. When you finish making your settings, click OK twice to save them.

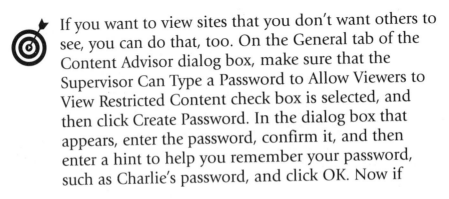 If you want to view sites that you don't want others to see, you can do that, too. On the General tab of the Content Advisor dialog box, make sure that the Supervisor Can Type a Password to Allow Viewers to View Restricted Content check box is selected, and then click Create Password. In the dialog box that appears, enter the password, confirm it, and then enter a hint to help you remember your password, such as Charlie's password, and click OK. Now if

you're logged on as the system administrator, you can get to any restricted site by using this password.

 To find rating systems that various organizations have created and apply them to Internet Explorer, click the Rating Systems button on the General tab. Here you can chose a system already shown there. Or, click Add; then, in the resulting Open Ratings System File dialog box, choose another system to apply.

Click a category

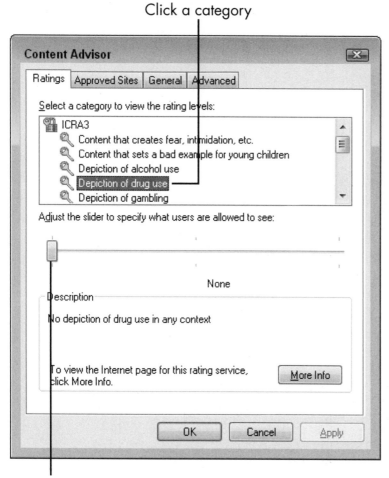

Then click and drag the slider

Figure 14-15

Enter a Web site address here

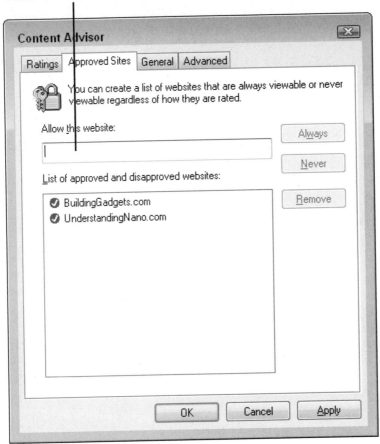

Figure 14-16

Keeping in Touch with E-Mail

An e-mail program is a tool you can use to send text messages to others. These messages are delivered to their e-mail *inbox*, usually within seconds. You can attach files to e-mail and even put graphic images within the message body. You can get an e-mail account through you Internet provider or through sites such as Yahoo! or Microsoft Live Hotmail. These accounts are typically free.

When you have an e-mail account, you can send and receive e-mail through the account provider's e-mail program online, or you can set up a program on your computer such as Microsoft Outlook, which comes with Microsoft Office, or Windows Mail, which is built into Windows to access that account. These programs typically offer more robust e-mail and contact management features than the programs that providers such as Yahoo! offer.

This chapter takes a look at these tasks:

➠ Choose an e-mail provider. Find out how to locate e-mail providers and what types of features they offer.

➠ **Manage your e-mail account.** Set up an e-mail account in Windows Mail and then create, modify, and add rules for your account to operate by.

➠ **Receive, send, and forward messages.** Deal with the ins and outs of receiving and sending e-mail. Use the formatting tools that Windows Mail provides to make your messages pretty.

➠ **Add information into the Address Book.** You can quickly and easily manage your contacts as well as organize the messages you save in e-mail folders.

➠ **Set up the layout of all Windows Mail features.** Use the Folder bar and Layout features to create the most efficient workspace.

Set Up An Internet-Based E-Mail Account

Your Internet service provider (ISP), whether that's your cable or phone company or a small local provider, probably offers you a free e-mail account along with your service. You can also get free accounts from many online sources, such as Yahoo!, AOL, and Windows Live Hotmail.

Here are some tips for getting your own e-mail account:

➠ **Using e-mail accounts provided by an ISP:** Check with your ISP to see whether an e-mail account comes with your connection service. If it does, your ISP should provide instructions on how to choose an e-mail alias (that is the name on your account, such as SusieXYZ@aol.com) and password and sign in.

➡ **Searching for an e-mail provider:** If your ISP doesn't offer e-mail, or you prefer to use another service because of features it offers, use your browser's search engine to look for what's available. Don't use the search term *"free e-mail"* because results for any search with the word *free* included are much more likely to return sites that will download bad programs like viruses and spyware on to your computer. Alternatively, you can go directly to services such as Yahoo, AOL, or Hotmail by entering their addresses in your browser address box (for example, www.aol.com).

➡ **Finding out about features:** E-mail accounts come with certain features that you should be aware of. For example, they each provide a certain amount of storage for your saved messages. (Look for one that provides 2 gigabytes or more.) The account should also include an easy to use Address Book feature to save your contacts' information. Some services provide better formatting tools for text, calendar, and to-do list features. Whatever service you use, make sure it has good junk mail features to protect you from unwanted e-mails. You should be able to control junk mail filters to place messages from certain senders or with certain content in a junk mail folder where you can review or delete them.

➡ **Signing up for an e-mail account:** When you find an e-mail account you want to use, sign up (usually there will be a Sign Up or Get An Account button or link to click) by providing your name and other contact information and selecting a username and password. The username is your e-mail address, in the form of UserName@*service*.com, where *service* is, for example, yahoo, hotmail, or aol. Some usernames might be taken, so have a few options in mind. Make sure your username is a safe one: Don't use your full name, your location, age, or other identifiers if possible. Such personal identifiers might help scam artists or predators to find out more about you than you want them to know.

Set Up Your E-Mail Account on Windows Mail

1. You can set up Windows Mail to access one or more e-mail accounts so you can manage your mail from one location. E-mail accounts are based on a type of server such as POP3 and IMAP. Don't worry about what these are: Just know that these two types of e-mail account can be set up to be accessed through Windows Mail. If you're unsure about what type of e-mail server your account uses, ask your e-mail account provider and then follow these steps to set up your account. Choose Start⇨All Programs⇨Windows Mail. In the Windows Mail main window that appears, choose Tools⇨Accounts.

2. In the resulting Internet Accounts dialog box, as shown in **Figure 15-1**, click Add.

3. In the resulting Internet Connection Wizard (see **Figure 15-2**), click E-mail Account and click Next.

4. In the following screen, enter the Display Name that you want to appear on your outgoing e-mails. You might use your full name or initials, for example. Click Next.

5. In the Internet E-mail Address window that appears, enter your e-mail address that you got from your account provider, such as **XYZ@aol.com**. Click Next.

Click Add

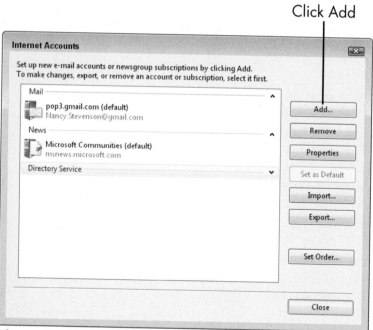

Figure 15-1

Select E-mail Account

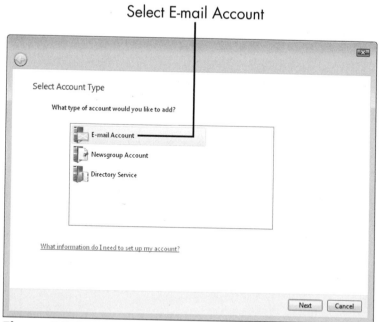

Figure 15-2

6. In the Set Up E-mail Servers window that appears, click the Incoming E-mail Server Type drop-down list and choose the format: POP3 or IMAP. (Note that though HTTP is still listed, if you select it, Windows Mail tells you it no longer supports HTTP.) If you're not sure about this, check with your e-mail account provider.

7. Enter the Incoming Mail Server and Outgoing Mail Server information in those two fields. Again, you must get this information from your e-mail provider. Click Next.

8. In the Internet Mail Logon window that appears, enter your E-Mail Username and Password in those fields and click Next. In the Congratulations window that appears, click the Finish button to save your account settings and download your e-mail.

Get to Know Windows Mail

Windows Mail (see **Figure 15-3**) is typical of many e-mail programs in that it includes both menus and tools to take actions such as deleting an e-mail, creating a new e-mail, and so on. There's also a list of folders on the left. Some typical folders are your Inbox where most incoming mail appears; your Outbox where saved drafts of e-mails are saved ready to be sent; and your Sent folder where copies of sent emails are stored.

Finally, the central area of the screen displays folder contents (in Figure 15-3, it's the Inbox folder with all incoming mail listed ready for you to open) and in some cases a preview pane that shows the contents of a selected message in the Inbox or other folder.

Folders | Menus | Messages in Inbox | Toolbar

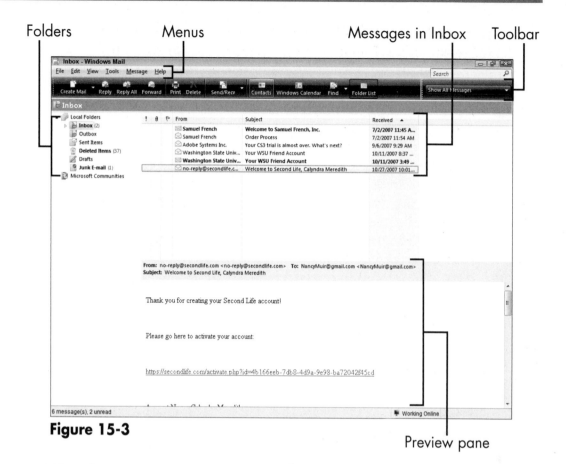

Figure 15-3

Preview pane

Open Windows Mail and Your Inbox

1. When you open your mail, one of the first things you are likely to do is check your inbox for new messages. Choose Start⇨All Programs⇨Windows Mail.

2. In the resulting Windows Mail window, press Ctrl+M to send any messages in the outbox and receive all messages from your e-mail account.

3. Click the Inbox item in the Folders list to view messages (see **Figure 15-4**). New messages sport a small closed envelope icon; those with attachments have a paper clip icon as well.

To organize messages in the Inbox, click any of the headings at the top, such as From (to sort the messages alphabetically by sender), Received (to sort by the date they were received), and so on.

Some e-mail programs such as Windows Mail limit the time that the program attempts to get mail from your server; if that time limited is exceeded the connection is said to be *timed out*. If you sometimes get a message that your connection timed out in Mail, choose Tools⇨Accounts, select your e-mail account, and then click Properties. On the Advanced tab, move the Server Timeout slider a bit to the right to allow for a longer time period before timing out.

Click Inbox

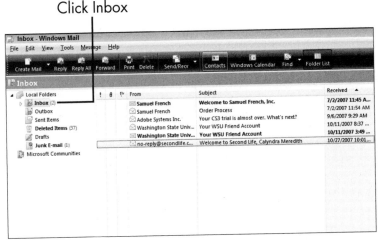

Figure 15-4

Manage E-Mail Accounts

1. You can set up more than one e-mail account in Windows Mail (for example, if you and your spouse each have your own account). If you have more than one account, you can choose to make one the default account that Windows Mail will use when you create a new message. You can also decide to delete an old account if you sign up for a different service. Choose Start➪All Programs➪Windows Mail. In the Windows Mail main window that appears, choose Tools➪Accounts.

2. In the resulting Internet Accounts dialog box, select an account on the left (refer to Figure 15-1) and do either of the following:

- To remove an account, click the Remove button on any of the tabs. A confirming message appears. To delete the account, click Yes.

- Select an account and click the Set as Default button to make it the account that Windows connects you to when you go online. In the case of the mail server, the default is the one used to send any message.

3. Click Close to close the dialog box.

Following the Internet Connection Wizard often requires that you provide certain information about your Internet service provider (ISP), such as its mail server or connection method. Keep this information handy!

4. When you finish setting up accounts, click the Close button to close the Internet Accounts dialog box.

Create and Send E-Mail

1. When you want to send a message to somebody else, you open a new e-mail form, address it, enter a subject line and your message, and then send it on its way. Choose Start➪All Programs➪Windows Mail.

2. Click the Create Mail button on the Windows Mail toolbar to create a new, blank e-mail form (see **Figure 15-5**).

In e-mail messages, you can use stationery that puts an attractive background behind your text. To create a new message with stationary, click the arrow on the Create Mail button in the Windows Mail main window and select a stationery option listed in the menu that appears.

3. Type one or more e-mail addresses of the recipient(s) in the To text box. You can also type an address in the Cc text box to send a copy of the message to somebody else.

 When creating an e-mail, you can address it to a stored address by using the Address Book feature. (See "Add Contacts to the Address Book" later in this chapter.) Just begin to type a stored contact in an address field (To or Cc), and it fills in likely options while you type. When it fills in the correct name, just press Enter to select it.

4. Click in the Subject text box and type a concise yet descriptive subject such as Club Meeting or Holiday Visit.

5. Click in the message text area and type your message (see **Figure 15-6**).

 Don't press Enter at the end of a line. Windows Mail has an automatic text wrap feature that bumps the cursor to the next line for you. Also, keep e-mail etiquette in mind as you type. For example, don't type in ALL CAPITAL LETTERS. This is called *shouting,* which is considered rude.

 E-mail does involve some etiquette. Do be polite even if you're really, really angry. Your message could be forwarded to just about anybody, just about anywhere, and you don't want to get a reputation as a hothead. Also, be concise because most people don't really like reading long messages on-screen. (It hurts the eyes.) If you have lots to say, consider sending a letter by snail mail (regular mail) or overnight delivery.

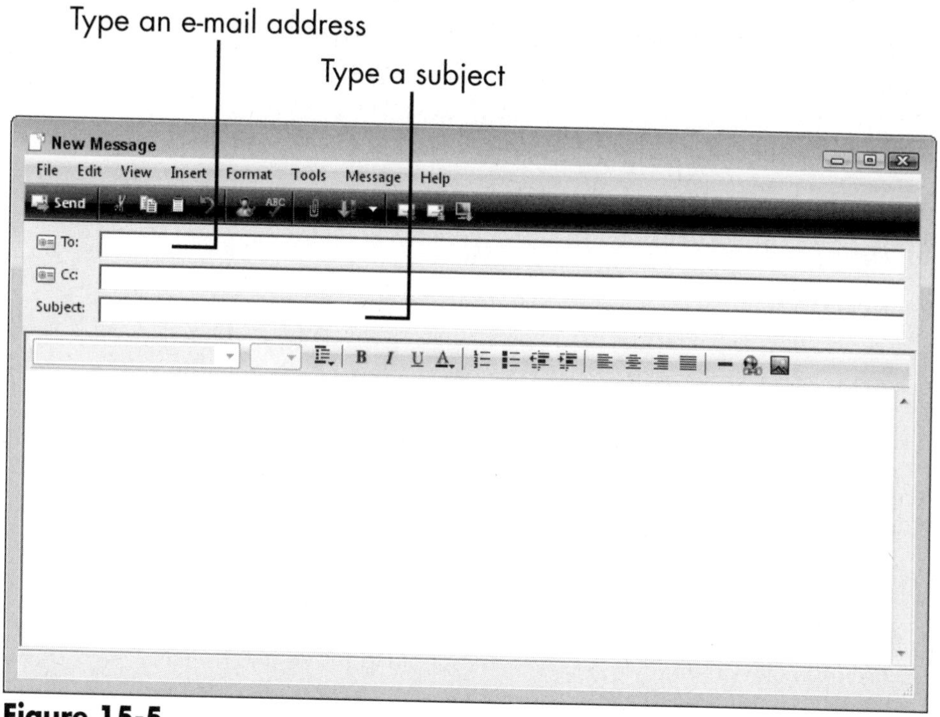

Type an e-mail address

Type a subject

Figure 15-5

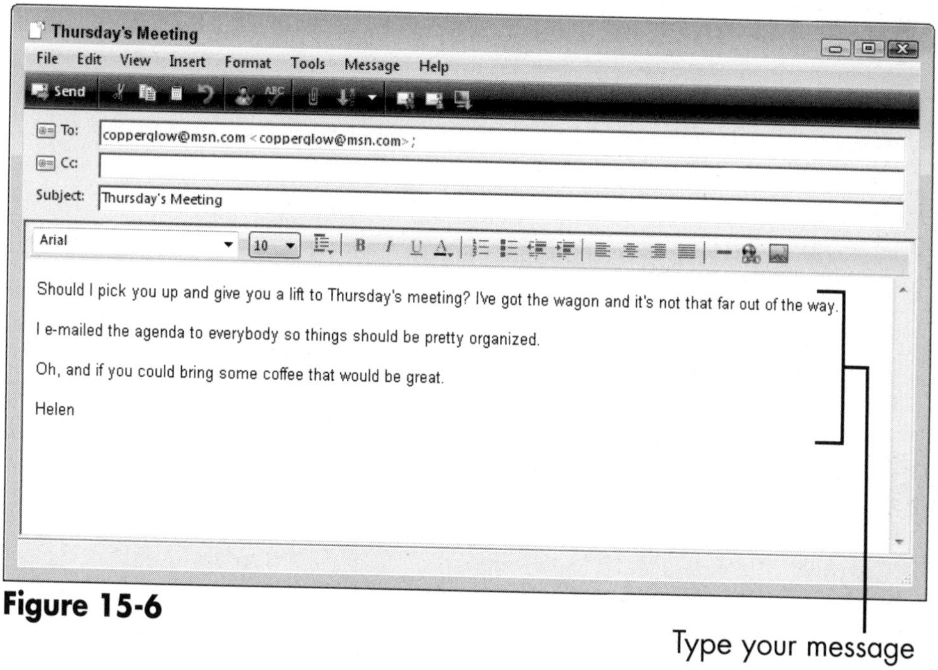

Figure 15-6

Type your message

6. When you finish typing your message, spell-check it (unless you're the regional state spelling champ). Click the Spelling button; possibly misspelled words get highlighted, and the Spelling dialog box appears (see **Figure 15-7**). At this point, you have some choices:

- Click the **Ignore** button to ignore this instance of the misspelling.

- Click the **Ignore All** button to ignore all instances.

- Choose a suggested alternative spelling and click the **Change** button to change that instance; or, click the **Change All** button to change all instances of the word.

- Click the **Add** button to add the current spelling of the word to the Spelling feature's dictionary so it's never questioned again.

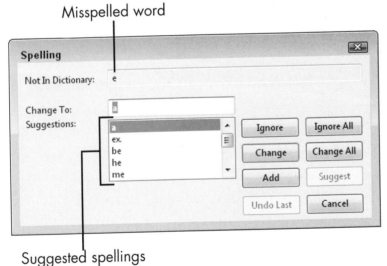

Figure 15-7

7. After you make one of the choices in Step 6, the Spell Check moves on to the next questionable word, if any, and you can make a new choice. When a window appears telling you the check is complete, click OK to close the Spelling dialog box.

8. Click the Send button. The message is on its way!

 You can also insert a picture in an e-mail. With the e-mail form open, choose Insert⇨Picture. Locate a picture in the Picture window that appears and click Open. The picture fills the background of the e-mail message area.

Send an Attachment

1. You can attach any file to your e-mail to send a document or picture along with your message. Create a new e-mail message, address it, and enter a subject.

 2. Click the Attach File to Message button.

3. In Open dialog box that appears (see **Figure 15-8**), locate the document or graphics file that you want and then click Open.

Select a file to attach

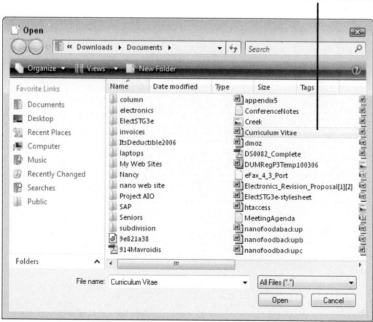

Figure 15-8

4. With the name of the attached file now in the Attach field text box (see **Figure 15-9**), type a message (or not — after all, a picture *is* worth a thousand words).

5. Click the Send button to send.

Attached file

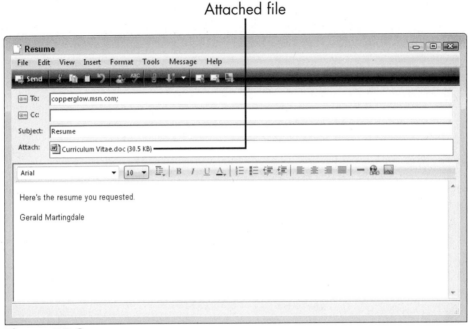

Figure 15-9

Read a Message

1. In your Inbox, unread messages sport an icon of an unopened envelope to the left of the message subject. Click an e-mail message in your Inbox or double-click it to open it in a separate window.

2. Use the scrollbars in the message window to scroll down through the message and read it (see **Figure 15-10**).

3. If the message has an attachment, a paper clip symbol is displayed next to the message in your Inbox; attachments are listed in the Attach box in the open message. To open an attachment, double-click it.

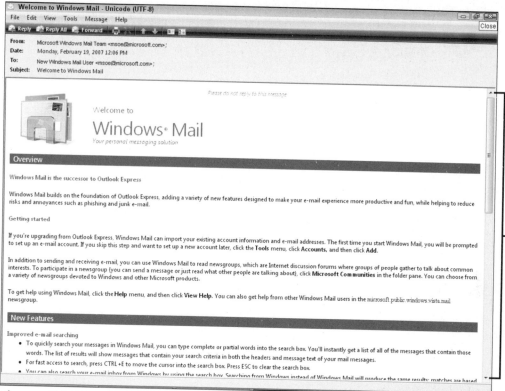

Figure 15-10

Use the scrollbar

4. In the resulting Mail Attachment dialog box (see **Figure 15-11**), click the Open button. The attachment opens in whatever program is associated with it (such as the Windows Photo Gallery for a graphics file) or the program it was created in (such as Microsoft Word).

 Instead of opening an attachment, you can save it directly to a storage disk or your hard drive. To do so, right-click the attachment name in the Attach field and choose Save As. In the Save as dialog box that appears, choose a location and provide a name for the file; then click Save.

E-mail attachments can be dangerous. They might contain viruses or other kinds of malicious software (called *malware*). Never open attachments from somebody you don't know. See Chapter 17 for more information about how to avoid malware.

Click Open

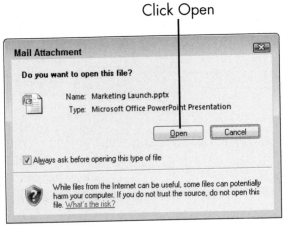

Figure 15-11

Reply to a Message

1. Open the message to which you want to reply and then click one of the following buttons, as shown in **Figure 15-12**:

   - **Reply:** Send the reply to only the author.

   - **Reply All:** Send a reply to the author as well as everyone who received the original message.

2. In the resulting e-mail form, enter any additional recipient(s) in the To and/or Cc text boxes and type your message in the message window area.

3. Click the Send button to send the reply.

Click Reply or click Reply All

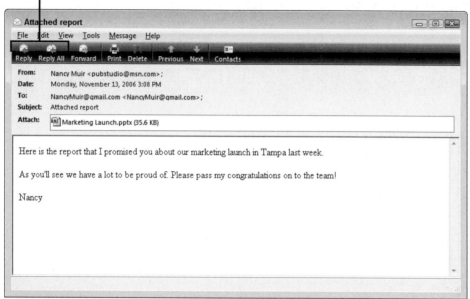

Figure 15-12

 If you don't want to include the original message in your reply, choose Tools➪Options and click the Send tab. Deselect the Include Message in Reply check box and then click OK.

Forward E-Mail

1. You might get a message that's just too good not to pass on. Passing on, or *forwarding*, e-mail to others is what sends jokes flying around the Internet in droves. Open the e-mail message that you want to forward.

2. Click the Forward button on the toolbar.

3. In the message that appears with Fw added to the beginning of the subject line, enter a new recipient(s) in the To and Cc fields and then enter any message that you want to include in the message window area, as shown in the example in **Figure 15-13**.

4. Click Send to forward the message.

Enter an e-mail address

Type a message

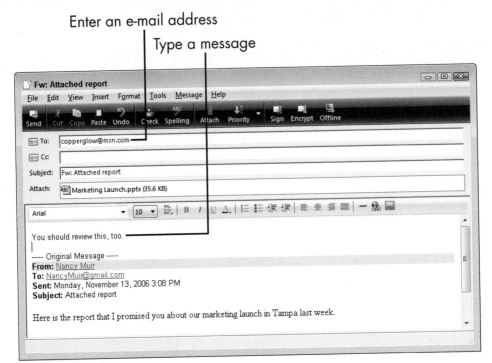

Figure 15-13

Create and Add a Signature

1. Just as you sign a letter *Sincerely yours,* followed by your name, you can add a signature to your e-mail messages. A signature might contain your full name and phone number or even your favorite saying. In Windows Mail, choose Tools⇨Options to open the Options dialog box. Click the Signatures tab (see **Figure 15-14**).

2. Click the New button to create a new signature and then enter your Signatures text.

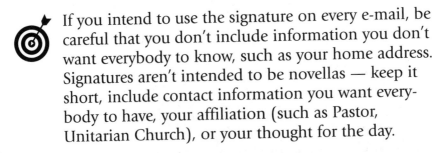 If you intend to use the signature on every e-mail, be careful that you don't include information you don't want everybody to know, such as your home address. Signatures aren't intended to be novellas — keep it short, include contact information you want everybody to have, your affiliation (such as Pastor, Unitarian Church), or your thought for the day.

Click the Signatures tab

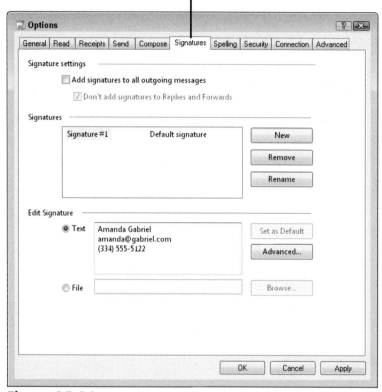

Figure 15-14

3. Select the Add Signatures to All Outgoing Messages check box and make sure that the signature is selected as the default. (*Note:* Select the Don't Add Signatures to Replies and Forwards check box if you want to add your signature only occasionally.)

4. Click OK to save the signature.

5. To manually add a signature to an open e-mail message, choose Insert⇨Signature and select a signature from the list that appears to insert it (see **Figure 15-15**).

 If you have different e-mail accounts and want to assign a different signature to each one, go to the Signatures tab of the Options dialog box. There, select a signature in the Signatures list box, click the Advanced button, and then select an account to associate it with.

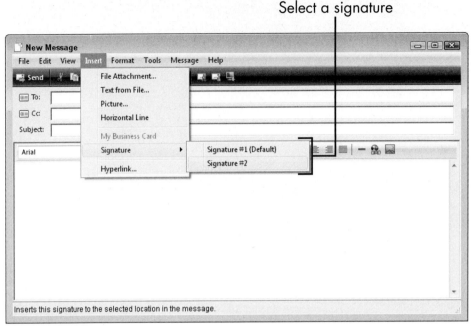

Select a signature

Inserts this signature to the selected location in the message.

Figure 15-15

Format E-Mail Messages

1. You can make text look attractive in a word-processed letter, and similarly you can format text in e-mails to use a certain font or use effects such as boldface type and underlining for emphasis. Create a new e-mail message or open a message and click Reply or Forward.

2. Select the text that you want to format (see **Figure 15-16**).

3. Use any of the following options to make changes to the font. (See the toolbar containing these tools in **Figure 15-17** and a message with various formats applied.)

- **Font drop-down list:** Choose a font from the drop-down list to apply it to the text.

- **Font Size drop-down list:** Change the font size here.

- **Paragraph Style button:** Apply a preset style, such as Heading 1 or Address.

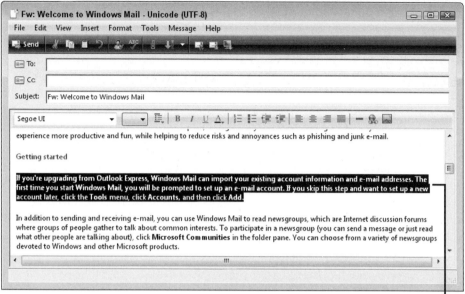

Figure 15-16

Select text to format

- **Bold, Italic, or Underline button:** Apply styles to selected text.

- **Font Color button:** Display a color palette and click a color to apply it to selected text.

- **Formatting Numbers or Formatting Bullets button:** Apply numbering order to lists or precede each item with a round bullet.

- **Increase Indentation or Decrease Indentation button:** Indent that paragraph to the right or move (decrease) it to the left.

- **Align Left, Center, Align Right, or Justify buttons:** Adjust the alignment.

- **Insert Horizontal Line button:** Add a line to your message.

Use the formatting tools

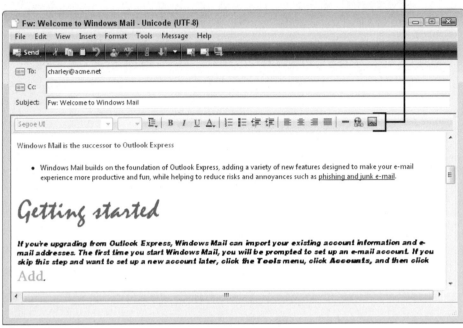

Figure 15-17

Add Contacts to the Address Book

1. Windows Mail (like most e-mail programs) contains an Address Book feature where you store information about your contacts. Contacts allows you to quickly address e-mail messages using stored e-mail addresses. In the Windows Mail main window, click the Contacts button to open your Windows Contacts window (see **Figure 15-18**).

2. Double-click a contact to view or edit information.

3. In the resulting Properties dialog box, as shown in **Figure 15-19**, go to the following options tabs to enter contact information:

- **Name and E-Mail tab:** Enter the person's name and e-mail address. (This is the only information you must enter to create a contact.)

Double-click a contact

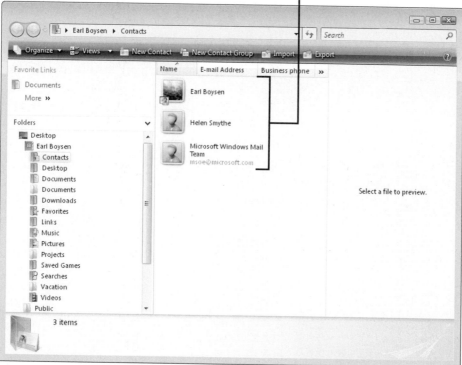

Figure 15-18

- **Home tab:** Enter the person's home and Web site addresses as well as phone, fax, and cell phone numbers.

- **Work tab:** Enter information about the company that the person works for as well as his job title and pager number. You can even add a map to help you find his or her office.

- **Family tab:** Enter the person's family members' names, as well as his or her gender, birthday, and anniversary.

- **Notes tab:** Enter any notes you like to in the form on this tab.

- **IDs tab:** Ensure secure communications. *Digital IDs* are certificates that you can use to verify the identity of the person with whom you're communicating. If somebody has provided you with a digital ID, you can store that information here so you can look it up when opening messages from that person.

4. Click OK to save your new contact information and then close the Contacts window.

You can create new folders to organize contacts. For example, you might want to divide your personal contacts from your business contacts. To do this, click the Organize button in the Contacts window and then choose New Folder. When you enter an address in an address area (To or Cc), Windows Mail looks in every folder of contacts that you have to find the addressee.

Select a tab and enter contact information

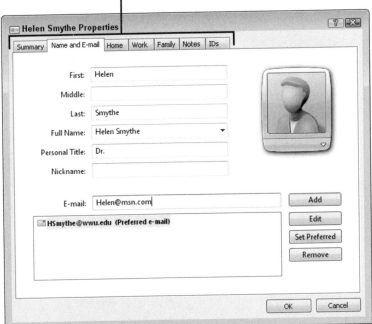

Figure 15-19

Customize the Windows Mail Layout

1. Choose View➪Layout to open the Window Layout Properties dialog box.

2. Select various check boxes in the Basic section, as shown in **Figure 15-20**, to select items to display in separate panes (see **Figure 15-21**), including

- **Folder Bar:** A bar near the top of the screen that includes a drop-down list of folders.

- **Folder List:** A pane containing a list of all folders.

- **Search Bar:** The bar that allows you to search your mail for keywords or other criteria.

Select items to display

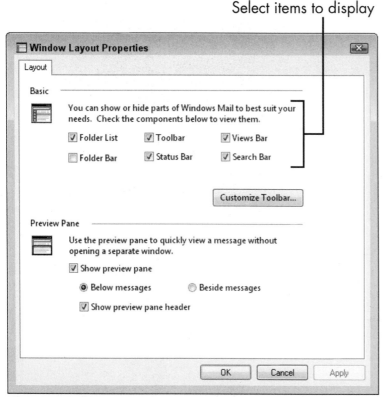

Figure 15-20

- **Status Bar:** The bar across the bottom of screen that lists the number of messages in all your folders and the number of unread messages.

- **Toolbar:** The bar containing tools you use to create and work with messages, such as Create, Reply, Forward, and Print.

- **Views Bar:** A bar under the toolbar containing a drop-down menu with three commands: Hide Read Messages, Hide Read or Ignored Messages, and Show All Messages.

3. Select various options in the Preview Pane section to preview a message selected in the Inbox, Outbox, Drafts, Sent Items, or Deleted Items folders.

4. Click OK to apply and save all your layout settings.

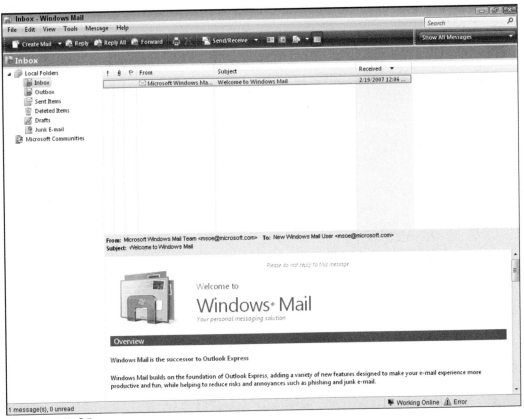

Figure 15-21

Create Message Folders

1. Being able to organize the messages you receive and even copies of messages you send is useful. Windows Mail allows you to use existing folders or create new folders that you can move messages into to find them more easily. Choose View➪Layout to open the Window Layout Properties dialog box.

2. Select check boxes to display the Folders list and Folder bar and then click OK.

3. In the Folders list, click any folder to display its contents.

4. Choose File➪New➪Folder (see **Figure 15-22**).

Choose File → New → Folder

Figure 15-22

5. In the resulting Create Folder dialog box (see **Figure 15-23**), select the folder that you want the new folder to be created in and then enter a new folder name.

6. Click OK.

Typically, you select the Local Folders item in Step 5 so that the new folder is at the same level as the Inbox, Outbox, and so on. Alternatively, you can select the Inbox item to place the new folder within the Inbox folder.

Name the new folder

Choose a location

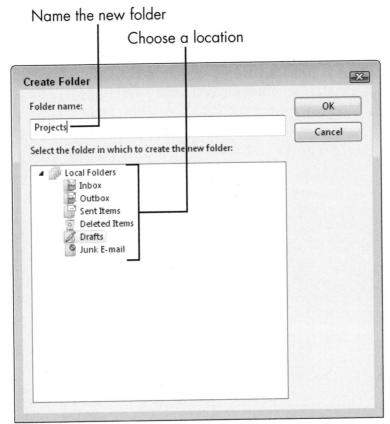

Figure 15-23

Organize Messages in Folders

1. After you've created folders, you should move messages into them to get your mail space organized. In the Folders list, click the arrow to the left of any folder to display its contents.

2. To place a message in a folder, you can perform one of these actions:

- With a folder (such as the Inbox) displayed, click a message and then drag it into a folder in the Folders list.

- With an e-mail message open, choose File⇨Move to Folder or Copy to Folder. In the dialog box that appears (see **Figure 15-24**), select the appropriate folder and click OK.

- Right-click a message in a displayed folder and choose Move to Folder or Copy to Folder. In the dialog box that appears, select the appropriate folder and then click OK.

Select a folder

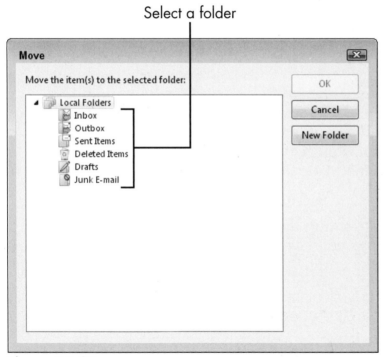

Figure 15-24

3. To delete a message, display the folder it's saved to, select the message, and then click the Delete button or press the Delete key.

If you try to delete a message from your Deleted Items folder, a message appears asking whether you really want to delete this message permanently. That's because when you delete a message from another folder, it's really not deleted; instead, it's simply placed in the Deleted Items folder. To send it into oblivion, you have to delete it from the Deleted Items folder, confirming your deletion so that Windows Mail is really convinced that you mean what you say.

Create Mail Rules

1. You can create rules for how Windows Mail handles messages. For example, you can create a rule that all message from your grandchildren be automatically placed in your Grandchildren folder. Choose Tools⇨Message Rules⇨Mail.

2. In the resulting New Mail Rule dialog box (see **Figure 15-25**), select a check box in the Select the Conditions for Your Rule area to set a Condition for the rule. For example, if you want all messages that contain the word *Sale* in the subject line to be moved to a Junk Mail folder, select the Where the Subject Line Contains Specific Words option.

3. Mark the Select the Actions for Your Rule check boxes to choose rule actions. In the example in Step 2, for instance, you would select the Move It to the Specified Folder option.

4. In the Rule Description area, click a link (the colored text). To continue the example shown in Figure 15-25, you click the phrase Contains Specific Words. Fill in the specific information for the rule in the dialog box that appears (see **Figure 15-26** for an example). For the second item in this example, click the word specified and select a folder for matching messages to be moved to.

5. Click OK to return to the New Mail Rule dialog box. Fill in the Name of the Rule text box with a name that you can recognize, and then click OK.

After you create a rule, open the Message Rules dialog box (choose Tools⇨Message Rules⇨Mail) and then click the Modify button in the Message dialog box to make changes to the rule, or click the Remove button to delete it.

Here are some rules that people find handy to create: Place messages marked as priority in a Priority folder or put messages with attachments in an Attachments folder. If a message is from a certain person, mark it with a color.

Set conditions for a rule

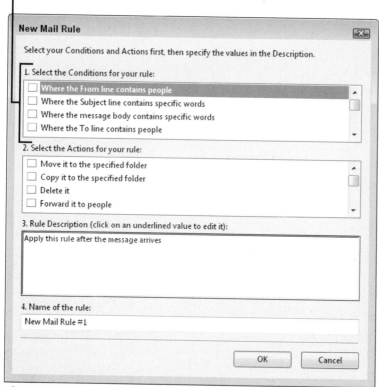

Figure 15-25

Specify rule details

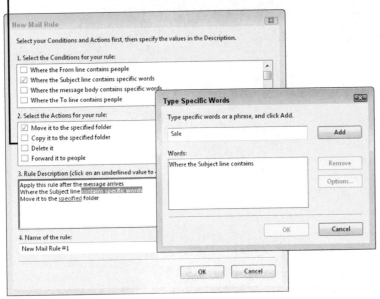

Figure 15-26

Connecting with People Online

Chapter 16

You grew up in a world where people held conversations in person, by writing letters back and forth, or over the phone, but the Internet has revolutionized the way people connect. Today, people can connect over the Internet in many ways. You can interact using a variety of technologies and with a variety of devices. You can enter text messages into your computer or cell phone that people receive immediately or whenever they get around to checking for messages. You can post an online journal called a *blog* (which stands for Web log) or read others' blogs. You can find people with like interests in a huge number of topics ranging from genealogy to investing to the best places to retire. When face-to-face communication just isn't possible, you will find the Internet a wonderful way to share ideas, information, and support.

In this chapter, you get advice about the following ways to interact with others online:

➡ You can communicate via text, voice, and video images.

➡ Post your thoughts to a discussion board or chat in real time in a chat room.

➡ Create your own online journal, called a *blog,* for others to visit.

➡ Become a member of a virtual community with your own online persona.

➡ Find Web sites that match your interests, from genealogy to pets or knitting.

Understand Instant Messaging

One way to connect directly with people who are online at the same time as you is by using an *instant messaging* (IM) program such as Windows Live Messenger, Yahoo! IM, or AIM, AOL's instant messaging program. Instant messaging is a text-based form of communicating over the Internet via your computer, cell phone, or other device. You enter a brief message and send it, and it appears instantly in an instant messaging program window on the other person's computer or other device. Your friend enters a reply, and you go back and forth holding a virtual conversation in *real time* (that is, you're both participating in the moment, not reading messages at a later time, as with an e-mail).

You can download instant messaging programs free from the Internet. (Search for these using the search tools discussed in Chapter 14.) Instant messaging is especially convenient for staying in touch with younger members of your family, who are likely to be hooked on IM, one of the primary communications methods for young people today.

Here are some of the ways you can use instant messaging:

➡ You create a list of people with whom you want to connect. This list is called a *buddy list* or *contact list* (see **Figure 16-1**). When you sign in to your IM program and your instant messaging window appears, it lets you know who's online. If any of your buddies are online, you can then send text messages back and forth to each other.

➡ In addition to text messages, you can share links to Web sites, videos, images, and even sounds.

➡ You can use settings in instant messaging programs to indicate to others that you aren't available for contact, even though you're online.

View contacts in Messenger

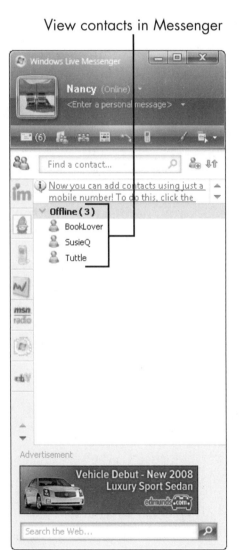

Figure 16-1

➠ You can often make phone calls from your instant messaging program. In addition, if you have a cell phone or other handheld device, you might be able to use it to send instant messages.

➠ Instant messaging also allows you to share files with other people, so you can transmit pictures or other items to each other.

 Consider who you allow on your IM contact list. Whoever is on that list knows every time you go online. Stick to friends and family and people you want to chat with on a regular basis.

Use a Webcam

Web cameras, referred to as *webcams*, are small devices that you can place near your computer to send images to other people over the Internet. For example, if you and another person each have a webcam pointed at you as you're interacting using a program such as NetMeeting or AOL Instant Messenger, you can see each other as you talk.

Here's what you should know about buying and using a webcam:

➠ **Purchasing a webcam:** Some computers, especially many laptop computers, have a webcam built in, but in most cases, you have to purchase a webcam from an office superstore or online site that sells electronics and computers. Prices start at around $25 in the U.S., or you can add a webcam to your system during the purchasing process if you buy a customized computer (see Chapter 1 for more about this).

➠ **Researching resolution:** Some inexpensive webcams provide a rather grainy, low-quality picture. If you want to use a webcam frequently, consider investing in one with higher resolution such as 1.3 megapixels, which will produce a better picture.

➡ **Factoring in features:** Some webcams can be used as motion detectors, helping you to keep an eye on your house when you're away. A model with a built-in microphone can also help you hear what's going on remotely. Also, look for wireless connection capabilities, and pan and tilt features (basically the ability to move the camera around to view different angles). Some of these features can cost several hundred dollars.

➡ **Putting your webcam to use:** When you have a webcam, using it is pretty simple. Using a program such as Windows NetMeeting, which you can download from www.microsoft.com, you plug your webcam into your computer (usually using a USB port, a small, rectangular slot), and the video feed is instantly detected. You can move the camera around to make sure it gets the best view. You then connect with another computer user using the tools of your meeting software, and the other person can see your image on his or her computer screen.

 Be careful about sharing images on the Internet. Share them only with people you know and trust. Unscrupulous people can take your image and manipulate it in ways that could embarrass you. If you have grandchildren who visit, supervise their use of the webcam to make sure they aren't sharing images with strangers.

Make VoIP Phone Calls

VoIP stands for Voice over Internet Protocol. You can use this technology to make calls to anywhere in the world from your computer. You can also use a webcam along with VoIP to create a video phone system.

Here are the basics you should know about VoIP:

➟ There are various VoIP providers, such as Skype and Vonage. Costs for signing up with these providers vary but are often much lower than paying a traditional phone company. Because there's no per call or per minute charge, the basic fee is usually paid for by your savings on long distance.

➟ When you sign up with a provider, you'll have to download software and make a test call using a microphone you connect to your computer.

➟ To use a VoIP service, you enter a list of contacts just as you do for instant messaging or e-mail. When you want to make a call, you choose a contact and click a button.

➟ You can make calls to other's computers equipped with VoIP or to a regular handheld or cell phone.

➟ VoIP services also offer features such as voicemail, caller ID, and call forwarding. If you don't want to be disturbed while working on your computer, you can block calls temporarily.

➟ Several sites, such as http://voipreview.org, can help you compare services before you sign up (see **Figure 16-2**).

Is your daughter living in another country? Check your provider's coverage area. Many allow international calls for no additional charges.

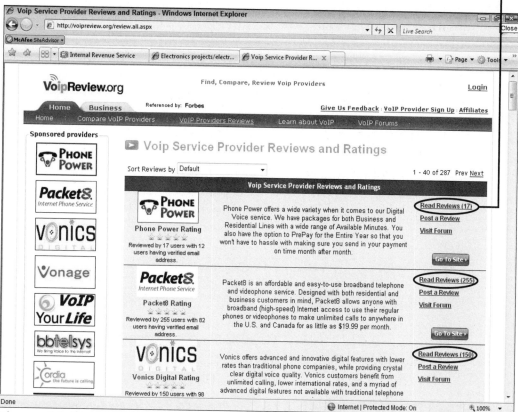

Figure 16-2

Participate in Discussion Boards and Chat

Two mainstays of online communication are *discussion boards* and *chat*. A discussion board is a place where you can post written messages on a topic and others can reply to you, or you can reply to their postings (and the postings might stay up there for years). A chat is an online space where people can talk back and forth via text; when the chat is over, unless you save a copy, the text is gone. The main difference between them is that discussion boards are asynchronous, which means that you post a message (just as you might on a public bulletin board) and wait for a response. Somebody might read it that hour or ten days or ten weeks after your posting. In other words, the response isn't instantaneous. With chat, the interaction is in real time (synchronous) and resembles a conversation in text. Chat takes place in virtual spaces called chat rooms.

The advantages of discussion boards are

➡ They allow you to give thought to your posting and spend time considering replies that others post to your discussion.

➡ They're organized in easy-to-follow *threads,* which organize postings and replies in an outline like structure (see **Figure 16-3**), and you can review the comments of various participants as they add their ideas to the entire discussion.

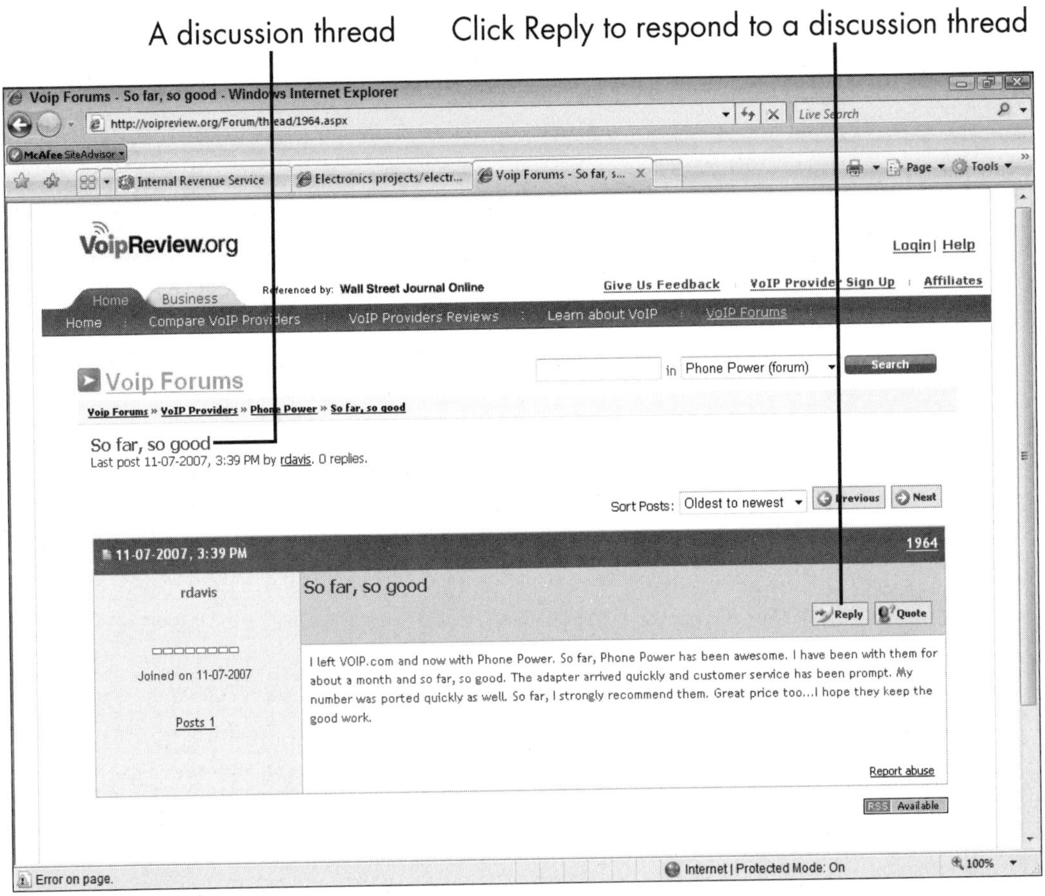

A discussion thread   Click Reply to respond to a discussion thread

Figure 16-3

Chat, on the other hand, has these advantages:

➟ You can interact with others right away. However, chat messages are usually rather brief to keep the conversation flowing.

➟ Several people can interact at once, though this can take getting used to as you try to follow what others are saying and jump in with your own quickly typed messages.

➟ You can invite others to enter a private chat room, which keeps the rest of the folks who wandered into the chat room out of your conversation.

Understand Blogs

The term *blog* comes from the phrase *Web log*. Blogs are essentially online journals or diaries in which people share their ideas and thoughts and others can comment on them. Both companies and individuals can create blogs. **Figure 16-4** shows a blog at www. look-both-ways.com, which discusses how to stay safe online

Here's some general advice about how to begin to explore the world of blogging:

➟ **Getting your own blog:** You can get a blog space from several sources, including your e-mail program such as Windows Live Hotmail or from a blog space service such as www.blogger.com. Creating a blog space is usually free, and the sign up process is simple.

➟ **Considering your access options:** Be aware of the settings you make when creating a blog. Allowing public access to the blog means that anybody can listen in to your thoughts and emotions and pick up private information about you from your blog entries. You might be safer setting up to provide access only to those you know. Even if you post blog entries anonymously, some folks have figured out how to find out your real name, so limiting access to your postings is the safest approach.

➡ **Designing your blog's appearance:** Blog sites typically provide tools to help you easily design your space. You can choose whether to post a picture of yourself, what colors and fonts to use, and organize the layout of postings, archives of older postings, and responses.

➡ **Interacting with the blogging community:** You can search blog sites to find people with like interests. If another person's blog is open to the public, you can read and respond to comments posted there.

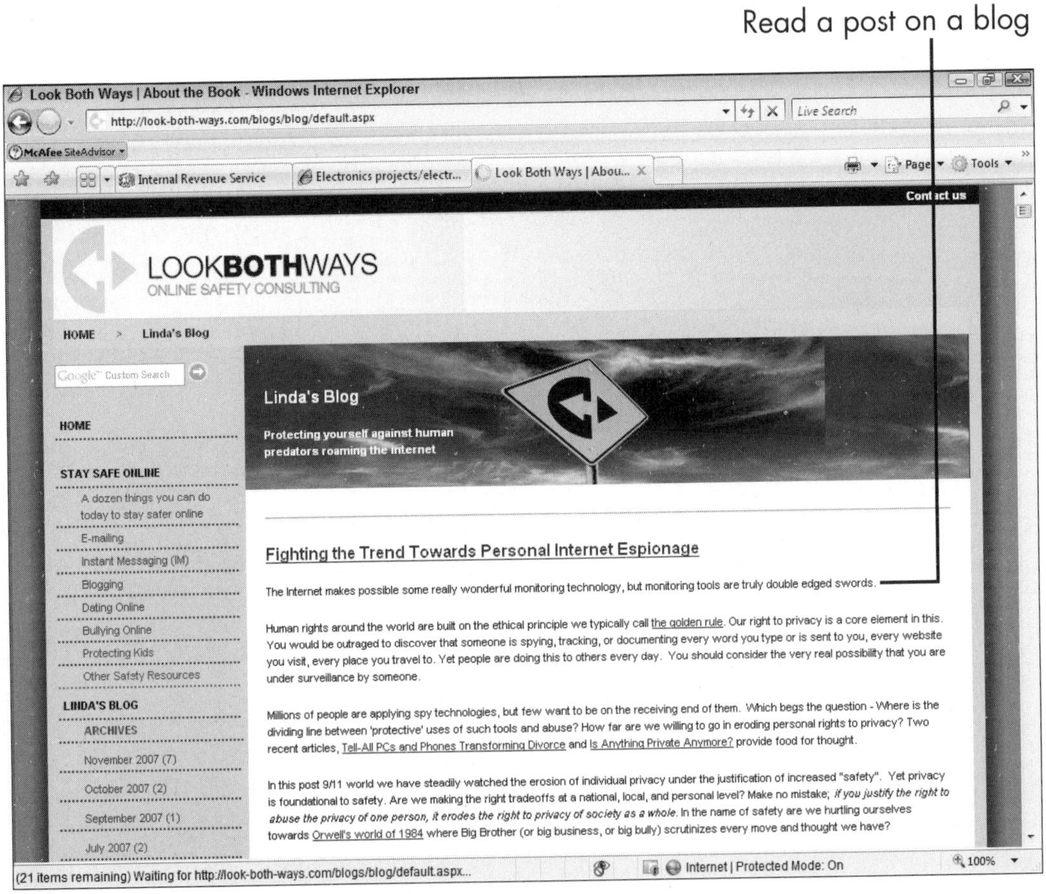

Read a post on a blog

Figure 16-4

Explore Virtual Worlds

You might have read about virtual world sites such as Second Life. These sites allow you to create an alter ego called an *avatar*, which is an on-screen character that represents you. You move around the world and interact with others in interesting ways.

Here are some guidelines to help you find your way around virtual worlds:

⟹ Virtual world sites such as Second Life (www.second life.com) and The Manor (www.madwolfsw.com) are free, but they also have a thriving economy. You can buy virtual clothing, props such as swords, and even virtual real estate.

⟹ These sites attract all kinds of people. You might run into very friendly folks who stop to chat as they explore the world, or people who run around with swords yelling at others. Be prepared to move along if somebody you don't care for approaches you. Also, remember not to reveal any identifying information about yourself to people you don't really know.

⟹ You can move all over these worlds, which often have many locations to explore. You can walk, run, fly, or teleport to other locations. Sites have maps to help you find your way.

⟹ Look for friendly characters, such as the tiger "Scotsman" in The Manor, which are there to help you out.

Be cautious about spending much money in virtual worlds. There have actually been incidents where shady characters have stolen people's possessions; however, it's difficult if not impossible to get law enforcement officials to do a thing about such a theft.

Find People with Common Interests

The Internet is full of sites that appeal to people with common interests. There, people chat and participate in discussion boards sharing their ideas. Everything from recipes to quilt patterns and home improvement projects might be posted online for you to try out. There are even support groups for those suffering from addictions or illnesses.

Here are some popular sites you might want to try out:

- Try www.genealogy.com or www.family search.org to get started finding your family roots.

- If you have a home project you'd like help with, go to www.doityourself.com or www.askthe builder.com.

- Support organizations for those with cancer include www.cancer.gov for information on financial help and hospices or www.cancerlinkusa.com to connect to The Cancer Information Network.

- For information and to connect with people dealing with Alzheimer's disease, go to www.alzheimer support.com.

- These sites cater to those who like sewing, knitting, or quilting: www.knittinghelp.com, www.sewing.org, and www.quilt.com.

- If you're intrigued by playing games online with others from around the world, try www.games.com (see **Figure 16-5**) or www.chess.net.

- If you're into classic cars, visit www.carclassic. com or www.dreamcarclassicsonline.com.

Click tabs to see different types of games

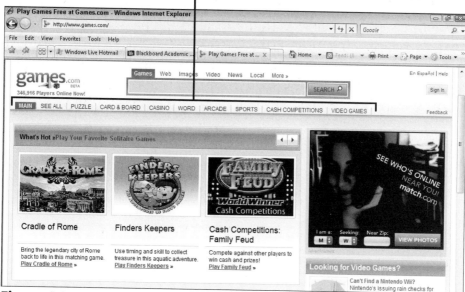

Figure 16-5

 Whatever your interest, you're likely to find others online who share it. Enter keywords in you browser's search field to find them. See Chapter 14 for more about how to search and browse online.

Part IV

Taking Care of Your Computer

The 5th Wave   By Rich Tennant

"Well, here's your problem. You only have half the ram you need."

Protecting Windows

*Y*our computer contains software and files that can be damaged in several different ways. One major source of damage is from malicious attacks that are delivered via the Internet. Some people create damaging programs called *viruses* specifically designed to get into your computer hard drive and destroy or scramble data. Companies might download adware on your computer, which causes pop-up ads to appear, slowing down your computer's performance. Spyware is another form of malicious software that you might download by clicking a link or opening a file attachment; spyware sits on your computer and tracks your activities, whether for use by a legitimate company in selling you products or by a criminal element to steal your identity.

Microsoft provides security features within Windows Vista that help to keep your computer and information safe, whether you're at home or travelling with a laptop computer.

In this chapter, I introduce you to the major concepts of computer security and cover Windows Vista security features that allow you to do the following:

➠ Understand computer security and why you need it.

➠ Run periodic updates to Windows, which installs security solutions and patches (essentially, patches fix problems) to the software.

➠ Enable a *firewall,* which is a security feature that keeps your computer safe from outsiders and helps you to avoid several kinds of attacks on your data.

➠ Work with Windows Defender, which is new in Windows Vista. Windows Defender is a built-in solution for managing all your security settings centrally.

➠ Protect yourself against spyware.

Understand Computer Security

When you buy a car, it has certain safety features built in. After you drive it off the lot, you might find that the manufacturer slipped up and either recalls your car or requests that you go to the dealer's service department to get a faulty part replaced. In addition, you need to drive defensively to keep your car from being damaged in daily use.

Your computer is similar to your car in terms of the need for safety. It comes with an operating system (such as Microsoft Windows) built in, and that operating system has security features. Sometimes that operating system has flaws, and you need to get an update to it to keep it secure. And as you use your computer, you're exposing it to dangerous conditions and situations that you have to guard against.

Threats to your computer security can come from a file you copy from a disc you insert into your computer, but most of the time the danger is from a program that you downloaded from the Internet. These downloads can happen when you click a link, open an attachment in an e-mail, or download a piece of software without realizing that the malware is attached to it.

There are three main types of dangerous programs (called *malware*) to be aware of:

➡ A **virus** is a little program that some nasty person thought up to spread around the Internet and infect computers. A virus can do a variety of things, but typically it attacks your data, deleting files, scrambling data, or making changes to your system settings that cause your computer to grind to a halt.

➡ **Spyware** consists of programs whose main purpose in life is to track what you do with your computer. Some spyware simply helps companies you do business with track your activities so they can figure out how to sell you things; other spyware is used for more insidious purposes, such as stealing your passwords.

➡ **Adware** is the computer equivalent of telemarketing phone calls at dinner time. Once adware gets downloaded onto your computer, you'll get annoying pop-up windows trying to sell you things all day long. Beyond the annoyance, adware can quickly clog up your computer, so its performance slows down, and it's hard to get anything done at all.

To protect your information and your computer from these various types of malware, you can do several things:

➡ **You can buy and install an antivirus, antispyware, or antiadware program.** Programs such as McAfee Antivirus, Norton Antivirus from Symantec (see **Figure 17-1**), or the freely downloadable AVG Free from Grisoft can help stop the downloading of malicious files, and they can detect files that have somehow gotten through and delete them for you.

Remember that after you install such a program, you have to get regular updates to it to handle new threats, and you need to run scans on your system to catch items that might have snuck through. Many antivirus programs are purchased by yearly subscription, which gives you access to updated virus definitions that the company constantly gathers throughout the year.

Choose a Norton Security product

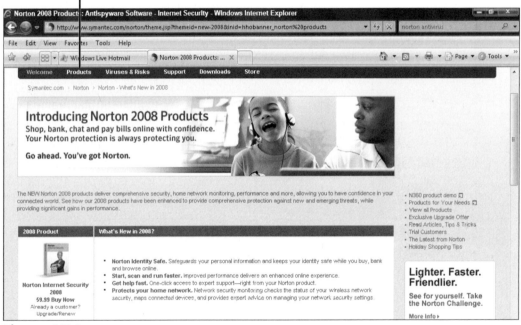

Figure 17-1

➠ **Some other programs such as Spyware Doctor from PC Tools combine tools for detecting adware and spyware.** Windows Vista has a built-in program, Windows Defender, that includes an antispyware feature. Windows Defender tools are covered later in this chapter.

➠ **You can use Windows tools to keep Windows up to date with security features and fixes to security problems.** You can also turn on a firewall, which is a feature that stops other people or programs from accessing your computer without your permission. These two features are covered in this chapter.

Understand Windows Update Options

When a new operating system like Windows Vista is released, it has been thoroughly tested; however, when the product is in general use, the manufacturer begins to find a few problems or security gaps that it couldn't anticipate. For that reason, companies such as Microsoft release updates to their software, both to fix those problems and deal with new threats to computers that appeared after the software release.

Windows Update is a tool you can use to make sure your computer has the most up-to-date security measures in place. You can set Windows Update to work in a few different ways by choosing Start⇨All Programs⇨Windows Update and clicking the Change Settings link on the left side of the Windows Update window that appears. In the resulting dialog box (see **Figure 17-2**), you find these settings:

➠ **Install Updates Automatically:** With this setting, Windows Update starts at a time of day you specify, but your computer must be on for it to work. If you've turned off your computer, the automatic update will start when you next turn on your computer, and it might shut down your computer in the middle of your work to complete the installation.

➠ **Download Updates But Let Me Choose Whether to Install Them:** You can set up Windows Update to download updates and have Windows notify you (through a little pop-up message on your taskbar) when they're available, but you get to decide when the updates are installed and when your computer reboots (turns off and then on) to complete the installation. This is my preferred setting because I have control and won't be caught unawares by a computer reboot.

➠ **Check for Updates But Let Me Choose Whether to Download and Install Them:** With this setting, you neither download nor install updates until you say so, but Windows notifies you that new updates are available.

➠ **Never Check for Updates:** You can stop Windows from checking for updates and check for them yourself, manually (see the following task). This puts your computer at a bit more risk, but it's useful for you to know how to perform a manual update if you discover a new update is available that you need to proceed with a task (such as getting updated drivers or a language pack).

Select update settings

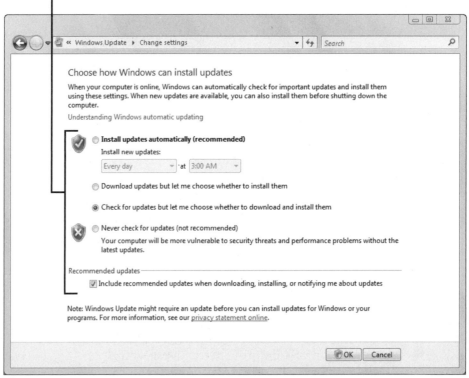

Figure 17-2

Run Windows Update

1. No matter which Windows Update setting you choose (see the preceding task) you can run a manual update at any time. To do so, choose Start➪All Programs➪Windows Update.

2. In the resulting Windows Update window, click Check for Updates. Windows thinks about this for a while, so feel free to page through a magazine for a minute or two.

3. In the resulting window, as shown in **Figure 17-3**, click the View Available Updates link.

4. In the following window, which shows the available updates (see **Figure 17-4**), select check boxes for the updates that you want to install. (It usually doesn't hurt to just accept all updates, if you have the time to download them all.) Then click the Install button.

5. A window appears, showing the progress of your installation. When the installation is complete, you might get a message telling you that it's a good idea to restart your computer to complete the installation. Click the Restart Now button.

You can set up Windows Update to run at the same time every day. Click the Change Settings link in the left pane of the Windows Update window and choose the frequency (such as every day) and time of day to check for and install updates.

If you set Windows Update to run automatically, be forewarned that when it runs it might also automatically restart your computer to finish the update installation sequence. Although it displays a pop-up message warning that it's about to do this, it's easy to miss. Then you might be startled to find that whatever you're working on shuts down and your computer restarts when you least expect it.

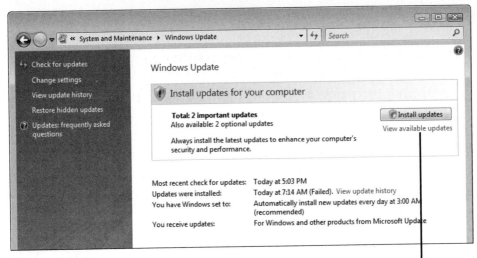

Figure 17-3

Click View Available
Updates

Check the box for each update you want to install

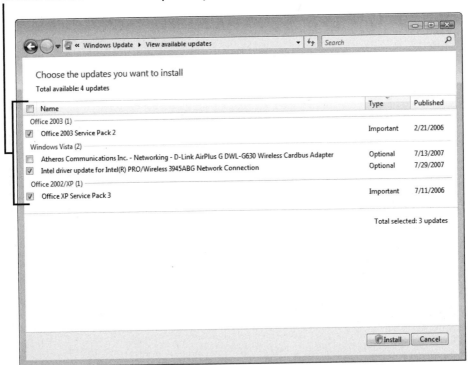

Figure 17-4

Enable the Windows Firewall

1. A *firewall* is a program that protects your computer from the outside world, preventing others from accessing your computer and stopping the downloading of dangerous programs such as viruses. With a firewall on, if you try to access sites or download software, you're asked whether you want to allow such access. Be aware, however, that you must turn on your firewall before you connect to the Internet for it to be effective. To turn on your firewall, choose Start⇨Control Panel⇨Check This Computer's Security Status.

2. In the Windows Security Center window that appears (see **Figure 17-5**), check that the Windows Firewall is marked as On. If it isn't, click the Windows Firewall link in the left pane of the window and then click the Change Settings link in the resulting dialog box.

3. In the resulting Windows Firewall window (see **Figure 17-6**), select the On button and then click OK.

Check that the firewall is On

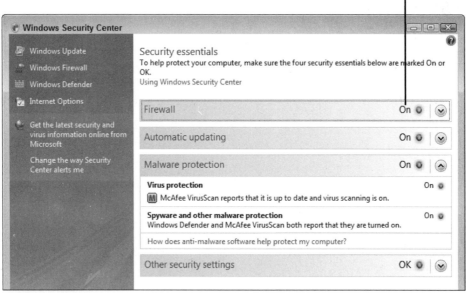

Figure 17-5

4. Click the Close button to close Windows Security Center and the Control Panel. Your firewall is now enabled and should stay enabled unless you go in and change the setting.

 Antivirus and security software programs might offer their own firewall protection and might display a message asking whether you want to switch. Check their features against the Windows Firewall features and then decide, but usually most firewall features are comparable. The important thing is to have one activated.

Select On

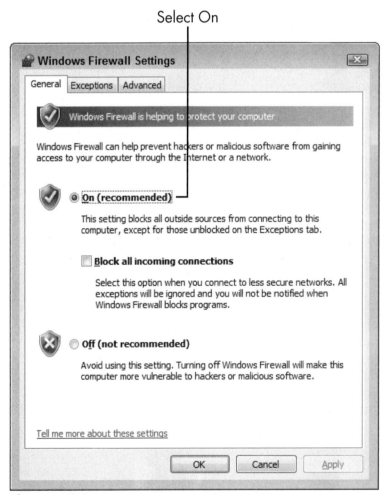

Figure 17-6

Run a Windows Defender Scan

1. If you use Windows Defender to detect spyware, you must run a *scan* of your computer system on a regular basis, which searches your computer for any problem files. You can run scans by setting up an automatic scan, or manually running a scan at any time. To make these settings choose Start⇨All Programs⇨Windows Defender.

2. In the resulting Windows Defender window, click the down-pointing arrow on the Scan button (see **Figure 17-7**). In the resulting menu, choose one of three options:

- **Quick Scan:** This runs a scan of the likeliest spots on your computer where spyware might lurk. In many cases, this quicker scanning process finds most, if not all, problems and is good choice for a daily automatic scan.

- **Full Scan:** This scan checks every single file and folder on your computer and gives any currently running programs the once-over. However, be aware that during a Full Scan your computer might run a little more slowly.

- **Custom Scan:** This scan allows you to customize where to scan. This is helpful if you suspect that a particular drive or folder is harboring a problem.

3. If you choose Quick Scan or Full Scan, the scan begins immediately. If you choose Custom Scan, you can click the Select button in the Select Scan Options dialog box that appears (see **Figure 17-8**). Then, in the Select Drives and Folders to Scan dialog box, select drives, files, and folders to scan. Click OK. Back in the Select Scan Options dialog box, click Scan Now.

4. When a scan is complete, a dialog box appears, listing any instances of spyware that were found and deleted or informing you that no spyware was found. Click the Close button to close the Windows Defender window.

Click to choose a scan option

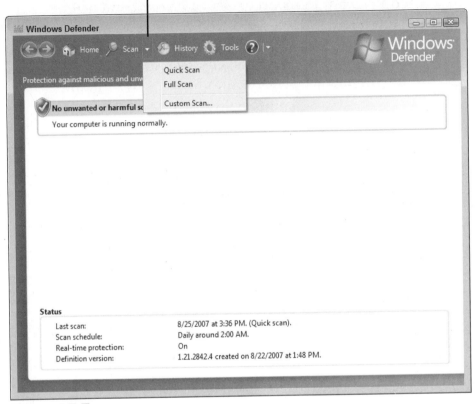

Figure 17-7

The History button in Windows Defender gives you a review of the activities and actions taken by Windows Defender. This is especially useful if you have chosen to run scans manually and don't remember whether you ran one recently. In that window, you can also view your settings for Microsoft SpyNet. By default, Windows Defender has set you up with a basic membership in SpyNet so that your computer automatically reports actions to remove spyware. An advanced membership is also available. Like the basic membership, it doesn't cost you anything, but it alerts you when new threats are detected and also provides Microsoft with more data about your computer, and some personal information might get through. Allowing reports on spyware activity can help

Microsoft prevent or stop such threats; however, if you don't want to report issues with your computer and spyware to Microsoft, you can choose not to join Microsoft SpyNet by clicking the Change Settings link in the History dialog box and clicking the I Don't Want to Join Microsoft Spynet At This Time radio button.

Click Select

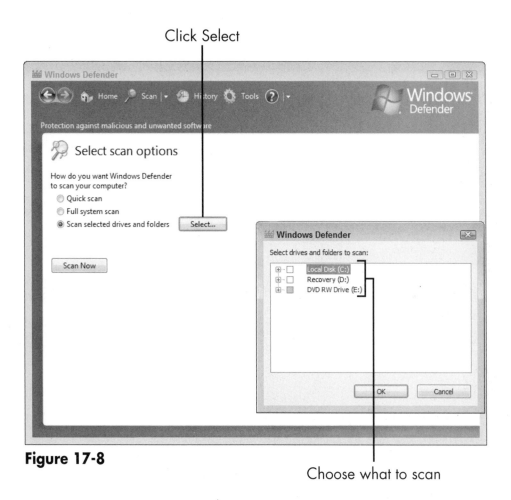

Figure 17-8

Choose what to scan

Set Up Windows Defender to Run Automatically

1. If you prefer to have Windows Defender run on its own so you never miss a scan, you can set it up to do so. Choose Start➪All Programs➪Windows Defender.

2. In the resulting Windows Defender window, choose
Tools⇨Options. In the Options dialog box that appears
(see **Figure 17-9**), select the Automatically Scan My
Computer check box if it's not already selected and then
choose the frequency, time of day, and type of scan from
the drop-down lists.

Select the check box

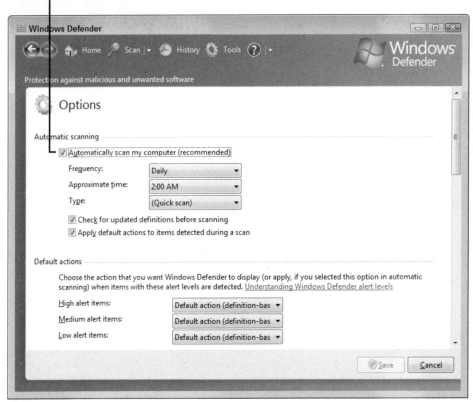

Figure 17-9

3. To ensure that your scan uses the latest definitions for *malware* (a kind of spyware with malicious intent), select the
Check for Updated Definitions before Scanning check box.

4. Scroll down to the bottom of the Options dialog box (see
Figure 17-10) and make sure that the Use Windows
Defender check box is enabled (selected) to activate the
program.

5. Click Save to save your settings.

 If you want to exclude certain files or locations from the regular scans, you can use the Advanced Options in the Windows Defender dialog box. Click the Add button and browse for the location or file you want to exclude.

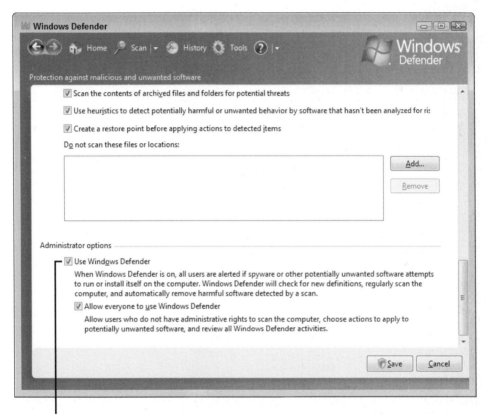

Make sure Windows Defender is enabled

Figure 17-10

Maintaining Windows

*T*his chapter covers tasks that are about as much fun as cleaning out your refrigerator. The fact is that computer maintenance might not be a barrel of laughs, but it keeps your computer running, so it has to be done. These are the types of tasks that help you keep your computer organized, in shape, and performing at its best.

The tasks in this chapter fall into two categories:

⟶ **Performing basic maintenance:** These tasks help you keep your Windows house in order. To keep your system in shape, you can *defragment* your hard drive (take small fragments of files and consolidate them to make accessing them more efficient) or free up space on the drive. These tasks optimize how files are stored on your hard drive to make sure that you get the best performance from your computer.

⟶ **Clearing up accumulated junk:** You can delete cookies and temporary files placed on your computer during online sessions to stop them from cluttering your hard drive. You can also schedule routine maintenance tasks to happen automatically so you don't have to remember to deal with them yourself.

Defragment a Hard Drive

1. When you store data to your hard drive (for example, when you save a file), that file isn't stored in one discrete section of the drive. Bits of it might be stored all over the place. Your computer uses a table to locate all those bits whenever you open the file. *Defragmenting* reassembles data on your hard drive to use the space more efficiently. Many people recommend defragmenting your hard drive on a regular basis to keep your computer performing at its best. Choose Start⇨Control Panel⇨System and Maintenance and then click Defragment Your Hard Drive (in the Administrative Tools section).

2. In the resulting Disk Defragmenter window (see **Figure 18-1**), to the left of the Defragment Now button is a note about whether your system requires defragmenting. If it does, or if you simply want to defragment your hard drive on a regular basis to play it safe, click the Defragment Now button. The message that appears (see **Figure 18-2**) tells you that Windows is defragmenting your drive and that it might take up to a few hours to complete. Windows shows you a progress window while you wait.

3. When the defragmenting process is complete, the Disk Defragmenter window shows that your drive no longer requires defragmenting. Click Close (the X in the upper right) to close the window.

Remember: Disk defragmenting can take a while. If you have energy-saving features active (such as a screen saver), they might cause the defragmenter to stop or delay, so you might want to turn off the screen saver feature. (Choose Start⇨Control Panel⇨ Appearance and Personalization and click the Change Screen Saver link.)

To keep defragmenting from interfering with your work, try running it overnight while you're happily dreaming of much more interesting things. You can also set up the procedure to run automatically at a preset period of time, such as once every two weeks by selecting the Run On a Schedule check box in the Disk Defragmenter window. A default schedule appears; to change it, click the Modify Schedule button and choose how often, what day, and what time to run the procedure.

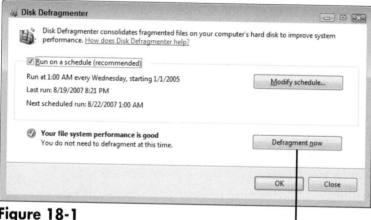

Figure 18-1

Click to run a defragment

Check the defragment status here

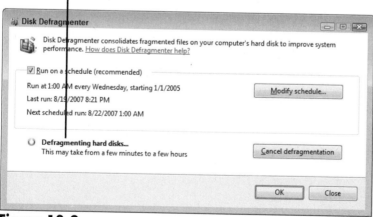

Figure 18-2

Free Up Disk Space

1. With all the little bits of data saved around your hard drive, there are some pieces that have become useless (little bits of files you deleted three years ago, for example). You can use a Windows tool to clean up your drive to remove that debris, which improves your computer's performance. Choose Start⇨Control Panel⇨System and Maintenance and then click Free Up Disk Space in the Administrative Tools.

2. In the dialog box that appears (see **Figure** 18-3), click the icon next to the kind of files you want to clean up. If you choose Files from All Users on This Computer, go to Step 3. If you choose My Files Only, choose the drives you want to scan from the Disk Cleanup: Drive Selection dialog box that appears and then proceed to Step 3.

3. The resulting dialog box shown in **Figure** 18-4 tells you that Disk Cleanup has calculated how much space can be cleared on your hard drive and displays the suggested files to delete in a list. (Those to be deleted have a check mark.) If you want to select additional files in the list to delete, click to place a check mark next to them, or deselect files if you want to keep them around. In most cases, whatever Windows proposes to delete is probably safe to delete, including fragments of long-gone files and otherwise corrupted data you haven't accessed in a long time.

Click an option

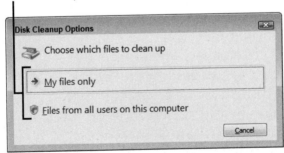

Figure 18-3

Check types of files to delete

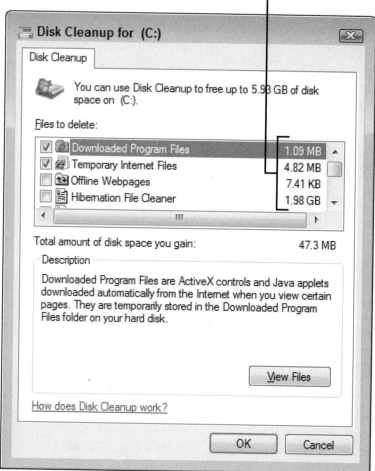

Figure 18-4

4. After you select all the files to delete (or accept the suggested files, which is probably just fine in most cases), click OK. The selected files are deleted.

 Though the Disk Cleanup process is pretty safe, if your computer starts behaving strangely after the cleanup, you might want to use the System Restore feature of Windows. This feature saves periodic backups of your system, and you can use it to restore your computer to an earlier time. Choose Start⇨Control Panel⇨Restore Files from Backup and then click the

Restore Files button. Follow the wizard screens that appear to restore files to the most recently backed up version before you ran Disk Cleanup.

 Click the View Files button in the Disk Cleanup dialog box to see more details about the files that Windows proposes to delete, including the size of the files and when they were created or last accessed.

Delete Cookies Using Internet Explorer

1. *Cookies* are tiny files that some businesses on the Internet place on your computer when you visit their sites. Cookies store information about you, such as your name and membership information, so that when you return to a site they can do personalized things like greeting you by name or suggesting products that might appeal to you. However, some people don't like the invasion of privacy that cookies can represent, and over time cookies pile up and take up space on your computer. To get rid of them, open Internet Explorer (choose Start⇨Internet Explorer).

2. From the menu bar, choose Tools⇨Internet Options.

3. On the General tab of the resulting Internet Options dialog box (see **Figure 18-5**), click the Delete button in the Browsing History section.

4. In the resulting dialog box, as shown in **Figure 18-6**, click the Delete Cookies button in the Cookies section.

5. A confirmation message asks whether you want to delete the files. Click Yes. Click Close and then click OK to close the open dialog boxes.

 There are pros and cons to allowing cookies to be saved on your computer. Cookies embed information about you and your Internet browsing habits on your computer, which Web sites can use to predict your buying interests. That information can be used to push annoying pop-up windows at you or simply to suggest products you might be interested in buying when you revisit a favorite online store. If you don't want to have cookies saved to your computer, change your privacy to a higher setting. (See Chapter 14 for more about this.)

Click Delete

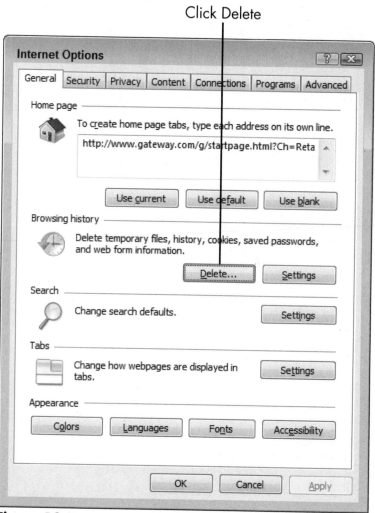

Figure 18-5

Click Delete Cookies

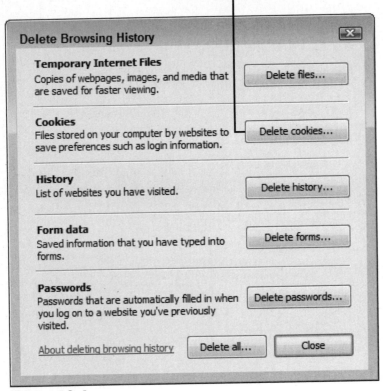

Figure 18-6

Set a Reminder for Maintenance Tasks

 1. If you'd like a reminder to perform regular maintenance tasks rather than schedule them to run automatically, you can use the Task Scheduler to display a message periodically to remind you. Choose Start⇨Control Panel⇨ System and Maintenance and then click Schedule Tasks under Administrative Tools.

2. In the resulting Task Scheduler dialog box, as shown in **Figure 18-7**, in the Actions pane click the Create Basic Tasks link.

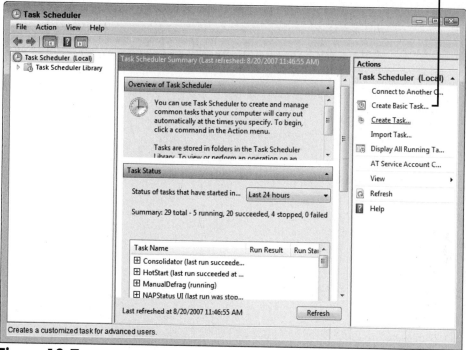

Click Create Basic Task

Figure 18-7

3. In the resulting Create Basic Task Wizard dialog box, as shown in **Figure** 18-8, enter a task name and description and click Next. For example, you might enter **Remind Me to Run Disk Cleanup**.

4. In the Task Trigger window that appears (see **Figure** 18-9), choose when to run the task such as Daily, Weekly, or Monthly. For most system maintenance tasks, Monthly is usually more than adequate.

Enter a task name

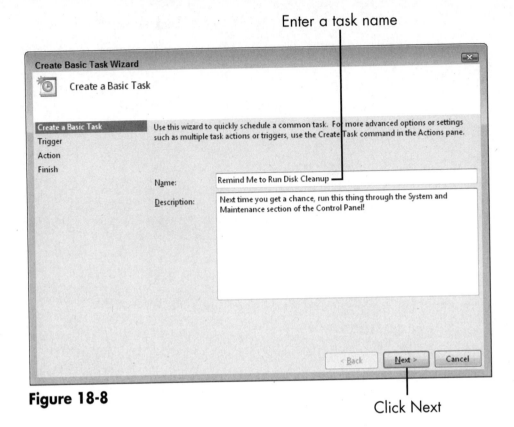

Figure 18-8

Click Next

5. Click Next. In the next wizard window that appears, choose a criteria from the Start drop-down list and use the Settings to specify how often to perform the task as well as when and at what time of day to begin. These options vary depending on what trigger you chose in Step 4. For example, if you chose Weekly, you can choose the day of the week and time to run the task. Click Next.

6. In the Action window that appears, select Display a Message and then click Next.

Choose when to run the task

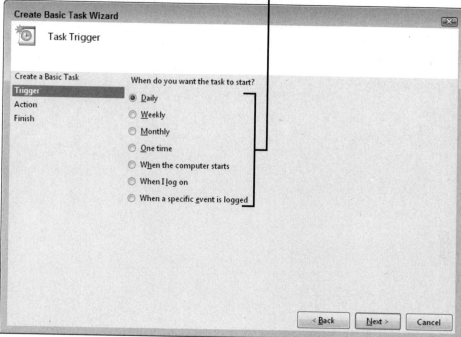

Figure 18-9

7. In the Display a Message window that appears (see **Figure 18-10**), enter the title and contents of the message you want to appear. For example, the title might be Disk Cleanup Reminder, and the contents might simply read, Run a Disk Cleanup Soon!

8. Click Next. A Summary window appears summarizing the task you have scheduled.

9. Click Finish, and you've finished the wizard. Click the Close button to close the Task Scheduler window.

Enter a title and message

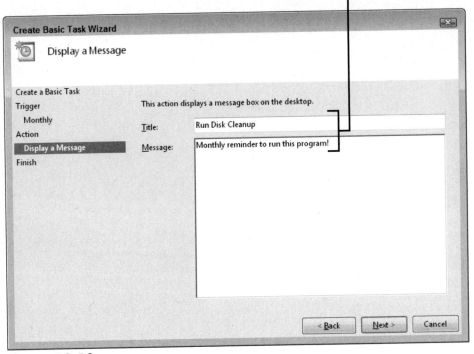

Figure 18-10

Index

● *G* ●